Gay Men and Feminist Women in the Fight for Equality

CULTURAL MEDIA STUDIES

Leandra H. Hernández and Amanda R. Martinez
Series Editors

Vol. 2

The Cultural Media Studies series is part
of the Peter Lang Media and Communication list.
Every volume is peer reviewed and meets
the highest quality standards for content and production.

PETER LANG
New York • Bern • Berlin
Brussels • Vienna • Oxford • Warsaw

D. Travers Scott

Gay Men and Feminist Women in the Fight for Equality

"What Did You Do During the Second Wave, Daddy?"

PETER LANG

New York • Bern • Berlin
Brussels • Vienna • Oxford • Warsaw

Library of Congress Cataloging-in-Publication Data

Names: Scott, D. Travers, author.
Title: Gay men and feminist women in the fight for equality: "what did you
do during the second wave, daddy?"/D. Travers Scott.
Description: 1 Edition. | New York: Peter Lang, 2020.
Series: Cultural media studies; vol. 2
ISSN 2641-1415 (print) | ISSN 2577-6231 (online)
Includes bibliographical references and index.
Identifiers: LCCN 2019052430 (print) | LCCN 2019052431 (ebook)
ISBN 978-1-4331-6280-0 (hardback: alk. paper)
ISBN 978-1-4331-6281-7 (paperback: alk. paper) | ISBN 978-1-4331-6282-4 (ebook pdf)
ISBN 978-1-4331-6283-1 (epub) | ISBN 978-1-4331-6284-8 (mobi)
Subjects: LCSH: Gay men. | Gay liberation movement. | Male feminists. |
Feminists. | Feminism. | Man-woman relationships.
Classification: LCC HQ76 .S39 2020 (print) | LCC HQ76 (ebook) |
DDC 306.76/6—dc23
LC record available at https://lccn.loc.gov/2019052430
LC ebook record available at https://lccn.loc.gov/2019052431
DOI 10.3726/b14795

Bibliographic information published by **Die Deutsche Nationalbibliothek**.
Die Deutsche Nationalbibliothek lists this publication in the "Deutsche
Nationalbibliografie"; detailed bibliographic data are available
on the Internet at http://dnb.d-nb.de/.

For Mike McGirr

Contents

Acknowledgments

This research was supported in part by the Clemson University Humanities Advancement Board, the Department of Communication at Clemson University, and a Clemson University Support for Early Exploration and Development Grant. Portions of this book have appeared, in different forms and context, in my doctoral dissertation and *Critical Studies in Media Communication*. My focus group participants provided crucial candor and willingness to explore the themes in this book. The staffs of the archives where I worked could not have been more helpful and congenial. I am deeply appreciative of everyone involved with the Louise Pettus Archives & Special Collections Women's History collections at the Winthrop University Dacus Library in Rock Hill, South Carolina, and the University of South Carolina Caroliniana LGBTQ Collection and South Carolina Pride Movement materials. I am very grateful to my research assistants in the MA in Communication, Technology, and Society program at Clemson University: Evan Lybrand, Jerrica Rowlett, Jessica Frampton Smith, and especially Sarah Arbogast, who provided perceptive insights and a great deal of trust in me that made getting this project under way possible. Many persons over the years provided suggestions, help, and feedback on this project, more than I can recall, so I thank them here collectively. The LGBTQ Studies Interest Group and the

Communication History Division of the International Communication Association supported the development of this work in conference presentations, as well as provided me ongoing intellectual homes. Sarah Banet-Weiser's teaching, mentorship, and friendship have been essential. Finally, this book offers respect to and gratitude for the gay men, feminist women, and all their entanglements and variations who paved the way, taught me, and continue to inspire me.

Introduction

"Why is it presupposed that the male feminist is a heterosexual man?"
                    —Craig Owens, "Outlaws: Gay Men in Feminism"

I am a gay male feminist. Feminism is a family issue for me. My maternal aunt, Carol (Rowell) Council, helped found the first women's studies program in the United States, at San Diego University in 1968, the year before I was born (Council, 2015; Orr, 1999). Although far away from where I grew up in Texas, she would send me feminist children's books for Christmas and, decades later, would share with me drafts of her memoir. Her grandmother, my great-grandmother, Luverna Jones, never used the word feminist to my knowledge, but was a strong woman who moved with her husband and children from Oklahoma City to the small South Texas town of Premont. There, she wrote, edited, and published a local newspaper, *The South-Press*. Her other grandchild, my biological mother, was fiercely independent, divorcing my father when I was young and heading out on a lifetime journey of discovery. Kay Council earned a graduate degree in folklore, researching Tex-Mex conjunto and norteña music, and then began interviewing South Texas curanderjas, or women folk healers.[1] Because of her, I grew up swing dancing in Latino honky-tonks and gazing in awe at the mysterious metal icons of desert folk shrines. My aunt remained independent as well, traveling to Italy for her graduate degree in art history. My mother roamed the United States, exploring and never setting down roots, often sharing with me her experiences as a woman dealing with sexism and gender roles, particularly in the conservative state of Texas.

These are only some of the women in my family whose strength and independence inspired and taught me. Independence, however, sometimes came with a price. Not all of their lives came to happy endings. But that is a different story, or set of stories. However, their examples helped give me the confidence to come out as a gay man, to be involved in gay activism and art, and to write popular articles and books exploring sexuality and gender (Scott, 1997, 1999, 2005, 2009).

Academics often speak of their training in familial terms, with advisors as parents and graduate students as children. My academic "mother," Sarah Banet-Weiser, is a feminist scholar and researcher with whom I studied at the University of Southern California. We went on to become great friends and colleagues in higher education.

Near the end of my time in graduate school, I asked her, "What gay men were involved with the women's movement?" Naively, I assumed that this was a well-documented history, the subject of several books or authoritative articles to which she could refer me. Sarah was never at a loss for readings to recommend.

"That's a good question," she said, quizzically. Now, in my tenth year as a college professor, I know all too well that "That's a good question" means "You should research that yourself."

A few years later, after I had graduated with my Ph.D. in Communication and secured a tenure-track job, a young graduate student in another department emailed me, asking if we could meet. She wanted to talk to me about "the relationship between queer theory and feminism." I welcomed the conversation, but still did not know of any authoritative sources to which I could now refer her. As a gay male scholar of identity and sexuality, as well as a published author of fiction and popular nonfiction on these topics, and participant in various forms of LGBTQ activism, I had encountered several views on how gay men and feminist women have related to one another. Some of these had been contradictory: gay men are naturally feminists; sexism is endemic among gay men. Others had been episodic: they worked together during the liberationist phase of second-wave feminism and early gay rights; they worked together to fight AIDS; feminism spawned gay civil rights; third-wave feminism incorporated LGBTQ issues. None of these scenarios satisfied me and, so, I set out to research it myself.

This book, the result of eight years researching the subject, does not claim by any means to be authoritative or comprehensive. It is, like many others' research projects, the result of nagging curiosity and a consequence of not being able to find answers in the existing literature. I began exploring the intersection between feminist women and gay men in their social movements for equality. Along the way, I stopped looking for answers and started listening to stories. This book is not an answer or series of answers, but a collection of stories. The stories are complicated, contradictory, and incomplete. This book is not the whole story. It is also, to a degree, the story of my search for these stories, a search for my political and intellectual family.

Feminist Women and Gay Men

Marginalized groups must speak to the mainstream—but also to each other. This book examines communication networks of women's and LGBTQ social movements, exploring how they communicated to and about each other. Given that these two groups share many obstacles, such as heteronormative gender roles and a patriarchal culture, when and under what conditions do they perceive each other as collaborative allies? Conversely, what has impeded these groups from working together? Has fluctuation in this dynamic been related to communication flows between and about the two groups? What insights can be found regarding communication and collaboration between other groups with shared goals?

This book aims to flesh out a largely unwritten but ongoing history of these two groups within the context of each other. Given the necessity of groups working together in efforts directed at social change, this book contributes a case study in realized and unrealized coalition-building. This project looks specifically at gay men in LGBTQ activism and their connections with feminist women in women's movements. It is motivated by the minimal popular and historic accounts of what would, ostensibly, seem to be two highly networked social movements. Furthermore, there is a lack of consistency and clarity in the material that does exist. One perspective, for example, suggests that one social movement absorbed the other: *The Rise and Fall of Gay Culture* explains that, in the 1960s, gay liberation "merged with" feminism (Harris, 1997, p. 243). Another common story has been the idea that mostly lesbian women connected these networks of social movements. To use a term from Manuel Castells' work, discussed below, lesbians have been thought of as the "switchers" who linked two social-change networks (e.g., during the first decade of the AIDS crisis). The concept of lesbian switchers appeared across a wide variety of my data sources. For example, New York City's 2001 *Directory of Lesbian, Gay, Bisexual and Transgender Services and Resources* (Hevesi, 2001) listed a few local chapters of the National Organization for Women (NOW) and described its main office in Washington, DC, as a "Feminist organization with focus on women's rights. Lesbian rights among top 4 priority issues."

The modern LGBTQ rights movement in the US is traditionally described as originating with the Stonewall riots in New York City in 1969. However, to compare the organized, recognized movement of first-wave feminist suffrage movements with what were contemporaneously only the most nascent LGBTQ rights efforts, and many outside of the US, would be too distinct of a difference in formulation. It would also present a challenge given that gay identity, as it is thought of today, was not widely diffused at that time. Therefore, I focus my research in this book as beginning with the contemporaneous periods of second-wave feminism and modern gay rights in the United States since the mid-twentieth century, continuing to the present. As research progressed, the driving questions of this project came into focus as:

- What stories have these groups told describing their experiences working together politically—or not?
- What stories do historical artifacts and other evidence tell?
- What stories do people in and outside of each group say about them?

This book is intended to resonate (Scott, 2013) a discursive formation. That is, I have taken the conceptual unit of "feminist women with gay men" and amplified it in a supportive manner. At times, I search for pre-existing associations of these two groups. Other times, as in the focus groups chapter, I push the two groups into thinking about and discussing each other.

Rather than attempting to write a single, authoritative history, I chose multiple research modes. Whereas multiple methods can be understood as an effort at triangulation, that approach is traditionally associated with a positivist approach to ascertaining and confirming truth through multiple corroboration (Biltereyst, Lotze, & Meers, 2012; De Laat, Lally, Lipponen, & Simons, 2007; Saukko, 2003). However, for more mixed-genre forms of research texts, Richardson (2000) suggests instead the concept of crystallization. Rather than the fixed geometric object of a triangle, researchers can approach validity using the concept of a crystal, which, while having structure, substance, and symmetry, is also dynamic, reflective, and refractive. This opens up validity to more than one possibility and also draws attention to additional, as yet unknown, possibilities. Ellingson (2014) extends crystallization as a research framework including multiple epistemological paradigms: postpositivist, constructivist, and creative/artistic. Crystallization leads us to greater knowing, including knowledge of what is not known, as well as different ways of knowing. Such is the goal of this project. The communicative relations between social movements of gay men and feminist women have multiple stories, only some of which are identified in this book. Others remain to be told.

I embrace such perspectives here in continuing my use of queer methodology (Scott, 2018). Queer methodology has, as perhaps expected, multiple definitions. In *Female Masculinity*, Halberstam (1998) used the term to describe combining interpretive and empirical qualitative methods in an attempt to "remain supple enough to respond to the various locations of information on female masculinity" (p. 10). This is, furthermore, positioned as a "disloyalty" or "form of refusal" (p. 10) to limit oneself to dominant definitions of a research topic but also dominant ways of producing and validating knowledge. Other approaches to queer methodology emphasize the research subjects over the epistemological paradigms. For example, the editors of a special issue of *Lambda Nordica* on queer methodology described it as "as empirically based designs of questions and methods in order to scrutinize heteronormative regimes and expose presences of queer interpretive potential" (Ambjörnsson, Laskar, & Steorn, 2010, p. 11). While this focus on queer subjects is relevant to the topics of this book, given their historic oppression by and exclusion from knowledge-making practices, the larger project of queer theory interrogates *all* subjects as inherently constructed and potentially unstable. In their book on queer methods and social science research, Browne and Nash (2016) make this explicit: "'Queer research' can be any form of research positioned within conceptual frameworks that highlight the instability of taken-for-granted meanings and resulting power relations" (p. 4). Queer research can be focused on experiences of non-normative gender, sexuality, and biological sex, but is not limited to those topics. However, "queer scholarship ... is anti-normative and seeks to subvert, challenge and critique a host of taken for granted 'stabilities' in our social lives" (p. 7). Such stabilities include those of researcher, researched, and research method(s). Ultimately, their collection suggests—but refuses to definitively answer—that there are no inherently queer or non-queer methods, individually or in combination, just as there are no specific, defined manners in which to study queer lives.

All of these perspectives inform my queer methodology here. Not only do I use multiple methods, with varying epistemological perspectives, to gain insight into multiple truths about my topics, but I also center the instability of those topics as well. Different types of data, using different qualitative methods, are employed to try and approach the topic from multiple perspectives and locations of knowledge. Not simply multimodal, this project presumes the instability of subjects and knowledge, and attempts to address that through a dynamic research design. The style of writing also intentionally varies with the book's form reflecting the variety and multiplicity of its content. Finally, this project is one of anti-normative destabilization. In addition to showing how knowledge about the social movements of feminist women and gay men vis-à-vis each other are inconsistent, contradictory, and fragmentary, the research subjects themselves destabilize and multiply over the course of the book. Here, I not only attempt to intervene in dominant understandings of these two groups, but also enact an intentional failure in attempting to force them into stable research subjects and myself as a researcher.

Theoretical Perspectives

This project draws on theoretical models of power and communication (Castells, 2001; 2009; Castells, Fernández-Ard'evol, Qiu, & Sey, 2007; Foucault, 1980, 1990; Foucault & Faubion, 1994), and is also informed broadly by critical historiography and post-structural feminist and queer theory. With Michel Foucault and Manuel Castells, I focus on power, communication, and networks: I conceive of the political movements of feminist women and gay men each as networks attempting to change their power relationships with dominant culture, through combined processes of communication and network reconfigurations. Within this process, my focus is on these two networks' communication to and about each other as their networks dynamically program and reprogram themselves with codes of cooperation or competition vis-a-vis each other.

Michel Foucault's Modern Power

From individual persuasion and influence to mass violence and threats of it, power has been theorized in a variety of ways and contexts. For the purposes of this project, I operate with a simplified, general conception of power as the ability to exert will over others. The classic, or what Foucault calls sovereign, model, would be a king exerting his will to have his army kill you or your community. This familiar model of power is centralized in an authority, which could also be a religious leader or other public figure, who controls and represses people, exerting power in a hierarchical manner.

While not denying the continued existence of this type of power, Foucault identifies more recent forms of power he calls *modern power*. Most significantly, he expands the concept of power in general to the linked concept of *power-knowledge*. This makes explicit the link between the two: not merely that one supports and informs the other, but that you cannot have one without the other. The connected concept of power-knowledge shapes dominant and competing *discourses*, which Faubion defines as "identifiable collections of utterances governed by rules of construction and evaluation which determine within some thematic area what may be said, by whom, in what context, and with what effect" (Foucault & Faubion, 1994, p. xvi). The type of power involved in bonding with knowledge and shaping discourses is not the simple control of others through threat of violence, nor exerting will through simply repressing those and that which deviate from one's will. Although these means did and do continue to exist—what Foucault calls sovereign, carceral, and pastoral forms of power—there are more recent dimensions of modern power that must be appreciated: it is productive, relational, multiple, mobile, reversible, and intentional.

For Foucault, modern power is *productive:* power creates, builds, and produces social knowledge, realities, and configurations. This is especially true in the production of subjects, in which various dominant and competing discourses create, shape, reproduce, and reconfigure ways in which we know ourselves or others as individuals and types of individuals—the discursive constitution of subjectivities. We cannot know ourselves or others as something—his most famous example, a homosexual person—if power-knowledge has not discursively constituted that subjectivity. We cannot know ourselves or others as something if we do not know that thing to begin with.[2]

In addition to being productive, Foucault sees power as a type of *relationship*, not a thing possessed—I have not "got the power," contra pop band Snap! and their dance hit from the 1990s. "Power" describes a type of relationship between individuals and groups. "Power is not a substance. Neither is it a mysterious property whose origin must be delved into. Power is only a certain type of relation between individuals" (Foucault, 2001, p. 324). Power is a modifier, not a noun. To try to contort it into common language, "a parent generally relates empoweredly over a child" or "the disempowering relationship of women toward medical expertise in the nineteenth century" or "the state disempowers same-sex relationships by denying them legal marriage."

If power, then, is a quality of relationships rather than a thing possessed, it cannot be entirely possessed by one person or group. Power cannot be locked up or fixed. Therefore, power relationships must be understood as *multiple* and *mobile*. While generally a parent relates powerfully over a child, should the child call a local social service agency and claim abuse, a competing power relationship is exercised against the parent, drawing on the child's power relationships with the state and society. The empowered relation of the privileged figure of the child is a discursive formation understood as needing protection by the state. The state's investment in its future citizens competes with and can trump the disempowered relationship a child has with a parent. And, as any parent knows, at times even a strategic public tantrum can invert the parent-child power relationship as well. Power relations are also *reversible*, therefore.

A final and crucial point in understanding Foucaultian power relations is that they are *intentional*. They are not forces of nature, like wind or gravity. When critics claim that Foucault puts power relations everywhere, and therefore nowhere, they are missing this aspect of intentionality. There is always some intention behind the exerting of power relations, whether dominant, resistant, or some in-between hybrid. If power is relational, it exists between actors (including the institutions and technologies they create). If the actors do not act, no power relationship is enacted. Dis-/counter-/em- powering is, therefore, always intentional. Where there is no intent, there is no exercise of power relation, and therefore power is not "everywhere and nowhere."

Of particular interest to this project is the challenging of dominant power relations, a shared goal of both feminist and gay political social movements. As Foucault famously states, "There is no power without potential refusal or revolt" (2001, p. 324). Keeping in mind the linkage of power-knowledge, challenges to power are challenges to truth. Challenges to power-knowledge initiate as critique. As Faubion cites Foucault,

> If government, then, is a "social practice of subjecting individuals by mechanisms of power which lay claim to truth," critique will be "the movement by which the subject assumes the right to question truth on its effects of power, and power on its effects of truth." (Foucault & Faubion, 1994, p. xxxix)

Social movements, then, can be understood as attacks on dominant power-knowledge and its discourses. Foucault lists feminism among other contemporaneous "anti-authority struggles," such as the youth movement and patients' rights, and suggests certain commonalities: they are international, they target power effects, they are focused on immediate conflicts and solutions, they question governmental regulation of the individual, they both reflexively examine their own identities and, in so doing, resist authorities that would determine their identities for them, and they struggle against privileged knowledge—"the way in which knowledge *circulates* and functions, according to its relations to power" (2001, p. 331, emphasis mine). Circulation of knowledge is communication; therefore, communication must be central to challenges to dominant power-knowledge and its discourses.

> Those wishing to establish a relation between what is known and the political, social, or economic forms that serve as a context for that knowledge need to trace that relation by way of consciousness or the subject of knowledge. It seems to me that the real junction between the economico-political processes and the conflicts of knowledge might be found in those forms which are, at the same time, modes of power exercise and modes of knowledge acquisition and transmission. (2001, p. 52)

In other words, if a government knows that women are of lesser intelligence and gays are criminal or sick, this knowledge forms a junction with economic and political actions: women are therefore ineligible to vote, and gays are therefore punished, jailed, and denied civil rights of marriage and parenting. The task for such groups on the short end of that power relationships is to change that knowledge; to bring the state knowledge in line with their own, different subjective experience: their knowledge of themselves as full and decent human beings. They must transmit or communicate their knowledge to the state.

Indeed, Foucault describes communication, much like power, as a type of relation, not a thing, and sees communication and power as distinct, yet overlapping and interrelated, types of major relations (the third being objective capacity or goal-seeking relations). "[Power] relations are specific," he writes, "that is, they have nothing to do with exchange, production, communication, even though they combine with them" (2001, p. 324).

Foucault notes that the relations of power and communication (and also his third area, objective capacities or goal-directed activities) are overall variable and unstable. They change and are diverse. And yet, they can have instances of consolidation: "There are also 'blocks' in which the adjustment of abilities, the resources of communication, and power relations constitute regulated and concerted systems" (2001, p. 338), such as at a particular educational institution.

> These blocks, in which the deployment of technical capacities, the game of communications, and the relationships of power are adjusted to one another according to considered formulae, constitute what one might call, enlarging a little the sense of the word, "disciplines." (2001, p. 339)

Different disciplines may connect elements differently, such as the discipline of apprenticeship giving priority to relationships of communication. I am interested in the overlapping communicative and power relations between feminist women and gay men: how they have consolidated or not into blocks, such as opposing or united disciplines. Or, in Castells' language, how their networks organize into cooperative or competitive relations. However, as will become apparent over the course of this book, such stable identities and tidy binary relationships will unravel and multiply.

In terms of the specific social movements under examination here, Foucault is not explicit, aside from his famous argument about the discursive constitution of the homosexual. His applicability and relevance are suggested however, by his adoption by feminist scholars (although not without controversy) and his influence on queer activism and theory. What I find useful here is that, in line with his conception of power relations as reversible, so are those between social groups. A stable power relationship can change into a destabilized struggle. Opposition and confrontation are destabilized power relationships seeking stabilization into new or pre-existing power relations.

> Every strategy of confrontation dreams of becoming a relationship of power …. In fact, between a relationship of power and a strategy of struggle there is a reciprocal appeal, a perpetual linking and a perpetual reversal. At every moment, the relationship of power may become a confrontation between two adversaries. Equally, the relationship between adversaries in society may, at every moment, give place to the putting into operation of mechanisms of power. The consequence of this instability is the ability to decipher the same events and the same transformations either from inside the history of struggle or from the standpoint of the power relationships. The resulting interpretations will not consist of the same elements of meaning or the same links or the same types of intelligibility, though they refer to the same historical fabric, and each of the two analyses must have reference to the other. (2001, p. 347)

This is what this project is attempting to do. However, I am not interested in the social groups discussed above as "dominant" and "dominated." It is easy to read that passage in such a way, even though Foucault notably does not specify that. What I want to bring into legibility is the unstable relation between two dominated groups. Gay men and feminist women can at times have a stable power relation: We are allies, we are enemies. You are part of the dominant power I am struggling against, or you are with me in struggling against them. However, those are both, positive and negative, stable relations. They can change into unstable struggles. And while we might not typically think of gay men and feminist women struggling directly against one another, I argue that particularly in overlapping relations of power and communication, there are mighty struggles of knowledge and understanding. What are you? To what degree and in what ways are you like or not like me? Struggling around this axis of communication and power, relationships can stabilize into those of coalition or opposition.

Clearly then, my perspective is not an ontological one. I am not asserting that gay men and feminist women are inherently allies or enemies, then proceeding from that point to ask, why they do or don't know, communicate, and act upon that knowledge of each other's being. I am, however, asserting that their places in the historical fabric can be interpreted in such a way as to perceive them as having similar or overlapping power relations with dominant culture. My intervention is to foreground this particular perspective, as I believe it has been neglected. From there, I ask, what happens? What has happened? What is happening now?

Manuel Castells: Communication and Power in the Network Society

Although Foucault's analyses tend to be more historical, generally stopping short of the twentieth century, I find his concepts nevertheless quite productive for the analysis of contemporary phenomena, as do many other scholars, including Castells, who draws on him in various ways. Castells offers conceptual tools for thinking about contemporary social structures that help connect these Foucaultian concepts to recent and contemporary social movements, and also offers a useful emphasis on communication. Indeed, it is central to his book, *Communication Power*. Drawing on Foucault and others, Castells conceives of power similarly as the ability to exert will over others, specifically, to change their minds and thereby actions. He is explicit, however, in specifying that this is accomplished largely through communication networks. He links mass-media messages and internal psychological process through cognitive neuroscience: Mass media shapes and frames messages, creates metaphoric understandings, and harnesses emotions in ways that are not merely literary descriptions of texts, but have biological counterparts in neurological functioning. This is how the communication of narratives, through media, has the power to affect people's actions. This is also the route that must be taken by social movements: "Social actors aiming to reprogram society must also go through the communication networks to transform consciousness and views in people's minds in order to challenge the powers that be" (2009, p. 53).

Indeed, Castells' hypothesis is that communication lies at the heart of global culture. However, by this he does not mean the communication of specific ideas or concepts, but the generalized, abstract processes of communication.

> *The common culture of the global network society is a culture of protocols of communication enabling communication between different cultures on the basis not of shared values but of the sharing of the value of communication.* ... The new culture is not made of content but of process. ... a culture of communication for the sake of communication. (2009, p. 38 emphasis original)

How does Castells conceive of power within this network society? Much like Foucault, Castells sees power as relational and multiple: "Power relationships are constructed in a complex interaction between multiple spheres of social practice" (2009, p. 5). After reviewing various theorizations of sources of social power—violence, discourse, coercion, persuasion, political domination, and cultural framing—he says these haven't really changed. What has changed is that power is now primarily organized in networks at local-global articulations, as opposed to local or national hierarchies: "Power is the relational capacity to impose an actor's will over another actor's will on the basis of the structural capacity of domination embedded in the institutions of society" (2009, p. 44). In Castells' more object-oriented language, "the power holders are networks themselves" (2009, p. 45).

Communication is centrally important to Castells' perspective on power, yet, in line with Foucault, he does not conflate power and communication. His titular concept is not communication-power or communication = power, but "communication power." In his native Spanish, the title is "Comunicación y Poder," communication *and* power. In English, communication modifies power; it is a type of power, not all power. It is, in Foucault's language, the cases in which power and communication relationships "overlap," "support," and "use each other"—cases Castells argue have become increasingly significant and even Foucault, writing decades ago, recognized as "exceedingly important." For example, note the communicative acts necessary for the networking power exercise of switching:

> Switching different networks requires the ability to construct a cultural and organizational interface, a common language, a common medium, a support of universally accepted value: exchange value. In our world, the typical, all-purpose form of exchange value is money. (2009, p. 52)

Ultimately, the most important area of communication and power, for Castells, is global media: "People make up their minds according to the images and information they retrieve from communication networks" (2009, p. 315).[3]

Castells summarizes his argument about communication and power thus:

1. Power is multidimensional and is constructed around networks programmed in each domain of human activity according to the interests and values of empowered actors. But all networks of power exercise their power by influencing the human mind predominantly (but not solely) through multimedia networks of mass communication. Thus, communication networks are the fundamental networks of power making in society.

2. Networks of power in various domains of human activity are networked among themselves. They do not merge. Instead, they engage in strategies of partnership and competition, practicing cooperation and competition simultaneously by forming ad hoc networks around specific projects and by changing partners depending on their interests in each context and in each moment in time.

3. The network of power constructed around the state and the political system does play a fundamental role in the overall networking of power. … While communication networks process the construction of meaning on which power relies, the state constitutes the default network for the proper functioning of all other power networks (2009, p. 425).

Entangling Foucault and Castells

Foucault famously theorizes identities as discursively constituted. Indeed, although my objects of study are feminist women and gay men, I am operating with the perspective of each of those four words and the concepts they invoke—identities and subjectivities political, gendered, sexed, and sexual—are not fixed, transhistorical stable essences but instead are historically and culturally contingent configurations of power-knowledge: there are discourses that shape our knowledge of each. Castells' network model is amenable to this. Unlike affiliations in traditional society (being born into a geographic region, family, clan, tribe, family business, etc.) network affiliations tend to be more voluntary and goal-directed. This perspective helps avoid the ontological thinking of whether gay men and feminist women are, essential and universally, allies or not, and the subsequent questions of why or why not they do or do not recognize and act upon this "fact" of their beings. Instead, it allows us to start from a position of instability, mobility, and fluidity—as is appropriate, given the fluid, mobile, and unstable nature of these very identity categories. A coalition model, as seen in social movement theory, presumes varying degrees of merging: either assimilating into a unified whole (as in the "melting pot" metaphor once used for American immigration) or joining together under a shared construct while maintaining distinction within it (the subsequent "mosaic" model). A network perspective sees the issue as, not of one of joining or merging, but of partnership or cooperation, which presumes nothing shared other than a shared goal, which may be very limited and contingent. Moreover, it also allows for a perspective that breaks the ally/enemy binary: The absence of cooperation does not necessarily imply antagonism.

For example, both Foucault and Castells frame communication and power generally in terms of relations between dominant and oppressed. How do groups in disempowering relations resist them and forge new relations with government and public opinion—how do they change the common-sense knowledge that drives representative democracy? How do they change what is known, specifically about them, in order to change the political and economic actions taken on them? This is of crucial importance. But my inquiry here is of a different component in this process, one I suggest is neglected in their power theorizations: the knowledge disempowered groups have of each other. A certain critical mass is necessary often to intervene in public knowledge. This can be attained by coalescing individuals around a cause or discourse. It can also be accomplished through coalitions, bringing groups together. This is the focus of my inquiry here: the knowledge disempowered groups have of each other. What are their fields of knowledge—their discourses—about each other, particularly in terms of relations to dominant power? Do they see each other and, if so, is it as similar or different, as enemies, allies, or something in-between? How do they transmit knowledge—how do they communicate—about and to each other to (re)form these knowledge, which is a necessary step in collectively challenging dominant knowledge?

While agreeing with Castells' idea that the state and political power form the default network, that is not my focus here. Both he and Foucault tend to focus on relations to and with dominant power and knowledge: government, mass media, public opinion, etc. I am in no way suggesting that these are not important, or even of primary importance. My interests here, however, are not primarily with the mass media, opinion, or government. This is not to disregard them, but merely to say I am here more often focusing on different parts of the process, on different actors and moments, ones that I feel have been neglected at times. As Castells writes, "The interaction between cultural change and political change produces social change. … Multiple changes proceed at different paces in a variety of groups" (2009, p. 300). By focusing on two disempowered groups and their relations of communication and power, I am not suggesting they alone can change society. I am saying they are part of the process. While not in dominant power relations, they are nonetheless power networks. They do not exist in a social vacuum.

Castells theorizes that power networks connect without merging, and how they cooperate without giving up their own realms, through programming and switching. My interest here is in how these two particular subordinate networks program and switch to and about each other: When the goals are programmed with shared objectives of social revolution, their networks switch power cooperatively. But part of this process is internally programming not only their own networks' goals, but also power-knowledge—shaping discourses of who and what another network is. To know whether or not your network would benefit from cooperating and switching power with another network, one has to know who and what that other network is: its goals, its constituents, etc. Thus, the formation of knowledge and truth is a crucial first step. How does one network produce knowledge of the truth of another? A precondition of switching, then, is internal programming or discursive formation of knowledge.

Castells adds concreteness and contemporary perspectives to Foucault. Foucault also addresses what I find to be a weak point in Castells. In *Communication Power*, Castells turns to cognitive science and linguistic political science to attempt to theorize the connection between communicating knowledge and social change. Castells links the analysis of "emotional language," such as scare tactics or bandwagon appeals, from mass communication and political science (and arguably, although not cited, rhetoric and literary studies) to contemporary neuroscience that supports understandings of emotion and similar aesthetic concepts, such as metaphor, as empirical biological activities in the brain. Drawing on the work of Antonio Damasio, he asserts that it has been

> demonstrated, experimentally and theoretically, the prominent role of emotions and feelings in social behavior. Emotions are distinctive patterns of chemical and neural responses resulting from the brain's detection of an emotionally competent stimulus (ECS), that is, changes in the brain and in the body-proper induced by the content of some perception (such as the emotion of fear when confronted with an image of, or evoking, death). Emotions are deeply wired in our brain. (2009, p. 140)

These are not merely emotions but also what are typically thought of as aesthetic techniques, such as metaphor. Here Castells turns to the work of George Lakoff and others, who have argued that

Our brain thinks in metaphors, which can be accessed in language but *are physical structures in the brain.* ... Metaphors are critical to connect language (thus human communication) and brain circuitry. It is through metaphors that narratives are constructed. Narratives are composed of frames, which are the structures of the narrative that correspond to the structures of the brain that resulted in the brain's activity over time. *Frames are neural networks of association that can be accessed from the language through metaphorical connections.* Framing means activating specific neural networks. (2009, p. 142, emphasis original).[4]

Similar turns to consciousness can be seen in various fields' appropriation of psychoanalytic theories and, more recently, theories of affect. Foucault, however, resists this turn to "changing hearts and minds":

The problem is not changing people's consciousnesses—or what's in their heads—but the political, economic, institutional regime of the production of truth. It's not a matter of emancipating truth from every system of power (which would be a chimera, for truth is already power) but of detaching the power of truth from the forms of hegemony, social, economic, and cultural, within which it operates at the present time. The political question, to sum up, is not error, illusion, alienated consciousness, or ideology; it is truth itself. (Power 132–133).

In other words, the focus should be not on how people choose what to believe, but how truth is produced—for truth does not require belief.

In sum, this project approaches the political activism of gay men and feminist women (acknowledged as discursively constituted subjectivities) each as networks of resistant social movements engaged in challenging dominant discourses that exercise disempowering relations with each of them. Although both are ultimately interested in trying to reprogram dominant networks, I am interested in the switching of these two networks, what they know and communicate about and to each other, and how they see each other as collaborators or competitors.

Manuel Castells suggests that power is the ability to change minds and thereby actions. This is accomplished largely through communication networks. Mass media shapes and frames messages, creates metaphoric understandings, and harnesses emotions in ways that are not merely literary descriptions of texts, but have biological counterparts in neurological functioning. This is how the communication of narratives through self-mass media has the power to affect a person's actions. "Social actors aiming to reprogram society must also go through the communication networks to transform consciousness and views in people's minds in order to challenge the powers that be" (2009, p. 53). An organized form of reprogramming would be social movements, which Castells conceptualizes as "social actors aiming for cultural change (a change in values)" (2009, p. 300).

Michel Foucault connects power and knowledge, which together shape dominant and competing discourses. Foucault describes modern power as productive—creating, building, and challenging social knowledge, realities, and configurations. Foucault also sees modern power as a type of relationship between and among individuals and groups. Power is a quality of relationships rather than a thing possessed and must be understood as multiple and mobile. Foucaultian power relations are intentional. They are not forces of nature, like wind or gravity. When critics claim he puts power relations everywhere, and therefore nowhere, they are missing this aspect of intentionality. When power is relational, it exists between actors (including the institutions and technologies they create). If the actors do not act, no power relationships are enacted. Where there is no intent, there is no power relation, and, therefore, power is not "everywhere and nowhere."

For this book, I conceive of the social movements of feminist women and gay men each as networks attempting to change their power relationships with dominant culture, through combined processes of communication and network reconfigurations. Within this process, my focus is on these two networks' communication to and about each other as their networks dynamically program and reprogram themselves with codes of cooperation or competition vis-a-vis each other. Such programming works to change the discursive formations of power-knowledge.

In simpler language, I am interested in what is known about feminist women and gay men, in relation to one another, and how that has been expressed through a variety of stories, especially their own.

Reflexive Positioning

Written by a feminist-identified, cisgender, gay man, of American-Anglo descent, I start with the presumption that, in patriarchal, heteronormative cultures, gay/queer/bisexual men share with women obstacles to equality, such as sexism, devaluation of femininity, violence, erotophobia, and binary dualisms of identity (e.g., MacKinnon, 1997; Owens, 1987; Radicalesbians, 1997; Rubin, 1997; Sedgwick, 1985). One of the key points of feminism has been that biology is not destiny. A woman is not naturally destined to be a mother or perform mothering. One of the core contributions of feminist thought is this conceptual separation of biological sex—categorization at birth as male or female, based on genitalia—from gender—the presumed-to-be-associated behaviors and attributes of masculinity and femininity. This, in turn, informs our understanding of sexuality. Sexual and romantic attractions are subsets of gender: the expected attributes and behaviors associated with biological sex. A man is expected to be masculine, and part of masculinity is being attracted to women. A woman is expected to be feminine, and part of femininity is being attracted to men. Such cisgender, heterosexual norms have reinforced conceptual binaries around these topics, but also neglected variations in terms of affection, relationships, presentation, perception, and other dimensions.

Feminism breaks the links in these chains of association, which is why, for me, feminist thought and political activism have been necessary foundations, whether acknowledged or not, to LGBTQ identities, political organizing, and scholarship. I could be a man who loves men without feminism, but, without feminism, I would not be able to think of myself as a gay man, let alone a gay, cisgender man who fluctuates from masculine to ironically fluid gender presentations.

I approach this project from a perspective of situated knowledge (Haraway, 1999). Rather than claiming an objective truth, I am acknowledging my specific perspective and position as a researcher. As this feminist perspective argues, a researcher should acknowledge their subjectivity, the experiences and insights that shape them and give them unique insights into their topics. Such transparency and reflexivity are in contrast to the traditional scientific notion of objectivity—what Haraway calls the "god trick" (1999, p. 177) of pretending to be able to rise above one's situated experience in the world. Feminist science studies scholar Daston (1999) has further denaturalized this scientific notion of objectivity by charting its historic and cultural contingencies.

An insistence on acknowledging contingency is central to post-structural and other forms of feminism, as well as queer theory more broadly. Simply put, categories of identity—such as sex, gender, and sexuality—but also race, nationality, and, as I focused on in my previous book, health (Scott, 2018)—are, to varying degrees, social constructs. The social meaning of femininity, for example, varies widely by time, place, and social group. The dynamic, fluid nature of identity categories is another presumed theoretical perspective of this book. The presumption of such categories as essential and stable inhibits potential coalitions: stereotypical, ideological perspectives prevent individuals and groups from seeing others as having the potential to become allies. They "are" what they are—fixed and unchanging—and this precludes the possibility of seeing what they (and we all) could be.

However, I fully acknowledge that this project risks reifying as natural and essential the identities and subjectivities of the categories of "man," "woman," "gay," and "feminist." It also at times runs the risk of erasing other identities, such as lesbian, transgender, bisexual, and others, and to generalize the wide variety of different types of feminisms. My choice to deploy these identity categories is a brute one: to force a juxtaposition between these two groups. I am not ignoring any of the complexities involved, but I am insisting on pressing the questions raised by putting these two groups side by side. As a critical scholar, my underlying perspective is that these two groups *should* work together for social change. By insisting on this conjuncture, I am trying to draw this perspective into the foreground. It cannot be all just left to lesbians, a perspective I will address more in a subsequent chapter. Research findings are determined by the questions asked. This project attempts to ask different questions, in hopes they might be productive in aiding future research and political action.

The power-knowledge of identity categories is dynamic. As feminist science scholar Karen Barad (2007) proposes in her philosophy of agential realism, we are not a universe of fixed, stable things or objects. We are all active, ongoing phenomena. We are each always changing and growing in a constant state of becoming and re-becoming. So, too, are material objects: a wooden door warps, a rock cliff erodes, and a glacier melts. So, too, are the objects of knowledge. "Marriage" in the United States is not what it was ten years ago. Meanwhile, to borrow a term from Barad, these phenomena, these ongoing processes of (re)becoming, are *entangled* with one another. As I age, I use the upper shelf in my closet less, delaying the day it breaks. My voice and breath enter the bodies of others. The increased summer heat from climate change warps my front door such that I sprain my wrist trying to wrench it free. In small and large ways, we entangle with one another's ongoing being.

This book is what Barad calls an *agential cut*. A cut is similar to framing, culling, bracketing, or editing, but with a crucial distinction: it acknowledges this as a process of boundary-making, and not a true, essential separation. It takes responsibility for the process of bringing phenomena and their patterns into legibility, but without presuming they are disconnected from all the other phenomena that make up the universe, including those making the cut.

This perspective of a universe of not objects and things, but active phenomena and processes—verbs, not nouns—brings me back to feminism, specifically, feminist art and process art. As an undergraduate student at the School of the Art Institute of Chicago, I was fascinated by feminist artists of the 1970s and 1980s, particularly those working in time-based media, such as performance, installation, video, film, sound, and even versions of painting and sculpture that foregrounded the experiential processes of their creation, rather than end products. I studied with women performance artists, such as Lin Hixson and Nancy Forest Brown. Lin directed engrossing, non-narrative events for her performance group, Goat

Island, which were incredibly physical series of real actions, not the metaphoric or expressive movements of dance. Nancy inhabited personas who staged real-life events or showed up at them, from a lesbian bar owner celebrating her and her lover's tenth anniversary to an attendee at a gallery art opening whose purse overflowed with viscera, possibly afterbirth. They introduced me to the work of artists such as Linda Montano, who did a series of life performances involving being tied or handcuffed to other persons for periods of time. This focus on art as, not taking place in a gallery or stage, but in one's daily life, resonated with the feminist adage, "the personal is political."

This book draws upon such traditions. Process is part of my methodology. The experience of searching for these stories is important in addition to the stories themselves. Finding data is too often neglected as a source of insight and information *in addition to* the data itself. This project, then, is one of performative scholarship. I am performing, enacting an interventionist juxtaposition between feminist women and gay men. My agential cut is not simply a research question, but also as provocation, and a personal journey for myself.

Themes

I turn now to introducing key themes of the relationships between gay men and feminist women. Throughout this project, several stories have reappeared. One is the presumption of an inherent *commonality* between gay men and feminist women. This could be evidenced, for example, in their shared enjoyment of certain entertainments and aesthetic cultures. For example, a 1968 women's discussion group on sex included this exchange:

> But you know, we miss out. We just kept so busy playing love object, we miss out on masculine beauty.

> You can see that in art, too. It's completely distorted. The only time masculine bodily beauty was celebrated was by the Greeks or Michelangelo, who were homosexual. That's the closest we've come to the female view of the world. ("Women Rap About Sex," 1968)

Commonalities could lead to *collaborations*, another narrative. A 1970 clipping from *Liberation News Service* described a coalition that included gay men gathering to protest the arrest of Angela Davis. "Hundreds of enraged people," the article states, "Black, brown, white, many gay—gathered in front of the Women's House of Detention in New York's Greenwich Village on October 13, [1970] within a half hour of Angela Davis' arrest in a midtown motor hotel" ("Angela," n.d.).

In seeming contradiction, however, were stories of inherent *conflict and opposition*. These included explicitly marking difference, describing how one group inhibits or oppresses the other directly, or how the two groups were in competition for social acceptance and progress in civil rights. For example, the minutes from a meeting of the 1970s radical feminist group DAR II assert a position on homosexuality that clearly distinguishes between men and women:

> The U.S. is an imperialist country with oppressive institutions (MALE SUPREMACY). Homosexuality is a response reaction to male supremist relations and institutions. Lesbianism is understandable because it is a reaction by women to male supremacy—Male homosexuality is the height of male supremacy. (Dykes for the Second American Revolution, 1975)

Demarcating anti-woman sexual practices was also applied, at times, to pornography, and also to fetish interests and other non-normative sexual practices. For example, *Majority Report* newsmagazine in 1977 published Ti-Grace Atkinson's address to the Eulenspiegel Society, the longest-running BD/SM education and support group in the United States. In "Why I'm Against S/M Lib," Atkinson declared that, "By no stretch of the imagination is the Women's Movement a movement for sexual liberation" (1977, p. 17). While speaking specifically about sado-masochistic practices, her opinion clearly had implications that positioned the women's movement as oppositional to all sexuality-based movements, including those of gay men. Finally, in addition to these ideological differences, opposition also appeared in the sense of *competition* between the two social movements, as in struggling against each other for media visibility, representation, and news coverage.

A more positive story was that of *intellectual contributions*. This theme dealt with how areas of academic disciplines, such as feminist theory, LGBTQ studies, women's studies, and queer theory, drew upon one another. They also entangled with similar phenomena in often overlapping activist movements, as well as with the way people looked at and interacted with the world in their daily lives. For example, women organizing against pornography, and what was thought to be actual footage of women being murdered in the film *Snuff* and others, looked to a gay example:

> A national alert system that focuses public attention on offensive programming, films, magazines, etc., is an important strategy. The National Gay Task Force has

organized such a system: members are encouraged to write letters, make calls, join demonstrations, and organize boycotts around particularly damaging or dangerous media portrayals of gays. They can effectively concentrate pressure on a specific target instead of wasting energy or uncoordinated efforts. Similar pressure tactics … could be used … to stop promoting movies like *Snuff*. (Friedman & Yankowski, 1976, p. 29)

These thematic narratives, and as well as others, will appear throughout this book. They multiply and grow more complex, ultimately pointing to future avenues for investigation.

Overview of Book

In the first chapter, "The Received View: Public Memory, Historiographic Discourses, and LGBTQ Media," I ask, what has been said about these two groups and their relations? Here I begin with a discourse analysis of historical and non-fiction books about the LGBT and women's social movements. I examine the frequency, extent, and content of these two groups' discussions of each other in them. This is used to establish a "received view" of what historical discourses say have been the two groups' conceptions of and interactions with each other. These historiographic discourses are approached as an institutional contributor to the foundation of emergent public memory about these two groups. Findings suggest that, while references between groups are common, they are brief and shallow. Analysis of the texts finds three major themes of commonality, opposition, and intellectual contributions. However, the books tend to marginalize one or the other: Gay male histories mostly only deal with feminism as it relates to working with or not working with lesbians. Similarly, feminist histories tend to address mostly the lesbian issue. No work has yet put these two groups side by side, front and center, staging this explicit juxtaposition. I turn, therefore, to a survey of LGBTQ popular magazines and publications for feminist-related articles. Arranged chronologically rather than thematically, I create a timeline in order to see the received view from an alternate angle. Combined, the discourses of historiographies and popular media present a background of the stories that have been told—the received view—against which the subsequent chapters of original research will be presented.

In "Networked Social Change: Feminism and LGBTQ Movements in South Carolina, USA," I move to broaden this received view with primary historical research. As a case study, I explore this state's archives of women's and LGBTQ activism since mid-century. Specifically, historic artifacts are examined to see how they, and the stories they suggest, support, contradict, or complicate the received view. My findings show a more complicated history of dynamic networks and shifting affinities, with the concept of network "switchers" expanded to include ad hoc "switching moments." Moreover, the use of South Carolina as a case study contributes original data to a region—the conservative and often rural US Southeast—that has been frequently neglected in feminist and LGBTQ histories and research.

Having examined nonfiction stories told by others about the two groups, then interpreted stories myself from historical artifacts, in the third chapter I turn to the stories these two groups have told about each other. "Representing Each Other: Gays in *The Second Wave*/Lesbians in AIDS Cinema" asks, how has each group depicted the other in internal cultural productions? The first part of this chapter focuses on the "liberation moment" of the late 1960s–1970s, an approximate time in which Western feminisms are categorized as in their "second wave," and the modern LGBTQ rights movement comes into being. Within the context of other equality- and justice-based social movements (civil rights, youth, environment, anti-war, etc.), this era is often described as one in which these movements are connected by a frequently, if not homogeneously, shared ethos of liberation. Broad revolutionary and explicit changes to social understandings and practices were the goals, rather than discrete accommodations through legislative changes. This is perhaps the period of greatest potential collaboration between feminists and gay men, as there were many shared aims, such as destroying patriarchy, undoing sexism, challenging heteronormative gender roles, and liberating sexuality from Puritanical shame.

To examine this era, I start by performing a close reading of a single collection of texts: *The Second Wave: A Reader of Feminist Theory* (Nicholson, 1997). This comprehensive and well-regarded collection of second-wave feminist writings presents perspectives including those of lesbian separatism, women of color, post-structuralism, and radical socialism. Across these varied voices gathered under the "second wave" umbrella, I examine the traces of presence, and often the glaring absences, of gay men and gay male sexuality. When mentioned, and almost never directly addressed, the positioning is a conflicting array of enemy and fellow traveler, yet they are never directly hailed as the audience of the writings. The call for collaboration one might imagine, during the second wave of all times, is nowhere to be found.

The second half of the chapter searches for lesbians in AIDS cinema. According to the lesbian switcher narrative, this was a moment of great collaboration between lesbian and gay men. If, as some accounts go, lesbians came rushing to the aid of gay men during the health crisis, making for a rare moment of women and gay men working together, how are they represented in AIDS dramas, documentaries, and docudrama? Looking for lesbians, I compile a list of AIDS films. While neither exhaustive nor absolute, my review finds lesbians rarely visible in AIDS cinema of any genre. Assessing common themes in the depiction of women in general, I group these narratives as depicting women who are either non-Western documentary subjects, Western narrative protagonists with AIDS, or caregivers to persons with AIDS. I then focus on four films produced by and/ or for gay men, about AIDS, which *do* have lesbians: *Chocolate Babies*, *The Normal Heart*, *How to Survive a Plague*, and *The Hours*. Each film presents a different take on lesbians during AIDS, from integral coalition members and subservient team players to unnamed faces and caregivers struggling with that role. None, however, focus on the lesbian switcher as its main narrative.

In "Talking Amongst Ourselves: Gay Men and Feminist Women (Before Trump)," the feminist women and gay men speak for themselves. In 2012—a time that felt far removed from second-wave feminism and AIDS but, as I reflect upon it now, feels also very far away from the present—I gathered four focus groups, two of feminist women and two of gay men. As part of their conversations, they were asked to reflect upon the women's and LGBTQ equality movements, and also their intersections with and ideas about each other. Their conversations were edited into excerpts and arranged into thematic groups, first the men, then the women, for comparison. However, I chose in this chapter to limit my analysis to these editorial acts and minor commentaries. My goal here is to let the participants speak for themselves. The resulting conversations are rich and varied, adding more layers and nuance to previous themes of commonality and conflict, ranging from resentment of the Gay Best Friend stereotype to a desire to center gender as the core concept of social action. Far from consensus, these optimistic and pessimistic stories offer insights into successful and failed coalitions, and also ways to think about future collaborations.

In the final chapter, I attempt to move beyond the discrete conversations of focus groups to the broader conversations online. In "Queering Networks, Entangled Platforms: Feminist Women and Gay Men in Online Media," two questions are central. The first moves from feminist women and gay men talking about themselves to examining them as the topics of broader conversations in the general public. How often do persons talk about feminist women and gay men together, at the same time, and, when they do, what is being communicated? The second question moves to an issue of communication networks, asking, how are online networks of feminist women and gay men connected? Given that the data-scraping and network analysis tools used in this chapter provided snapshots of a moment in time, I chose to queer these network portraits by repeating them seven years later, after having completed the other research components of this project. Revisiting the original conversations, networks, and influencers shows consistency in what people are saying, but rapid change in the communication platforms. The dynamism of social media is explored here as having strengths and weakness, something important to consider with regards to the stability of professional political organizations. Finally, an ironic decay is found in which the networked links of feminist women and gay men end up leading to the pages of their far-right ideological enemies.

I conclude in a reflexive mode, contemplating the initial goals of this project and its findings from the context of the era of US President Donald J. Trump. Considering the current states of feminism and LGBTQ politics, as well as the instability of those identity categories, I re-examine lesbian separatism as a potential way to rethink identity and identity politics.

Notes

1. While attempting to avoid language which essentializes biological sex, gender, and sexuality, or collapses their distinctions, at times I will choose to use terms as encountered in their source materials or my original experience. This is to avoid imposing too strong of a presentism on a historical project primarily, retaining respect for my sources and reflecting the ways in which biological, sex, gender, and sexuality were understood and expressed at that time or in that school of thought.

2. Of course, this is misrepresented as a form of extreme nominalism that suggests this thing—e.g., homosexual persons—did not exist prior. This is a specious misrepresentation. The actual argument is that while, of course, many people throughout history had homosexual acts and relationships, but they did not know themselves as nor were they known as "a homosexual" in our modern understanding of the category because, as a point of knowledge, it did not yet exist.

3. This assertion neglects the ability of audiences, to some degree at least, to make up their minds in opposition or negotiation to mass media, which Castells positions as, if penetrable, nevertheless still the dominant communication network. However, this does not address issues of near or relative invisibility. What if the issue one is making one's mind up about is not represented in mass media? Alternative or specialty media? What if it is only marginally represented, say, in infrequent negative stereotypes? Arguably, one would agree with those stereotypes. Unless, however, one is also in the position of invisibility or misrepresentation in media. From such a position, then,

akin to double-consciousness or standpoint, one would have a fundamental distrust of media representations, particularly those that were limited, marginalizing, and negative as the representations of your own network were. In such cases, I argue other sources of information and images—alternative, independent, and community media; word of mouth, art—become even more important.

4. Castells' move here is to biologize, make empirical, and thereby validate centuries of textual scholarship. From classical rhetoric and literary studies to mass communication and cultural studies, scholars have analyzed how techniques of storytelling (producing narratives that harness and evoke emotions, articulate relationships through metaphors, and frame the issues being discussed in particular ways) change people's minds. Whether named persuasion, argumentation, identification or propaganda, it is not a new model. And it, and the interpretivist, subjectivist, textual realms it inhabits, have been dismissed and criticized by scientists as having a faulty gap: they do not explain how narrative content causes change in the mind. Bodies of theory, such as psychoanalysis and recent studies of affect (noticeably missing from Castells' survey of scholarship on emotion), have attempted to fill in this gap. Critical theorists argued that media was simply powerful enough and audiences weak, anesthetized, distracted, and/or uneducated enough for it to just happen. The modern field of communication, particularly its social science wing, begins with the early twentieth-century propaganda studies attempting to prove this scientifically in laboratory experiments—what today often goes by the name media effects and focuses more on the effects of violent, stereotypical, or sexualized media content on audiences' thinking, values, and behaviors. I find such cognitive work reductive and misplaced. Bestowing too much power on the media, as many before me have argued, diminishes our understanding of human agency. Much like structural linguistics, they veer into universalizing arguments I try to avoid. Laboratory experiments and neural scans neglect the complicated web of social factors and contexts that play into attitude formation and opinion change over time. The focus on responses to stimuli, such as narratives, neglects questions over the limits of how and in what ways narratives can be shaped, shared, and populated with ideas. This is not to say that any of these perspectives are wrong; for my purposes, they simply focus on an unproductive area. Suffice to say, information (be it factual, associative, or emotional) plays a significant role in our formation of the knowledge upon which we act in our lives. The sharing and transmission of this information is communication. Therefore, communication influences our actions. I am not interested in pursuing the specific mechanisms of cognitive knowledge formation, be they neurolinguistic or psychoanalytic. To use Castells' example, I am repeatedly confronted with images not merely evoking death but explicitly depicting it. Some may provoke fear, but, in the genre of horror films of which I am a fan, far more provoke bored comparisons to better depictions, others provoke laughter and glee. The endless parade of sexualized female imagery to which I am inundated in media provoke precious little pupillary dilation, palm perspiration

or penile tumescence. Indeed, as a gay man born in 1969, and even more so the gay men that came before me, our sexual and romantic predilections stand in stark contrast to the power of a media that has almost entirely until recent years depicted us negatively if at all and endlessly and vehemently asserted the joy and goodness of our opposite. As a more subjective, critical scholar, I am content to believe that stories are powerful.

References

Ambjörnsson, F., Laskar, P., & Steorn, P. (1). (2010). Introduction. *Lambda Nordica, 15*(3–4), 9–14. Retrieved from https://www.lambdanordica.org/index.php/lambdanordica/article/view/289

Angela. (n.d.). Liberation News Service, possibly from the feminist news publication. *Off Our Backs*. Retrieved from http://scriptorium.lib.duke.edu/wlm/angela/

Atkinson, T. (1977, Sept. 29). Why I'm against S/M lib: Address to Eulenspiegel Society. *Majority Report*, p. 17.

Barad, K. (2007). *Meeting the universe halfway: Quantum physics and the entanglement of matter and meaning*. Durham: Duke University Press.

Biltereyst, D., Lotze, K., & Meers, P. (2012). Triangulation in historical audience research: Reflections and experiences from a multimethodological research project on cinema audiences in Flander s. *Participations: Journal of Audience and Reception Studies 9*(2), 690–715.

Browne, K., & Nash, C. J. (2016). Queer methods and methodologies: An introduction. In C. J. Nash & K. Browne (Eds.), *Queer methods and methodologies: Intersecting queer theories and social science research*. New York: Routledge.

Castells, M. (2001). *The Internet galaxy: Reflections on the Internet, business, and society*. New York: Oxford University Press.

Castells, M. (2009). *Communication power*. Oxford, UK: Oxford University Press.

Castells, M., Fernández-Ard'evol, M., Qiu, J., & Sey, A. (2007). *Mobile communication and society: A global perspective*. Cambridge, MA: The MIT Press.

Council, C. R. (2015). *The girl at the fence*. Morgan Hill, CA: Bookstand Publishing.

DAR II (Dyke for the Second American Revolution). (1975). Revolutionary Union. Meeting minutes from January 19. Retrieved from http://scriptorium.lib.duke.edu/wlm/darii/darii-01.19.75.html

Daston, L. (1999). Objectivity and the escape from perspective: In M. Biagioli (Ed.), *The science studies reader* (pp. 172–188). New York: Routledge.

De Laat, M., Lally, V., Lipponen, L., & Simons, R. J. (2007). Online teaching in networked learning communities: A multi-method approach to studying the role of the teacher. *Instructional Science, 35*(3), 257–286.

Ellingson, L. L. (2014). "The truth must dazzle gradually" Enriching relationship research using a crystallization framework. *Journal of Social and Personal relationships, 31*(4), 442–450.

Foucault, M. (1980). *Power/knowledge: Selected interviews and other writings, 1972–1977*. New York: Pantheon.

Foucault, M. (1990). *The history of sexuality Volume One An introduction*. New York: Random House.

Foucault, M. (2001). *Power*. New York: The New Press.

Foucault, M., & Faubion, J. D. (1994). *Michel Foucault, power, essential works of Foucault*. New York: Penguin.

Friedman, D., & Yankowski, L. (1976, Fall). Snuffing sexual violence. *Quest Magazine, 3*, 2, 24–29.

Halberstam, J. (1998). *Female masculinity*. Durham, NC: Duke University Press.

Haraway, D. (1999). Situated knowledges: The science question in feminism and the privilege of partial perspective. In M. Biagioli (Ed.), *The science studies reader* (pp. 172–188). New York: Routledge.

Harris, D. (1997). *The rise and fall of gay culture*. Westport, CT: Hyperion.

Hevesi, A. G. (2001, June). *Directory of lesbian, gay, bisexual and transgender services and resources*. New York City: Office of Community Relations.

MacKinnon, C. A. (1997). Sexuality. In L. Nicholson (Ed.), *The second wave: A reader in feminist theory* (pp. 158–180). New York: Psychology Press.

Nicholson, L. J. (Ed.). (1997). *The second wave: A reader in feminist theory*. New York: Psychology Press.

Orr, C. M. (1999). Tellings of our activist pasts: Tracing the emergence of women's studies at San Diego State College. *Women's Studies Quarterly, 27*(3/4), 212–229.

Owens, C. (1987). Outlaws: Gay men in feminism. In A. J. a. P. Smith (Ed.), *Men in feminism* (pp. 219–232). Methuen.

Radicalesbians. (1997). The woman identified woman. In L. Nicholson (Ed.), *The second wave: A reader in feminist theory* (pp. 153–157). New York: Psychology Press.

Richardson, L. (2000). Writing: A method of inquiry. In N. K. Denzin & Y. S. Lincoln (Eds.), *Handbook of qualitative research* (2nd ed., pp. 923–943). Sage.

Rubin, G. (1997). The traffic in women: Notes on the political economy of sex. In L. Nicholson (Ed.), *The second wave: A reader in feminist theory* (pp. 27–62). New York: Psychology Press.

Saukko, P. (2003). *Doing research in cultural studies: An introduction to classical and new methodological approaches*. Sage.

Scott, D. T. (1997). *Execution, Texas, 1987: A novel*. St. Martin's Press.

Scott, D. T. (1999). *Strategic sex: Why they won't keep it in the bedroom*. Cleis Press.

Scott, D. T. (2005). *One of these things is not like the other*. Suspect Thoughts Press.

Scott, D. T. (2009). *Love hard: Stories 1989–2009*. Queer Mojo.

Scott, D. T. (2013). Intertextuality as 'resonance': Masculinity and anticapitalism in pet shop boys' score for Battleship Potemkin. *Music, Sound, and the Moving Image, 7*(1), 53–82.

Scott, D. T. (2018). *Pathology and technology: Killer apps and sick users*. Peter Lang Publishers.

Sedgwick, E. K. (1985). *Between men: English literature and male homosocial desire*. Columbia University Press.

Williams, W. W. (1997). The equality crisis: Some reflections on culture, courts, and feminism. In L. Nicholson (Ed.), *The second wave: A reader in feminist theory* (pp. 71–92). New York: Psychology Press.

Women rap about sex. (1968). Retrieved from http://scriptorium.lib.duke.edu/wlm/notes/#sexrap

1

The Received View: Public Memory, Historiographic Discourses, and LGBTQ Media

This chapter researches the formation of public memory around LGBTQ and feminist social movements. By performing a historiographic discourse analysis of nonfiction works on these two movements, I analyze their references to and about each other in order to determine the received view of the relations between the two groups. The historiographic discourse is approached here as an institutional contributor to the foundation of emergent public memory.

The formation of popular memory involves an interplay between individuals, groups, publics, and institutions. This is an ongoing process of creation, maintenance, and contestation on many fronts. A synchronic approach to memory studies can examine a relatively fixed or stabilized popular memory and assess its contours, connections, or construction. However, a more diachronic approach can examine the processes of memory construction, and memories that have yet to solidify or gain wide, public awareness. This chapter examines an as-yet-unformed public memory: the relation between gay men and feminist women across their respective social movements. This is a topic about which there are several small competing memories, often contradictory, but they have yet to coalesce. My investigation is into a particular stage of the process of forming public memory: the writing of a public record that can serve as a foundation to public memory, and support—or discredit—various competing narratives as the 'legitimate' memory.

Approaching historiographic writings as components of forming the public memory of the topic, I performed a discourse analysis of nonfiction works about the histories of gay men and feminist women. I was specifically interested in feminist women writ large—not merely lesbian feminists, who are often presumed to be the bridge between the two movements. My intention was to avoid potentially obscuring heterosexual female feminists and gay male feminists. My focus on gay men is not to erase the work of lesbians (who are not all necessarily feminists) in LGBTQ social movements, but to examine the work done elsewhere. In a sense, I am trying to *not* suggest that lesbians did all the work. Furthermore, for this stage of the project, I did not search for explicit mentions of trans or intersexed persons. Working with a graduate student, we examined books on gay male history, memoir, and politics, as well as similar works on feminism and women's movements, looking for references in each for the other. What emerged were frequent but very brief references, and three main themes of commonality, opposition, and intellectual contributions.

Beginning in the 1980s, much work from feminist, post-structuralist, and queer theorists sought to interrogate and destabilize the constructedness of key subject categories, such as man, woman, or gay. Despite being in debt to such work and supportive of it, in the spirit of Spivak's strategic essentialism (1999), here I work with such terms, not as if they were stable, but reflecting the stability with which they have been treated in various historiographies.

Finally, to resist imposing a presentist view upon the past, I also reflect differences and similarities as they are discussed in my artifacts. Some circles suggest we are in a post-gay or postfeminist culture, where these issues no longer matter. Others see a perhaps utopian vision of Millennials and Generation Z having embraced feminism and LGBTQ rights as part of a unified package of progressive social issues. However, I aim here to present discourses as expressed in my artifacts, with their varying degrees of concern and progress.

Public Memory

Multiple definitions, contestations, and alternatives appear in the literature on public memory. A recent study (Segesten & Wüstenberg, 2016) of memory scholars assessed that the field as at "a mid-level state of development" (p. 1) in its professionalization and institutionalization. As such, it is highly multidisciplinary and, if no longer nascent, still somewhat amorphous.

Public memory has been described as one of many terms used to unify a broad and diverse array of approaches to studying collective or group memory, which have been criticized for potentially reifying a singular group mind and/or every related phenomenon involved in its constitution (Olick & Robbins, 1998). Attempts at greater precision include Schudson's (1997) call for reprioritization of collective memory studies from intentional memorialization, including such self-conscious creators of shared memory as monuments and textbooks, to unintentional process of collective memory creation. He urges memory scholars to make their priority instead unintentional processes, such as changes in language—whose origins are forgotten, but words persist—lived experiences, such as trauma and legislation. Olick and Robbins (1998) offer a focus on social memory studies, which they describe as "a general rubric for inquiry into the varieties of forms through which we are shaped by the past, conscious and unconscious, public and private, material and communicative, consensual and challenged" (p. 112). Other scholars have taken the approach of focusing inquiries on specific institutional sites involved in memory creation. One wide area of study has been the contribution of news and media to public memory construction (Gamson, Croteau, Hoynes, & Sasson, 1992; Patterson, 2014; Zelizer, 1992). Museums have been the focus of memory construction, in both virtual (Fitzmaurice, 2014) and physical (Maurantonio, 2015) forms. Havel (2005) argues for defining public memory as that which is related to official public or State memory, constituted largely through legislation and policy, and which attempts to preserve social structures and obscure challenges to it. However, he also acknowledges that educational institutions contribute to this form of public memory.

Such an institutional focus can be limited to institutions of the past, but can also be applied to contemporary institutions involved in contributing to discourses about the past. As Schudson writes, "The structures, interests, and organization of knowledge in the present construct the past" (1997, p. 4). This reminds us that memory-making occurs in time. Zelizer (1992) also reminds us that memory is not a static thing but an ongoing process. Indeed, this process includes contestations of memory, which include institutional actors. Ryan (2010) describes individual or group challenges to collective memory as "mnemonic resistance" (p. 154), which can include, for example, publishing a counter-historical book that runs against public memory. Olick and Robbins (1998) acknowledge the social power of memory construction in their quotation from Michel Foucault: "Memory is actually a very important factor in struggle ... if one controls people's memory, one controls their dynamism" (p. 126).

This project approaches public memory as a dynamic process and chooses as its focus an institutional site of memory production: nonfiction publications such as textbooks, memoirs, and historiographies. These are framed as contributing to a particular moment within the process of memory construction, a stage before memorialization. Whereas, for example, Browne (1999) performed a similarly historiographic effort in looking at speeches, debates, and news leading up to the Crispus Attucks Memorial, this project investigates the background of something which has yet to be memorialized. Memorials exist to gay men in LGBTQ social movements, and to women in the feminist social movements, but the intersection has yet to be memorialized. Who can easily name a gay male leader in women's rights? In contrast, white leaders of abolitionist and civil rights movements, such as Susan B. Anthony and Robert F. Kennedy, spring more readily to mind. Dunn (2015) explored an as-yet-unformed transgender public memory through the documentary *Paris Is Burning*; this project investigates an as-yet-unformed public memory about the relations between two social movements.

Indeed, this mutable, temporal perspective can be seen in research involving public memory of feminism. Fitzmaurice (2014) analyzes how the National Women's History Museum, an online cybermuseum, attempts inclusivity and diversity in its memorializing of women's history in ways that traditional museums cannot, yet their financial and political alignments privilege the practices of memorialization in the strictly material world. In examining contemporary public memory of Italian second-wave feminism, Hajek (2016) focuses on the role of social media to argue that "past events play a crucial role in the (re)construction of collective identities of protest movements in the present" (p. 130). Individual feminist figures have been explored as well, such as Mandziuk and Fitch's (2001) analysis of the representation of Sojourner Truth by historians and critics, arguing her case illustrates the various transformations and transfigurations of historical figures through historiography and criticism, thereby influencing public memory. Rosenberg (2003) reflects the perspective of public memory as an ongoing, temporal process in her analysis of public memory of the 10th anniversary of the Montreal mass shooting targeting feminists, which she finds to be marked by great ambivalence. However, in this ambivalence, she argues there is a potential resource, and that re-examination of the event and its memory can potentially spur thinking about future feminist memorialization and activism.

Such mutability can be seen in LGBTQ memory research as well. Dunn (2011) exemplifies a seemingly traditional approach to public memory, if there can be said to be one, in his visual analysis of a statue of Canada's "gay pioneer," Alexander Wood. Yet, he extends his analysis to the ongoing acts of decoration and graffiti that the local queer community performs to challenge the institutionalized public memory with their own counter-memories regarding Wood. Indeed, the material world is in a mutually constitutive relationship with memory, as Van Doorn (2016) argues in his examination of leather subcultures in Baltimore's gay community. Elsewhere (Scott, 2011), I have explored the interplay between past and present in gay men's gendering of athletic shoes. Mutability can also mean disappearance. As a historically oppressed group, like women and feminists, gay men are subject to erasure and forgetting, even within their own communities. Castiglia and Reed (2012) argue that gay culture was particularly subject to "unremembering," beginning with the onset of the AIDS epidemic and a powerful variety of forces that urged separation from what had come previously. They cite the work of Vincent Doyle (2008), who similarly describes the professionalization of the media-monitoring nonprofit, Gay and Lesbian Alliance Against Defamation, as a mainstreaming effort that produced amnesia regarding earlier gay liberation activism and perspectives.

Method

For this chapter, I wanted to ascertain what knowledge of gay men and feminist women would an average researcher would come across, starting in a university library collection. I approached this as a discourse analysis in the Foucaultian sense of attempting to unearth the field of knowledge around a topic (Fairclough, 1992; Foucault, 1998, 2012). That is, I sought to map the horizons of what was known. This was, in itself, a form of historiography: compiling and documenting what has been written (if not in chronological order). From my past experience, I expected there would not be an abundance of rich, detailed data. Therefore, I operated with an understanding of historiography as involving scraps, clues, or traces that the historiographer (or historiographic discourse analyst) must stitch together in a process that is inherently interpretive (de Certeau, 1988; Ginzburg, 1980; Gomez-Barris & Gray, 2010; Sterne, 2010). Schudson describes the elements that the past leaves with and in individuals as "residue" (1997, p. 5), which shape understandings of past, present, and, in turn, influence attitudes and actions.

In order to map out this residue, I set out to review indices of feminist/women's and gay histories for listings of the other, then analyze the pages indicated. I worked with a research assistant to identify nonfiction books in a university library dealing with these two social movements. Texts that turned out to be fiction, or to have not had a main focus on gay men or feminist women, or were not indexed, were excluded. After narrowing them down, we kept 25 gay-male-centric books and 27 feminist books, for a total of 52. The indices for each were checked for gay and feminist terms. Use of these terms excluded pages in which the mentions were simply citations of a book or article titles. After cataloging these pages, the pages themselves were examined for content and contexts, taking notes on emergent themes and identifying salient quotes. Constant comparison for naturalistic inquiry (Fram, 2013) was practiced throughout this process between my research assistant and myself, in which the data was examined and re-examined, with reflections on our processes and understandings, to identify, refine, and consolidate themes. In revising this chapter, some additional books were incorporated, bringing the total to 63.

The Received View

Minimal Mentions

The first overall finding was that the two groups did acknowledge each other in ways that related them, but not regularly. Indeed, many books that seemed ripe for the topic had relatively little material. For example, the collection *Homosexuality: Power and Politics* sports a back cover that reads, "What all the authors share is a commitment to developing a radical politics in which the gains of the women's and gay movements will be fully integrated." However, there is no listing for "feminism" in the index. In the book, the chapters do address women's lesbian and gay politics, but there is not much integration. Sue Carteledge's "Bringing It All Back Home: Lesbian Feminist Morality" has no mention of gays, nor does Margaret Jackson and Pat Mahoney's "Lesbian, Socialist, Feminist." Only two contributors connect the two. One chapter, which I will discuss later, addresses a lesbian activist's move from feminist to LGBTQ politics. The other was Keith Birch's "The Politics of Autonomy." In it, Birch asserts differences between gay and women's movements but the two factors "fundamental to both" are "a stress of self-activity, on the individual level and as an autonomous movement, and secondly the assertion of a wider kind of politics, amounting to a redefinition of what had become understood by the term" (1980, p. 86–87). Birch, in describing autonomy as separation from political parties, writes at length about how the "personal is political" but doesn't attribute it to feminism, describing it more as a broadly socialist/leftist idea. He credits women's and gay movements for instigating discussions and analysis of ideology, culture, consciousness, and sexuality, and mentions lesbian and gay men working with women's organizations and other groups.

Overall, of the gay male books, about two-thirds explicitly mentioned feminism and feminists. Of the feminist books, almost all explicitly mentioned gay men. (Again, I refrain here from using exact figures, as these samples of books are examples, not representative.) However, this turned out to be a very limited amount of references within each book. The number of pages indexed with gay- or feminist-related keywords within these books was quite small relative to the total number of pages in each book. Of the gay male books that did mention feminism, they only mentioned feminism on about two percent of the pages within their entire text. The amount of gay mentions was a larger percentage of pages in the feminist books, but still quite small, averaging three percent of the pages in the books that mentioned gay men. In some books this was particularly striking, such as *Men and Feminism* (Tarrant, 2009). Given the book's title, the frequency with which gay rights and women's rights are articulated, and the author's own description of a popular perception that gay men are feminists, they are only mentioned in nine percent of the book's pages.

Individuals and Events—Not Movements

In studying historiographic discourses of these two groups, their intersections typically are described in terms of individuals or events. Individuals include activists who advocated for both, such as Emma Goldman and Shelby Knox, or theorists, such as Judith Butler, Eve Kosofsky Sedgwick, or Gayle Rubin. However, these are described more as exceptional cases; generalizations occur more around events, with two major ones reappearing. The first is the "liberation moment" of the late 1960s and early 1970s, when a spirit of revolutionary change at the societal level linked (and perhaps reductively conflated) social movements of women, sexual and gender minorities, racial minorities, youth, environmentalists, peace activists, and other radicals and progressives (e.g., Baumgardner, 2011, pp. 37–38, 61, 247, 251; N. Miller, 2008, pp. 339–365). The second common event is the AIDS crisis and its grass-roots activism and caregiving involving gay men and lesbians (e.g., Baumgardner, 2011, p. 183; Moore, 2004).

Feminists, Lesbians, and Gays: The Venn Diagram

As I will describe throughout this book, often discussions of feminists and gay men are reduced to lesbians. During the "liberation moment," the issue is where lesbians throw their support: with feminism, where they encounter homophobia and racism; with gay rights, where they encounter sexism and racism; or with separatist movements (e.g., Bunch, 1987; Combahee River Collective, 1997;

D'Emilio, 1989, p. 472; N. Miller, 2008, pp. 344–348). During AIDS, lesbians are the prodigal queers, returning to the gay-rights fold after years in the wilderness.

If you imagine a Venn diagram of overlapping circles, feminist women are one circle, gay men are the other, and lesbians are the circles' overlap. As mentioned previously, a common narrative is that lesbians acted as links or, to use Castells' (2009) term, switchers, between networks of feminist women and gay men. In this narrative, lesbians had been involved in second-wave feminism to varying degrees, but with the rise of lesbian separatism, abandoned gay rights. However, the onset of AIDS brought them back.

In feminist and gay narratives, this often results in a focus *only* on lesbian-feminism, or lesbians within feminist movements, or lesbians within LGBTQ movements. For example, in an early work from 1971, suggestive of the coalition mindset of the times, the two groups are situated squarely in the book's subtitle. *Angelo D'Arcangelo's Love Book: Inside the Sexual Revolution: From Women's Lib to Gay Power* is a follow-up to the author's *The Homosexual Handbook*, released the year prior. Given its cocktail of memoir, gonzo journalism, reprints, essays, sketches, and rants, I would describe this book today as exceptionally queer, particularly given its camp and funny tone. However, in the author's interview with Claudia Dreifus, a writer for *EVO*, an underground weekly paper, about the women's movement, there is a complete change in tone. Their serious discussion covers topics from clitoridectomies to the journalistic profession. However, he never asks her about a connection between the women's movement and all homosexuals; he asks her about lesbians:

d'A: What about lesbianism? What about lesbians in Women's Lib? Is there an attitude within the Movement about feminine homosexuality?

CS: The goal of Women's Lib is to let women be themselves. So, yes. Homosexuals, as a group, have been dumped on and fucked with all along. And if it was bad for male homosexuals, it was twice as bad for female homosexuals.

d'A: Simply because they are women. (p. 151)

Although she at least acknowledges male homosexuals, the conversation never progresses to discussing related concerns of women's liberation and all homosexuals. Indeed, despite being joined in the book's subtitle, women's liberation and gay power are never linked in the book itself.

The next year saw the release of a more scholarly collection, *Out of the Closets: Voices of Gay Liberation* (Jay & Young, 1972), containing 52 reprints and other essays. None, however, have an explicit gay male-feminist focus, although there is a section titled "Lesbians and the Women's Liberation Movement," with six essays. The book also includes "A Selected Gay Bibliography" listing 62 titles of fiction, nonfiction, and periodicals. Of these, there are some identified as "Related Readings in Feminism," but these are only three titles: Vivian Gornick and Barbara K. Moran's *Women in a Sexist Society: Studies in Power and Powerlessness*, Kate Millett's *Sexual Politics*, and Robin Morgan's *Sisterhood is Powerful*.

In an unusual example I noted earlier, gay men are presented as an appealing alternative to feminism for lesbians and, perhaps, a more authentic feminism. Amber Hollibaugh's (1980) "Right to Rebel" essay in *Homosexuality: Power and Politics* describes, in San Francisco in the 1970s, her having grown uncomfortable with separatist feminism. However, she writes

> My political confusions began to resolve themselves when I began to work in the gay caucus in the organizing committee for the July 4th anti-bicentennial in 1975–6. I chose to work in the gay caucus as opposed to the women's caucus, a moderately scandalous choice. I was the only woman with eleven gay men, mostly political white gay men. My experience with them was good. It gave me a sense that there were men committed to struggles against sexism: men who were as moved by feminism in their own way as I had been. Not because they were guilty about being men, being oppressors, but who were moved by the idea of a new way to be men. I hadn't met men like them before: I'd met gentle straight men but wasn't convinced. I hadn't met men before who passionately identified with parts of feminism as their own. I got a real sense of feminism reaching out beyond women, and touching and changing men and how they wanted to be, and impelling them to work against sexism. Feminism was bridging the gaps between lesbians and gay men, and I began to spend more time in the Castro. (1980, p. 211–212)

Note, however, that this narrative maintains feminists and gay men as separate groups, with the lesbian moving from one to the other, not forming a link between the two.

This reduction of gay men and feminist women to lesbians is problematic in several ways. While such narratives have aspects of truth and significance to them, there is also problematic discursive work here: the possibilities for feminist women's and gay men's intersections or coalitions is typically reduced to the bridge figure of the lesbian. This places an undue and unrealistic burden upon lesbians— they must be the locus for the battles for women's and homosexual rights (which in turn, provides justification for their continued marginalization when they fail to live up to this responsibility). It also excuses non-lesbian feminist women and gay men from the responsibility of understanding each other and working togeth-er, as if "the lesbians will take care of that." If it's all up to lesbians, then women's rights are not an issue for gay men, and gay rights are not an issue for heterosexual feminists. It creates separations, not coalitions.

The focus on the figure of lesbians is also an act of erasure, with bisexual, asexual, intersexed, transgender, and other persons left out of the spotlight. It also serves to maintain invisibility of such persons, who likely have relevant if not uniquely useful insights in these matters.

Additionally, it also at times tends to discredit or marginalize feminism. When the focus is limited to gay men and lesbians, and why or why not they worked together (arguably a version of the catfight cliché that reinforces stereotypes of feminine competitiveness and disagreeability), often feminism becomes framed as a *problem* for the LGBT rights movement (Miller, 2008, p. 321). That is, a reason why it doesn't do better: feminism breaks up the potential combined power of gay men and lesbian women.

My intervention with this book is to resist that reduction, to argue through an investigation of a forced juxtaposition of the two that there are more persons involved here than lesbians.

Commonality

Themes of commonality included explicit mentions of how the two groups shared common experiences and at times directly collaborated. This was the most com-mon theme in both groups, appearing in about half of the books examined.

Common experiences included, but were not limited to, shared oppression. *No Turning Back: The History of Feminism and the Future of Women* (Freedman, 2002) describes the alignment of gay men with feminism due to shared experi-ences such as job discrimination. Others saw shared experiences of homophobia. In *Socialist Feminism: A Strategy for the Women's Movement* (1972), the Chicago Women's Liberation Union, Hyde Park Chapter, wrote:

> As the women's movement developed, the gay movement, too, has grown. The gay movement has more forcefully brought the issue of sexuality into the politi-cal arena with an analysis of the oppression suffered by gay people in our society. Hating the conditions that shunt us and loving women with whom we find new strength and new room to be weak, many of us come into lesbian relationships. The gay liberation movement has brought people together collectively to bring an end to that oppression. Gay or straight lives are joined in that these struggles affect us as women.

Sexism and misogyny were discussed as extended to hostility toward feminine behaviors in certain gay men. Valenti (2008), in *He's a Stud, She's a Slut: And 49 other Double Standards Every Woman Should Know*, notes how a South Carolina prison forced sexually active male prisoners to wear pink jumpsuits, branding them with a feminine stigma as punishment. She goes on to note how feminine scapegoating occurs not only in mainstream culture, "but also in the queer community, where 'effeminate' gay men have been accused of 'holding back' the gay rights movement" (p. 64). In *Sweet Tea: Black Gay Men of the South* (Johnson, 2011), one interviewee relates, "It was not okay to be a smart boy. Like, I also find interesting for like, conventional feminist arguments … second-wave feminists are arguing, like, girls can't be smart in class" (p. 47). In his experience, although there was a sexist prejudice against girls being intellectual, there was also a somewhat contradictory sexism that associated excess intellectualism in boys with compromised masculinity. A more internalized version of this could be seen when a gay male self-identified as also a feminist (Fellows, 1998).

Another type of shared experience frequently discussed was common positive experiences of fandom, entertainment, and aesthetic culture. Among feminists, objects of affection shared with gay men included the television programs *Dynasty* (Hollows, 2000) and *Will and Grace* (Jervis & Zeisler, 2006), musician Madonna (Zeisler, 2008), and the magazine *Sassy* (Douglas, 2010; Zeisler, 2008). Arguably, this could be due to the importance of popular culture and media studies in feminist research, particularly third-wave feminism. The gay books examined here were less focused on popular culture, although one forged an interesting architectural connection between the camp aesthetic of gay interior decor in certain films and the drawings of fantasy homes in a feminist quarterly publication (Castiglia & Reed, 2012).

Arguably, shared experiences could lead to collaborations, the other subset of the commonality theme. *Feminism: A Paradigm Shift* (Tandon, 2008) notes feminist Emma Goldman's support for homosexual rights. *Feminism: A Reference Handbook* (Harlan, 1998) notes within its timeline NOW including lesbian and gay rights among its list of feminist issues in 1971, the National Women's Conference in 1977 listing them in the top three feminist issues, alongside the Equal Rights Amendment (ERA) and abortion rights, and, finally, noting that third-wave feminism explicitly includes gay rights. *The Essential Feminist Reader* (Freedman, 2007) includes gay couples' right to adopt as part of the third-wave feminist conception of reproductive rights. Moore's (2004) *Beyond Shame: Reclaiming the Abandoned History of Radical Gay Sexuality* notes that the activist group AIDS

Coalition to Unleash Power (ACT UP) incorporated both feminist and gay concerns (although he suggests this was a new experience for many of its members).

More recently, Lillian Faderman's exhaustive history of the American gay rights movement mentions feminists, lesbians, and gay men together in a chapter on AIDS. Faderman mentions gays and lesbians as both being at demonstrations, and notes lesbian Amy Bauer using her experience from working with radical peace organizations to train members of ACT UP. The group's media advisor, Ann Northrop, is described as a feminist and lesbian. Women's groups, such as abortion activists Women's Health Action and Mobilization (WHAM), are noted as participating in some events. She also describes heterosexual Dr. Iris Long providing instruction on the science of AIDS to ACT UP. However, one reviewer of the book demonstrates the emphasis again on lesbians, even when missing:

> One quibble I have with this book is the elision of lesbians from this section. While Faderman notes the work of Jean O'Leary, lesbians, especially those of us in New York City at the time, were deeply engaged in the fight against HIV/AIDS. That is missing here. (Brownworth, 2015, ¶26)

This is not to say that the presence of lesbians in AIDS activism was not significant. I will address this later, and, indeed, one can find it noted by other scholars. For example, Kathy Rudy (2001) writes in the journal *Feminist Studies*, that, in contrast to feminist groups,

> Queer communities are much more open to racial, class, and ethnic differences and are infinitely more successful than separatists in building coalition across a wide variety of social issues, especially around concerns of race and class. Partly as a result of the AIDS crisis, lesbians in the last decade have united with gay men and many different people of color to build a strong community of political resistance in Durham [North Carolina]. (p. 216)

However, I suggest again that the dividing of feminists/lesbians/gay men reduces the complexities of actual roles played, people involved, and, most importantly, conceptual and political links among these people.

Opposition

The second major theme was opposition, which included explicitly marking difference, describing how one group inhibits or oppresses the other directly, or how the two groups were in competition for social acceptance and progress in civil rights. This theme was less prevalent in both groups, appearing in about a fifth of the books. In terms of marking difference, in *Being Homosexual: Gay Men and Their Development*, Isay (2009) proposes that sexual orientation is hard-wired in gay men to a greater degree than in women, who (he claims) demonstrated their greater ability to "choose" their sexual orientation when they adopted same-sex relationships upon discovering feminism, but then stopped when they became disenchanted with the women's movement. Such a perspective arguably exhibits a gay male sexism or misogyny that is, significantly, described within both gay male and feminist books as how gay men oppress women. For example, Moore (2004) cites feminist John Stoltenberg criticizing the gay movement for abandoning its wider revolutionary goals for a narrow push for civil rights as men within a male-dominated culture, rather than trying to change that culture. In *Gay and Gray: The Older Homosexual Man*, Berger (1996) suggests that, despite their common oppression and goals, gay male leaders are unsympathetic toward feminist movements. Tarrant (2009), in *Men and Feminism*, similarly notes the logical intersection of gay and feminist interests, but claims there is a stereotype that all gay men are feminists, and questions this association in light of gay male misogyny. In *Gay Masculinities* (Nardi, 2000), several authors cite gay male misogyny as inhibiting the potential for gay-feminist alliances. One author (Ward, 2000) also addresses the idea that gay men have "specialized knowledge about women's oppression and feminism" (p. 9).

Others point out ways in which their political agendas are at odds. *Why Feminism? Gender, Psychology, Politics* (Segal, 1999) critiques the depoliticized aspects of queer identity and how celebrations of a "gay gene" subvert feminist principles. D'Arcangelo, mentioned previously, writes, "I have watched the Gay Liberation movements carefully, allowing general admiration to grow despite particular skepticism and noticed the natural, strengthening and inevitable alliance with Women's Lib. And I am not unaware of the consequences of this alliance" (1971, p. 9). Referring to his previous book, he later clarifies, "If you remember my chapter on WOMEN, I clearly stated that the main trouble with them is *getting rid* of them" (p. 39, emphasis original). He is not however, entirely gynophobic, as he later writes approvingly of a gay friend having sex with a woman for the first time: "For many homosexual men there is an enormous amount of time and effort wasted in the attempt to compensate for or compete with the feminine gender in absentia. Pressures build up out of carnal ignorance of the feminine body, and content for the feminine soul" (p. 130).

Opposition in the sense of competition appeared, for example, in the sense of sharing media visibility. In *Feminism, Femininity and Popular Culture* (Hollows, 2000), the gay male character on the television melodrama *Melrose Place* is described as playing the "ideal mother" role, suggesting gay male incursion on spaces for female visibility. Another sense of competition is vying for favor in the public sphere. In *Well-behaved Women Seldom Make History*, Ulrich (2007) describes the familiar moment of NOW co-founder and first President Betty Friedan's fear that perceived homosexuals within the women's movement would limit its appeal, choosing to fight sexism over homophobia. Typically, this "lavender menace" is framed to explain her resistance to lesbian feminists, but Ulrich clarifies it was not just lesbians: Friedan was threatened by the Stonewall Riots and gay movement in general.

Faderman (2015) also describes the homophobia within mainstream second-wave feminism, as well as an essentialist attitude toward men as the enemy that would spur departures of lesbians from feminism (in contrast to Hollibaugh's experience). Lesbians who had joined the radical Gay Liberation Front, for example, after the Stonewall riots, had quickly felt ostracized from male leadership:

> By the time GLF was six months old, they concluded that they'd been radicals long before they hooked up with radical gay men; and they needed to put their radicalism into lesbian issues, women's issues. They'd meet on their own, without the men. (p. 229)

Furthermore, a new generation of lesbians, inspired by radical politics, were impatient with the political caution of their elders. Additionally, there was also, Faderman recounts, a position from various corners that lesbianism was the highest form of feminism, and that any woman could choose to be a lesbian.

> There were probably more lesbians in America in the 1970s than at any time in history. The new lesbians have no connection to old-school lesbians … those who thought that if only lesbians would mind their manners, they'd be given a place at the table. The new lesbians didn't want to place the table—they aimed to trash the whole dining room. They'd fought side-by-side with leftist men against society's oppression of underdogs; but when they became feminists, they saw that women, too, were underdogs; and men on the Left were as much to blame for it as men on the Right. Refusing to sleep with the oppressor, they became newly minted lesbians. The fervor they'd once put into ending racism or the war in Vietnam, they now put into lesbian-feminism. Thousands of them took their radical lesbian-feminism the giant step further. (p. 240–241)

Faderman describes how, inspired by the Nation of Islam, they developed a philosophy of lesbian separatism, and "Lesbian separatists had no interest in the fight for gay and lesbian civil rights. They'd create 'Lesbian Nation' instead" (p. 241).

Indeed, in 1980, Adrienne Rich, in her influential essay "Compulsory Hetero-sexuality and Lesbian Existence," wrote of a "lesbian continuum," which includ-ed but was not limited to romantic and sexual relations between women. The continuum included all women-centered or women-identified experiences, even without romance or physical intercourse per se.

Intellectual Contributions

The third theme was that of intellectual contributions. These references dealt with how areas of academic disciplines, such as feminist theory, LGBTQ studies, women's studies, and queer theory, drew upon one another. This theme was more prevalent in the gay books, appearing in about a third, but in only about a fifth of the feminist books.

What looked at first to be a notable example among the books examined was Tim Edwards' *Erotics & Politics: Gay Male Sexuality, Masculinity and Feminism* (1994). The author positions himself as a feminist-identified gay man, one who is looking to bring insights from feminism to gay men. He expresses frustration with other gay men that do not see the potential. And yet, feminism is only listed six times in the index. It appears slightly more than that in the actual text, but comes and goes in and out of the discussion. Sometimes Edwards shifts to talking about lesbians, other times he focuses on gay male issues, such as chapters on public sex and AIDS. Despite the subtitle, feminism of any school is not a sus-tained intellectual project or social movement put in conversation with gay male politics or identities. Postmodernism is more directly engaged with as a school of thought. Only in his conclusion, when Edwards addresses his notions of "erotic politics," does it read like a true synthesis of feminist and LGBTQ thought. Ed-wards calls for

> A politics of sexuality that recognizes racism, sexism and ageism as part of sexu-ality, as opposed to separate issues and, in addition, recognizes and supports the rights of sexual minorities. … Many more recent feminist and gay studies have gone some way to doing this, as does the new politics of postmodernity. The process still has to move much further. (p. 158)

This is, however, on the last page of the book, the culmination of its reflection and exploration.

Although several other gay authors credit feminist activism, thought, or schol-ars as informing their work, none examined attempt to elevate it to a central argu-ment or idea (Bech, 1997; Clum, 2000; Kennedy, 2013; Rauch, 2004; Reynolds

& Sullivan, 2003). Some do describe specific feminist concepts they applied. For example, Eric Rofes, in *Reviving the Tribe* (2013), uses feminist writer Susan Griffin's concept of emotional shutdown to explore the psychosocial impact of AIDS on gay men. Nardi (1999) applies Marilyn Friedman's concept of friendship being the "cement … of the various historical waves of the feminist movement" (quoted p. 199) to similar bonds in the gay rights movement. *Gaydar Culture: Gay Men, Technology and Embodiment in the Digital Age* (Mawlabocus, 2010) applies Kappeler's feminist research on pornography as part of his theoretical framework for examining gay male digital culture.

Among feminist books, Segal (1999) explicitly notes the feminist influence on LGBT theorizing and political movements. In *Feminism and Pop Culture*, Zeisler (2008) calls for a research agenda into media share of lesbians, gay men, bisexuals, and other alternate sexualities. Also evoking the "cement" concept, Mohanty (2005) calls for an integrated perspective in *Feminism without Borders*:

> Within the context of the history of feminist struggle in the United States, the 1980s were a period of euphoria and hope, friendship being the "cement" for feminists of color, gays and lesbians, and antiracist, white feminists. Excavating subjugated knowledges and histories in order to craft decolonized, oppositional racial and sexual identities and political strategies that posed challenges to the gender, class, race, and sexual regimes of the capitalist nation-state anchored the practice of antiracist, multicultural feminisms. (p. 175)

From a historiographic perspective, Brodkey and Fine (in Giroux, 1991) call for an archive of feminist intellectual activism, including "arguments for developing gay men's and lesbian women's studies programs" (p. 117).

The Potential of a Pre-Formative Stage

The sparsity and variety of findings described above demonstrates that the historic record is far from solidified. This suggests, in turn, that public memory on the topic is far from fixed. The potential malleability of public memory still in the process of being formed means that contributions to historiographic discourses can make an impact. The discourse analysis of historiographies suggests that, thus far, institutions of education and publishing have contributed to the process of creating a foundation, albeit thin, for public memories of gay and feminist social movements.

Furthermore, the three main themes—commonality, opposition, and intellectual contributions—suggest, I argue, not contradiction and fracture so much as healthy complexity. For, indeed, there have been misogynist gay men and feminist gay men, as well as homophobic feminists and ally feminists. There has also been a robust mutual influence across academic disciplines as these social movements have drawn on and fed back into the academy.

However, this research suggests that these threads have not tied together. Almost no book examined exhibited all three themes together. The relative absence of such complexity can be seen to potentially amplify and resonate negative stereotypes. For example, although two works reacted to a *perceived* stereotype of the inherently feminist gay man (Tarrant, 2009; Ward, 2000), no direct examples of this stereotype were found in the books examined. While several books articulated links between gay men and feminists, or argued for why they should connect or collaborate or be viewed together, none presented an example of or made an argument for an assumed, 'natural' gay male feminist actually existing. A simplified view of impossible enemies or natural allies not only mars the historic record, but, more importantly here, can lead to creating a pessimistic public memory regarding future coalition-building among social movements. At different times, gay men and feminist women worked together or were at odds. Understanding the complexity involved, and how each group progressed to successes as well as missed opportunities, can be an important lesson for their own and other coalitions of social movements.

Michael Schudson urges the study of memory-making as it occurs in time, reminding us that "the past seeps into the present whether or not its commemoration is institutionalized" (1997, p. 15). This chapter thus far has presented an exercise in identifying foundational historiographic discourses as part of the process of building public memory. In addition to identifying what the received view is thus far of gay men and feminist women in their respective social movements, I have aimed to demonstrate a broader reminder of how the process of building or reshaping public memory is ongoing, and scholars have an important institutional role to contribute to that, particularly when foundational discourses are still in their early or sparse stages.

The convenience sampling for this project may not accurately represent the most influential works in gay and feminist history. However, I argue that it replicates the experience of a researcher as well as the library as an institutional site of memory construction. The collections of any library, and the order and way they are searched and utilized, are never universal. While common titles may appear, such as Betty Friedan's *The Feminine Mystique* in our convenience sample, many other less-known or marginal works may take up equal shelf space, such as our inclusion of Will Fellow's *Farm Boys*. As a queer scholar, I suggest this is not such a bad thing. I am wary of canonization and do not want to suggest such a list in this project. Moreover, looking to the current practice of researching online, even more various types of artifacts become available, in ever more disparate juxtapositions, and even search engine rankings or citation counts do not enforce a clear standardization.

During this process, a suspected methodological finding that was confirmed was the inadequacy of indexes. When a random selection of books was double-checked online through electronic keyword searches using tools such as those within Amazon.com, Barnes and Noble, and Google Books, additional mentions were found of gays and feminists not listed in their indices. Given that the initial design of this chapter was to replicate the experience of researching within hard copies of books—the traditional manner, which, over the past decades, can be argued to have had a large impact on the construction of historiographic discourses and knowledge—the page counts and analyses from printed indices were maintained, although notes were taken on content beyond the indexed pages. While these pages did provide additional examples and qualitative information, they did not contradict or drastically change the overall findings of this project.

Although I did not exhaust the archive, as a Foucaultian genealogy might prefer, the sample of book-length works provides significant insight. As saturation was beginning to appear in the texts, confining the project to those at this educational institution was deemed sufficient for establishing a received view. As research continued on other aspects of this project, some additional works were incorporated due to the useful examples they provided, bringing the total to 63.

Ideological Practices in LGBTQ Media

I switch approaches now to studying from below, looking at the stories of feminism in LGBTQ independent media. In this section, rather than distill texts into themes, I present them in a timeline. This is intended to show how the themes described previously appear and reappear chronologically. Books take often years to write, and many of the ones discussed above contained reprints of articles previously published. Others are histories looking back and describing the past. Here, I attempt to let the past speak for itself. My primary resource is the *Advocate*, the nation's longest-running LGBTQ publication, although it has typically skewed in its coverage to gay, white men, especially in its early years. However, its continual publishing allows for a longitudinal view. I have augmented it with examples from other LGBTQ publications as well.

Stuart Hall (1985) specifies that "the terrain of ideology [is not] constituted as a field of mutually exclusive and internally self-sustaining discursive chains" (p. 104), but ideologies are multiple, contested, and in constant articulation and re-articulation, which is amenable to how Foucault describes modern power relations and competing discourses (in contrast to a monolithic "dominant ideology"). Drawing on Althusser, Hall reminds us to think of ideologies as not mere ideas, but practices. He clarifies that ideas are inscribed in material practices and effects as ideology, but this does not mean that ideas do not exist (1985, pp. 99–100). He argues that one of the areas that most needs investigating is how, in liberal democracies that afford freedom of the press and freedom of speech, journalism and news tend to reproduce the ideologies of the State. He asserts that "language and behavior are the media, so to speak, of the material registration of ideology, the modality of its functioning" (1985, p. 99).

However, Hall's analyses tend to be based on a more unified concept of the media, as suggested by the title of the essay "The 'Unity' of Current Affairs Television" (Hall, Connell, & Curti, 2007). Although they challenge a simplistic, top-down, conspiracy view of the media, their perspective is nevertheless rooted in a context of limited, state-run, public broadcasting and pre-cable and pre-satellite multichannel media consumption. Not only does this lack the contemporary feedback and production aspects of internet and social media, it also lacks the realm of alternative and independent media.

In "The Problem of Ideology: Marxism Without Guarantees," Hall (1986) articulates a more ideal bridge between the two:

> The *problem* of ideology is to give an account, within a materialist theory, of how social ideas arise. … By ideology, I mean the mental frameworks—the languages, the concepts, categories, imagery of thought, and the systems of representation—which different classes and social groups deploy in order to make sense of, define, figure out and render intelligible the way society works.

The problem of ideology, therefore, concerns the ways in which ideas of different kinds grip the minds of masses, and thereby become a "material force" (1986, p. 28–29, emphasis orig.).

Hall (1986) demonstrates his openness for thinking through marxism without the determinism of necessary or predicted effects. Demonstrating similar openness, Hall writes approvingly of the notion of "extra-discursivity" in Foucault's discourse theory, signaling an understanding of Foucauldian materialism. Hall writes that although Foucault "skirts the difficult question of determination," his breaking down the dichotomy between social practices and ideological representations in discourses and knowledge regimes "opened up again the problem of 'representation' itself, on which so many theories of ideology and symbolic representation have been based" (2003, p. 25).

The reference to Foucault "opening up" suggests what McRobbie refers to as "an endless openness" (2005, p. 27) in Hall's work. My "reading an ideological field" here can be understood as comparable to a Foucauldian mapping of a discourse. If, for Foucault, a discourse is a field of knowledge, then one can think of reading an *ideological* field of knowledge.

LGBTQ Media

In reviewing close to 500 of these periodicals, in chronological order, I noticed several general points of interest. These are anecdotal observations, however, not a formal content analysis. One was that, over time, there seems to be an increase in racial inclusion and intersections of LGBTQ and racial identities, such as "Gay Latino," but a decrease in explicit alignment with women and feminism. Another was steadily increasing coverage of celebrities and allies. It was not total, but, as I looked through one magazine after another, I began to feel that the increase in straight celebrities and politicians on the covers had come at the price of fewer representations of ourselves. Furthermore, this emphasis on allies, straight celebrities, straights we love, and straights playing gay roles in media, would seem to be an opportunity to include NOW or other women's leaders and organizations, but it did not. However, in the 1990s, coverage of women's issues *did* seem to increase, due to current events such as the Anita Hill testimony and rape trials of Mike Tyson and William Kennedy Smith. In most of the publications that were not lesbian-specific, though, women were presented as LGBTQ or individual female allies and celebs, but not representatives of an organized feminist movement. For example, the column "Mo'Nique Gets the Last Word," in the July 2006 issue of *Instinct*, describes her body-positive beauty contest show, *Mo'Nique's F.A.T. Chance*:

> Gay men and heavier women are friends because we're both the underdog and because we want to be accepted so bad and we find acceptance in each other. You fight because you're gay. I fight because I'm fat. Put us in a room together, we're friends. (p. 88)

Whether from anti-feminist backlash or basic neoliberal individualism, the LGBTQ publications frequently exhibited disconnection from organized social movements completely, be they feminism or civil rights.

As you will see below, some variants appeared from the historiographic themes. Missing below, however, are topics that seemed to be lost opportunities, such as articles and even an entire magazine devoted to gay parenting and adoption, which never addressed the vast amount of relevant work and experience on these topics from the women's movement.

Feminism in LGBTQ Media: An Incomplete Timeline

1982

The Advocate #335, Jan. 21. "The Year in Review" Photo: Six women outside a Washington, DC, courthouse, smiling, three raising fists in power salute. Caption: "Feminists took the lead in connecting gay issues with other causes. These six women, some of whom are lesbians, were convicted of disrupting U.S. Senate hearings on an antiabortion amendment to the Constitution" (p. 20).

The Advocate #350, Sept. 2. Cover: "Reaching Out to Other Issues: Beyond Gay."

"ERA Reintroduced" (1982) notes that "among those supporting reintroduction of the constitutional amendment [guaranteeing equal rights for women] was Rep. Phillip Burton (D-Calif.). ... Burton is a co-sponsor of the national gay rights bill and has lobbied extensively to sign up new co-sponsors for this bill" (p. 10).

In "Lesbians and Gay Men Join the Antinuclear Family" (Has, 1982) interviewees describe a decrease in homophobia in progressive activist groups. "Probably the women's movement has contributed the most to the change in attitudes evident today among political activists" (p. 25). One female anti-nuke activist "feels gay men identify their gayness as a sexual issue, whereas lesbians identify lesbianism as a political issue" (p. 53). She suggests gay men are less political because one does not see organizations such as specifically gay male anti-nuke groups. Another female activist says gay men won't get involved with other political issues because activism could threaten their male privilege. A gay man suggests gay men's greater economic status may limit their political action compared to women, who generally have less resources or income.

"Women and Terrorism" (Jay, 1982) describes media coverage suggesting that women in radical groups drove out the heterosexual men, or that radical philosophies could drive straight men to celibacy or homosexuality. It describes radical alliances in the 1960s, when "revolution appeared to be the inevitable consequence of the awareness by blacks, Puerto Ricans, Chicanos, Native Americans, Asian Americans, women, gay men and lesbians that they were all being oppressed by the system" (p. 22).

1984

Advocate #391, April 3. In "Face to Face Women React to AIDS," Califia (1984) writes that "AIDS is not just a men's issue. It is an issue for women, too" (p. 26). Califia, who identified and presented as a butch lesbian cisgender woman at the time, describes women, lesbian and heterosexual, involved in AIDS activism, research, caregiving, volunteering, and other areas. Although not discussing feminism, the article remains unusual even today for its inclusiveness, discussing lesbian, heterosexual, bisexual, and transgender women.

Advocate, June 26. "National Organizations Boost Gay Cause" (1994) lists the National Organization for Women among 20 ally organizations.

1985

Advocate #419, April 30. "Homophobia" (Giteck & Daniels, 1985) includes an interview with heterosexual female sociologist and sex researcher Sue Kiefer Hammersmith. She and the authors link homophobia against gay men to sexism against all women, as both are coming from straight men being unused to giving up power and perceiving that their personal space was violated.

Advocate #428, Sept. 3. In the cover story "See No Evil: The Anti-Porn Movement," Califia (1985) goes into detail on feminist anti-pornography legislative efforts (see discussion in Chapter 3). Califia does not demonize feminists but documents the split between feminists on the issue of pornography, and articulates its relevance for LGBTQ persons (e.g., police raids on porn palaces, obscenity laws' disproportionate impact on LGBTQ literature, and overall criminalization and desexualization).

1990

San Francisco Lesbian/Gay Freedom Day Parade & Celebration guidebook contains a quarter-page advertisement for a "Feminist Psychology" degree from the New College of California, Valencia (1990, p. 33).

1991

Advocate #573, March 26. In "Justifying Our Love? The Evolution of Lesbianism Through Feminism and Gay Male Politics," Alice Echols presents her take on several aspects of the received view. She reiterates the conflict of sexism:

> In the wake of Stonewall, some lesbians did attempt to work with gay men. For most lesbians, this was a short-lived partnership, in part because of the sexism

they encountered. ... Gay men's eroticization of power relations epitomized to many lesbians all that was wrong with male sexuality. This was an issue as early as 1969 in New York's Gay Liberation Front, and it remained a major issue into the '80s. (p. 52)

Echols also presents the "prominence of antiporn feminists" as a possible factor alienating young women from feminism in postfeminist culture, and the feminist 'sex war' debates on BD/SM alienating young lesbians from feminism, so they looked instead to gay men for strategies and tactics of embracing sexual pleasure. AIDS, she writes, brought gay men and women together, but drained energy from feminism. Among current politics, she admires the energy of Queer Nation, but finds its dominance by white gay men "depressingly familiar." She writes:

> Just as the rhetoric of sisterhood failed to make it a reality in the feminist movement (and often functioned instead as a way of obscuring differences arising from class, race, and sexual preference), talk of nationhood will fail as well unless queerness is broadly defined. In fact, this may be happening already, since women in the Boston chapter of Queer Nation have found it necessary to form a caucus. ... Feminism is still reeling from its debilitating love affair with 'woman-identified' thought, sex, and behavior. It would be a shame to see Queer Nation follow in feminism's footsteps. ... among the most obvious lessons to be learned from the '60s are that no one group—blacks, women, lesbians and gays, Latinos, or Asians—can do it alone. (p. 53)

As one of the co-founders of the Chicago chapter of Queer Nation, I can testify to Echols' prescience. Queer Nation was an attempt at broadening coalition, both in the sense of dealing with issues other than AIDS/HIV and also in deploying the umbrella term "queer" to be more inclusive than LGBT. Although we protested, for example, the homophobia, sexism, and racism of comedian Andrew Dice Clay, and the biphobia and misogyny of the film *Basic Instinct*, we did not form lasting coalitions with women's groups or racial minority groups. Kiss-ins at malls and protests at anti-gay Cracker Barrel restaurants focused on same-sex relations, and queers groused about appropriation of the term by persons in opposite-sex relationships. Echols' article presents an excellent example of how communication between gay men and feminist women, not exclusively or solely lesbians, offered important lessons, even if they were not heeded. Queer Nation could have learned much from the de-centering of white feminism, the intervention of global and postcolonial feminists, and the feminist debates around sexuality. We did not.

1992

10 Percent. Winter. Premier issue. In "Seven Great Minds: Books for the '90s" (1992), Urvashi Vaid lists feminist author Susan Faludi's *Backlash*.

Advocate #603, May 19. Cover story "Gloria Steinem v. Sally Quinn" (Minkowitz, 1992) examines the public debate spurred by novelist Sally Quinn, who, in a *Washington Post* editorial titled "Who Killed Feminism?" argued that lesbianism keeps feminist issues on the fringe. Popular feminist writers such as Naomi Wolfe describe pressure from media and publishers to reassure the public they are heterosexual, creating a divide-and-conquer technique of splitting straight and lesbian feminists. Patricia Ireland, who had come out the previous fall, claims that the burst of articles bashing NOW as a lesbian group were part of a White House spin campaign in the wake of the Clarence Thomas nomination hearings. "Gloria Steinem, Feminist Luminary" (1992) asks her, "Will the gay and lesbian and feminist movements unite more in the future?" She replies:

> I think we have united to a remarkable degree, when you consider the enormous pressure to divide. I'm rather proud that we have not knuckled under. We need a deeper understanding of the shared root of the problem. It's not simply a civil rights issue. As long as patriarchy tries to direct all sexuality into the rearing of children who can inherit property, women and gay men are going to be anathema. (p. 35).

1993

Christopher Street #207, Nov., features a cover story "Is Political Correctness Destroying the Gay Civil Rights Movement?" (Miller, 1993), which complains that "progressive feminists (lesbian and straight), influenced by academic feminist theory" (p. 36) are male bashing and attacking white men. "There are the lesbian feminists who argue AIDS has received too much attention compared to breast cancer," writes Stephen Miller (p. 37). He cites the Michigan women's music festival as an example of "female chauvinism" and claims that the first wave of gay activism (between Stonewall and AIDS) was "hampered (and in some places undone)" by leftist ideology (p. 37).

1995

San Francisco Pride Access. The official guide to the city's 25th annual LGBT pride celebration included an advertisement for Homeless Women's Project (1995,

p. 24) and a photo of a woman carrying a sign that reads, "AIDS not just a man's issue—Women's AIDS Network" (p. 21).

The "Resource Directory" (1995) includes several women's organizations: SF Women Against Rape, Old Wives Tales & Women's Visions and Books, Sister-spirit Women's Bookstore/Coffeehouse, Radical Women National Office, Women Against Imperialism, Women's Feminist Alternative, Young Women's Rap Group, but not a separate women's section.

"Pride Calendar" (1995) includes the National Women's Music Festival in Bloomington, IN, and other women's events.

New York Native #657, Nov 20. Stephen H. Miller (1995) strikes again in "Family Matters," this month's installment of his column "Culture Watch." "The so-called feminist men's movement," he writes, "tends to condemn manhood and masculinity (and, for that matter, any recognition of gender distinctions) as part of evil patriarchy" (p. 18).

Advocate #695, Nov 28. "Howard Stern: The *Advocate* Interview" with Camille Paglia (1995): "You have an undeserved reputation among feminists and gay activists for misogyny and homophobia," she tells him (p. 56). "Heterosexual men have a very taunting, jeering, and to me stimulating way of talking to each other. A lot of women and gay men find it too harsh and get their feelings hurt" (p. 65).

Lesbian News vol. 21 #1, Aug. The "world's largest monthly lesbian magazine" includes a full-page ad for AIDS Walk LA (p. 16).

Cover-story interview quotes "honorary lesbian" Ramona Ripston of the ACLU saying, " 'Whether we're straight women or lesbians, we have the same problems,' Ripston said. 'Males still dominate in society. And gay men and lesbians have the same struggle that straight women have with straight men' " (Frazier, 1995, p. 40).

"Sexism: Lesbians v. Gay Men" describes reverse sexism when "gay men are often overcharged at lesbian bars and many men who work directly with lesbians are subjected to the kind of insults and harassment one is more likely to associate with male-on-female sexism of the world at large" (Shoemaker, 1995, p. 56). The article describes hostility and harassment experienced by a male bartender and male patrons of a women's bar: " '(Gay men) totally disgust me,' one lesbian bar regular complained. 'They're tramps in heat, without a doubt. They don't even care enough about each other to be safe' " (p. 57). The article also presents several examples of gay men and feminist women working together:

> Women, in unprecedented numbers, participated in this year's California AIDS Ride fundraiser; many gay men work for and support women's rights. A few men even joined in June's L.A. Dyke March as it made its way down Santa Monica Boulevard. This new unity is a far cry from the separatism that many lesbians practiced in the '70s. Nowadays most lesbians see gay men as their brothers in oppression, co-warriors in the battle against prejudice and hate. And many gay men turn to women and lesbians for support and nurturance that isn't always available to them in the world of men, gay or straight. (p. 56)

New York Native #638, July 10. Another Stephen H. Miller (1995) rant, "Pride Potpourri," relates stories that New York City Pride was "dominated by lesbians with a penchant for confrontational vulgarity and an obsession with their genitalia" (p. 18). Citing reverse discrimination again, he says that men wouldn't be allowed to do the same thing. In what sounds today like an incel or alt-right man blaming of feminism for emasculating men, he describes a "gender-war feminist lesbian attack on strong men" in which the intellectual contributions between feminist women and gay men are seen as a negative:

> Strong, dynamic male leaders seem to have disappeared from the scene. Assertive gay men, especially masculine men, are not politically correct unless they are ultra-left-wing and/or 'of color' (and even that's no guarantee). They are condemned by both feminist theory (which demands power be wrested from the white male 'class') and its sibling, academic 'queer theory' (which considers masculinity the root cause of patriarchy, which, in turn, underlies capitalism and other forms of 'oppression'). (p. 18)

1998

Out, Feb. After cringing through three Stephen Miller essays, it was heartwarming to read "Angela at Our Table" (Miles, 1998). Angela Davis talks about being inspired by ACT UP, and how it has helped her see how private issues, such as disease or domestic violence, can be organizing points for movements. "She has also found common ground with feminists and lesbian and gay activists" (p. 67), the article states, describing her joining a group of black feminists to speak out on the sexism of the Million Man March, and addressing homophobia more in her public speaking.

1999

Advocate, #776–777, Jan. 19. "Man in the Hot Seat" presents lesbian author and ACT UP member Sarah Schulman (1999) interviewing conservative gay writer Andrew Sullivan, both revealing conflicts. In promoting his new book about promiscuity and intimacy, he asserts a belief in biological differences between male and female sexuality that played out among gay men and lesbian women. Schulman replies, "So you're rejecting the 30-year argument of the feminist movement that biology is not destiny." Sullivan states that "[Biology] is simply part of what makes one who one is, and ignoring that will lead you to all sorts of frustrations and an inability to understand what is going on." Schulman replies that "the biological determinism argument is mostly embraced by gay men. Lesbians have a long history of arguing for their sexuality as a choice" (all p. 88).

Curve, May. "Lesbians & NOW—Mending the Rift." Patricia Ireland (1999) writes that "Surely every feminist—of whatever sexual orientation—was offended and outraged by the attacks on the LGBT community this past year. Congress attacked through legislation; the right wing attacked in the media; and hate attacked Matthew Shepard, taking his life." She announces that NOW will be hosting a Lesbian Rights Summit for third time, "a feminist strategy session for lesbians and allies" (all p. 35).

The Harvard Gay & Lesbian Review v6 #3, Summer. "State of the Struggle" (Billard, 1999) a roundtable discussion, includes Urvashi Vaid, former Executive Director of the National Gay and Lesbian Task Force. "I was active in the feminist movement from 1975 on," she says, "and that's when I started to read about gay and lesbian history" (p. 17). Rather than an oppositional or problematic relationship, she suggests a mutual influence.

2000

Advocate, June 6. "Trailblazers" (2000) article lists Cris Williamson and Leisha Hailey as women's music pioneers, mentioning the "struggle of lesbian-feminist artists."

2001

Genre #99, Dec. "Is Gay Liberation Dead?" (Gierach, 2001) has as its first quoted source Ivy Bottini, "a long-time activist with the National Organization for Women (NOW) and gay and lesbian causes" (p. 44). She doesn't specifically address women's LGBTQ coalitions but talks of general complacency, commercialization, and assimilation, and not being able to turn out numbers for events as they had in the past. Martha Matthews, an ACLU attorney says, "Every movement struggles with the progression of professionalism beyond the grass roots—the black civil rights movement, the women's movement, labor, all of them" (p. 45).

2015

Advocate, March 10. "15 Women Who Stood Up for LGBT People" (2015) photo essay includes—and names—two feminists. Bella Abzug is shown in a photo "speaking to her friend and fellow feminist Robin Morgan, [and] was a member of Congress from 1971 to 1977; in 1975 she and Rep. Ed Koch (who many believe was a closeted gay man) introduced the first federal gay rights bill, the predecessor of today's still-pending Employment Non-Discrimination Act." Audre Lorde's photo caption reads, in part, "She spoke out against racism, sexism, homophobia, and economic injustice in her poems, prose, and activism. She also called out her fellow feminists for largely ignoring race and class issues."

Although certain familiar themes appear in the LGBTQ media and the historiographic books, there are also significant differences. I have kept them separate here, and written about them using different styles, to resist a false sense of coherence. The stories of feminist women and gay men are varied, both when told at the time and when retrospectively historicized. In the next chapter, I will alternate from this difference and diffusion to focusing on a single case study: feminist women and gay men in the US state of South Carolina, a region of the country historically neglected in these wider national conversations.

List of Titles Examined

Ball, S. (1998). *The HIV-negative gay man: Developing strategies for survival and emotional well-being.*
Beasley, C. (1999). *What is feminism? An introduction to feminism.*
Bech, H. (1997). *When men meet: Homosexuality and modernity.*
Bell, D., & Valentine, G. (1995). *Mapping desire: Geographies of sexualities.*
Bennett, J. M. (2006). *History matters: Patriarchy and the challenge of feminism.*
Berger, R. M. (1996). *The older homosexual man.*
Berubé, A., D'Emilio, J., and Freedman, E. B. (Eds.). (2011). *My desire for history: Essays in gay, community, and labor history.*
Bullough, V. (1976). *Sexual variance in society and history.*
Butler, J. (1990). *Gender trouble: Feminism and the subversion of identity.*
Castiglia, C., & Reed, C. (2012). *If memory serves: Gay men, AIDS, and the promise of the queer past.*

Clum, J. M. (2000). *Still acting gay: Male homosexuality in modern drama.*

Cochran, P. D. H. (2005). *Evangelical feminism: A history.*

Cory, D. W. (1951). *The homosexual in America.*

D'Arcangelo, A. (1971). *Angelo D'Arcangelo's love book: Inside the sexual revolution: From women's lib to gay power.*

Douglas, S. J. (2010). *Enlightened sexism: The seductive message that feminism work is done.*

Ellis, A. L. (2001). *Gay men at midlife: Age before beauty.*

Faderman, L. (2015). *The gay revolution: The story of the struggle.*

Fellows, W. (1998). *Farm boys.*

Freedman, E. B. (2002). *No turning back: The history of feminism and the future of women.*

Freedman, E. B. (2007). *The essential feminist reader.*

Friedan, B. (2001). *The feminine mystique.*

Gay Left Collective (Eds.). (1980). *Homosexuality: Power and politics.*

Gerassi, J. (1966). *The boys of Boise.*

Gideonse, T., & Williams, R. (2006). *From boys to men: Gay men write about growing up.*

Giroux, H. A. (1991). *Postmodernism, feminism, and cultural politics: Redrawing educational boundaries.*

Hall Carpenter Archives. (1989). *Walking after midnight: Gay men's life stories.*

Hall, S. (1985). Signification, representation, ideology: Althusser and the post-structuralist debates. *Critical Studies in Media Communication, 2*(2), 91–114.

Hall, S. (1986). The problem of ideology-Marxism without guarantees. *Journal of communication inquiry, 10*(2), 28–44.

Hall, S. (2003). Cultural studies and the centre: Some problematics and problems. In Hall, S., Hobson, D., Lowe, A., & Willis, P. (Eds.). (2003). *Culture, media, language: working papers in cultural studies, 1972–79*, (pp. 12–45). Routledge.

Hall, S., Connell, I., and Curti, L. (2007). The "unity"of current affairs television. In *CCCS Selected Working Papers*, (pp. 342–380). Routledge.

Harlan, J. (1998). *Feminism: A reference handbook.*

Havel, B. F. (2005). In search of a theory of public memory: The state, the individual, and Marcel Proust. *Indiana Law Journal, 80*(3), 605–726.

Hollows, J. (2000). *Feminism, femininity and popular culture.*

Hooks, B. (2000). *Feminism is for everybody: Passionate politics.*

Isay, R. A. (2009). *Being homosexual: Gay men and their development.*

Janssen, V. (2002). *Homosexual men in action, 1890–1930.*

Jay, K., & Young, A. (1972). *Out of the closets: Voices of gay liberation.*

Jervis, L., & Zeisler, A. (2006). *Bitchfest: Ten years of cultural criticism from the pages of* Bitch Magazine.

Johnson. P. E. (2011). *Sweet tea: Black gay men of the south.*

Jones, R., & Bego, M. (2009). *Macho man: The disco era and gay America's "coming out."*

Kaiser, C. (1997). *The gay metropolis: History of gay life in America.*

Kenealy, A. (1920). *Feminism and sex-extinction.*

Kennedy, H. C. (1999). *The ideal gay man: The story of Der Kreis.*

Mallon, G. (2004). *Gay men choosing parenthood.*

Martin, C. E., & Sullivan, C. J. (2010). *Click: When we were feminists.*

Mawlabocus, S. (2010). *Gaydar culture: Gay men, technology and embodiment in the digital age.*

Moller Okin, S., & Mansbridge, J. (1994). *Feminism: Volume I.*

Moore, P. (2004). *Beyond shame: Reclaiming the abandoned history of radical gay sexuality.*

Nardi, P. M. (1999). *Gay men's friendships: Invincible communities.*

Nardi, P. M. (2000). *Gay masculinities.*

Rauch, J. (2005). *Gay marriage: Why it is good for gays, good for straights and good for America.*

Reynolds, R., & Sullivan, G. (2003). *Gay men's sexual stories: Getting it!*

Rofes, E. (1996). *Reviving the tribe.*

Sadownick, D. (1997). *Sex between men: An intimate history of the sex lives of gay men postwar to present.*

Schneir, M. (1994). *Feminism: The essential historical writings.*

Scott, J. W. (1996). *Feminism and history.*

Seely, M. (2007). *Fight like a girl: How to be a fearless feminist.*

Segal, L. (1999). *Why feminism? Gender, psychology, politics.*

Staal, S. (2011). *Reading women: How the great books of feminism changed my life.*

Talpade Mahanty, C. (2003). *Feminism without borders: Decolonizing theory, practicing solidarity.*

Tandon, N. (2008). *Feminism: A paradigm shift.*

Tarrant, S. (2009). *Men and feminism.*

Valenti, J. (2007). *Full frontal feminism: A young woman's guide to why feminism matters.*

Valenti, J. (2008). *He's a stud, she's a slut: And 49 other double standards every woman should know.*

Walters. (2005). *Feminism: A very short introduction.*

Woog, D. *Friends & family: True stories of gay America's straight allies.*

Ziegler, A. (2008). *Feminism and pop culture.*

References

15 women who stood up for LGBT people. (2015, Mar. 10). *Advocate.* Retrieved from https://www. advocate.com/women/2015/03/10/15-women-who-stood-lgbt-people?fb_comment_id=112 0076044684596_1120295367995997

AIDS not just a man's issue Women's AIDS Network. (1995). Photo in *SF Pride Access 1995 official guide 25th annual SF LGBT pride celebration,* 21.

AIDS Walk LA. (1995, Aug.) Advertisement. *Lesbian News 21*(1), 16.

Baumgardner, J. (2011). *F'em! Goo goo, gaga, and some thoughts on balls.* Berkeley, CA: Seal Press.

Bech, H. (1997). *When men meet: Homosexuality and modernity.* Chicago: University of Chicago Press.

Berger, R. M. (1996). *Gay and gray: The older homosexual man.* New York: Psychology Press.

Billard, B. (1999, Summer). State of the struggle. *The Harvard Gay & Lesbian Review 6*(3), 17–20.

Birch, K. (1980). The politics of autonomy. In Gay Left Collective (Ed.) *Homosexuality: Power and politics* (pp. 85–92). Brooklyn, NY: Verso Books.

Brodkey, L., & Fine, M. (1991). Presence of mind in the absence of body. In H. A. Giroux (Ed.), *Postmodernism, feminism, and cultural politics: Redrawing educational boundaries* (pp. 100–118). Albany, NY: SUNY Press.

Browne, S. H. (1999). Remembering Crispus Attucks: Race, rhetoric, and the politics of commemoration. *Quarterly Journal of Speech, 85*(2), 169–187.

Brownworth, V. A. (2015, Oct.). A 750-page journey through gay American history. *Slate.* Retrieved from https://slate.com/human-interest/2015/10/the-gay-revolution-by-lillian-faderman-reviewed.html

Bunch, C. (1987). Learning from Lesbian Separatism. In C. Bunch (Ed.), *Passionate politics: Feminist theory in action* (pp. 182–191). New York: St. Martin's Griffin.

Califia, P. (1984, Apr. 3). Face to face: Women react to AIDS. *Advocate* #391, 26–27, 30–31.

Califia, P. (1985, Sept. 3). See no evil: The anti-porn movement. *Advocate* #428.

Castiglia, C., &Reed, C. (2012). *If memory serves: Gay men, AIDS, and the promise of the queer past.* Minneapolis: University of Minnesota Press.

Clum, J. M. (2000). *Still acting gay: Male homosexuality in modern drama.* Macmillan.

Combahee River Collective, T. (1997). A black feminist statement. In L. Nicholson (Ed.), *The second wave: A reader in feminist theory* (pp. 63–70). New York: Psychology Press.

D'Emilio, J. (1989). Gay politics and community in San Francisco since World War II. In M. V. Martin Bauml Duberman & George Chauncey (Eds.), *Hidden from history: Reclaiming the gay and lesbian past* (pp. 456–476). New York: Penguin.

De Certeau, M. (1988). *The writing of history.* New York: Columbia University Press.

Douglas, S. J. (2010). *The rise of enlightened sexism: How pop culture took us from girl power to girls gone wild.* New York: Macmillan.

Doyle, V. (2008). "But Joan! You're my daughter!" The gay and lesbian alliance against defamation and the politics of amnesia. *Radical History Review, 100,* 209–221.

Dunn, T. R. (2011). Remembering "a great fag": Visualizing public memory and the construction of queer space. *Quarterly Journal of Speech, 97*(4), 435–460.

Dunn, T. R. (2015). Historical trans-cription: Struggling with memory in *Paris Is Burning.* In J. Capuzza & L. G. Spencer, (Eds.), *Transgender communication studies: Histories, trends, and trajectories* (pp. 217–231). Washington, DC: Lexington Books.

Echols, A. (1991, Mar. 26). Justifying our love? The evolution of lesbianism through feminism and gay male politics. *Advocate,* #573, 48–50.

Edwards, T. (1994). *Erotics and politics: Gay male sexuality, masculinity and feminism.* New York: Routledge.

ERA reintroduced. (1982, Sept. 2). *Advocate* #350, 10.

Fairclough, N. (1992). *Discourse and social change.* Cambridge, UK: Polity Press.

Fellows, W. (Ed.). (1998). *Farm boys: Lives of gay men from the rural Midwest.* Madison: University of Wisconsin Press.

Fitzmaurice, M. I. (2014). Re(place)ing space: Privilege and public memory in the National Women's History Cybermuseum. *Feminist Media Studies, 14*(3), 520–523.

Foucault, M. (1998). On the ways of writing history. In J. Faubion, (Ed.), *Michel Foucault: Aesthetics, method, and epistemology* (pp. 279–296). New York: The New Press.

Foucault, M. (2012). *The archaeology of knowledge.* New York: Vintage.

Fram, S. M. (2013). The constant comparative analysis method outside of grounded theory. *The Qualitative Report, 18*(1), 1–25.

Frazier, C. (1995, Aug.) ACLU. *Lesbian News (21),* 1, 40–41.

Freedman, E. (2007). *No turning back: The history of feminism and the future of women*. New York: Ballantine Books.

Gamson, W. A., Croteau, D.,Hoynes, W., & Sasson, T. (1992). Media images and the social construction of reality. *Annual Review of Sociology*, 18, 373–393.

Gierach, R. (2001, Dec.) Is gay liberation dead? *Genre #99*, 42–45.

Ginzburg, C. (1980). Morelli, Freud and Sherlock Holmes: Clues and scientific method. *History Workshop Journal*, 9, 5–36.

Giteck, L., & Daniels, M. (1985, Apr. 30). Homophobia. *Advocate #419*, 26–27.

Gloria, S.. (1992, May 19). Feminist luminary. *Advocate #603*, 32–35.

Gomez-Barris, M., & Gray, H. (Eds.). (2010). *Towards a sociology of a trace*. Minneapolis: University of Minnesota Press.

Hajek, A. (2016). Feminist impact: Exploring the cultural memory of second-wave feminism in contemporary Italy. In A. Hajek, C. Lohmeier, & C. Pentzold, (Eds.), *Memory in a mediated world* (pp. 129–141). New York: Palgrave Macmillan.

Haraway, D. (1999). Situated knowledges: The science question in feminism and the privilege of partial perspective. *Feminist Studies, 14*(3), 575–599.

Harlan, J. (1998). *Feminism: A reference handbook*. Santa Barbara, CA: Abc-Clio Incorporated.

Has, R. (1982, Sept. 2). Lesbians and gay men join the antinuclear family. *Advocate #350*, 20–21, 25, 53.

Hollibaugh, A. (1980). Right to rebel. In Gay Left Collective (Ed.) *Homosexuality: Power and politics* (pp. 205–215). Brooklyn, NY: Verso Books.

Hollows, J. (2000). *Feminism, femininity and popular culture*. Manchester, UK: Manchester University Press.

Homeless Women's Project. (1995). Advertisement. *SF Pride Access 1995 official guide 25th annual SF LGBT pride celebration*, 24.

Hyde Park Chapter. (1972). *Socialist feminism: A strategy for the women's movement*. Chicago: Chicago Women's Liberation Union.

Ireland, P. (1999, May) Lesbians & NOW—Mending the rift. *Curve*, 35.

Isay, R. (2009). *Being homosexual: Gay men and their development*. New York: Vintage.

Jay, K. (1982, Sept. 2). Women and terrorism. *Advocate #350*, 22–24.

Jervis, L., & Zeisler, A. (2006). *BITCHfest: Ten years of cultural criticism from the pages of Bitch magazine*. New York: Macmillan.

Johnson, E. P. (2011). *Sweet tea: Black gay men of the South*. Chapel Hill: University of North Carolina Press.

Kennedy, H. (2013). *The ideal gay man: The story of Der Kreis*. New York: Routledge.

Mandziuk, R. M., & Fitch, S. P. (2001). The rhetorical construction of Sojourner Truth. *Southern Communication Journal 66* (2), 120–138.

Maurantonio, N. (2015). Material rhetoric, public memory, and the Post-It Note. *Southern Communication Journal 80* (2), 83–101.

Miles, S. (1998, Feb.). Angela at our table. *Out*, 62–67.

Miller, N. (2008). *Out of the past: Gay and lesbian history from 1869 to the present*. Los Angeles: Advocate Books.

Miller, S. (1993, Nov.). Is political correctness destroying the gay civil rights movement? *Christopher Street* #207, 36–37.

Miller, S. (1995, July 10). Pride potpourri. *New York Native* #638, 18–24.

Minkowitz, D. (1992, May 19). Gloria Steinem v. Sally Quinn. *Advocate* #603, 30–37.

Mo'Nique. (2006, July) Mo'Nique gets the last word. *Instinct*, 88.

Mohanty, C. T. (2005). *Feminism without borders: Decolonizing theory, practicing solidarity.* Shahpur Jat, New Delhi, India: Zubaan.

Moore, P. (2004). *Beyond shame: Reclaiming the abandoned history of radical gay sexuality.* Boston: Beacon Press.

National organizations boost gay cause. (1994, June 26). *Advocate*, 41–49.

Nardi, P. M. (1999). *Gay men's friendships: Invincible communities.* Chicago: University of Chicago Press.

Nardi, P. M. (2000). *Gay masculinities.* Thousand Oaks, CA: Sage Publications.

New College of California. (1990, June 24). Feminist psychology. Advertisement in *SF Lesbian/Gay Freedom Day Parade & Celebration Guide*, 32.

Olick, J. K., & Robbins, J. (1998). Social memory studies: From "collective memory" to the historical sociology of mnemonic practices. *Annual Review of Sociology 24*(1), 105–140.

Paglia, C. (1995, Nov. 28). Howard Stern: The *Advocate* interview. *Advocate* #695, 55–67.

Patterson, J. R. (2014). Public memory and political history: news media and collective memory construction after the deaths of former presidents (Doctoral dissertation). University of Texas-Austin.

Pride Calendar. (1995). *SF Pride Access 1995 official guide 25th annual SF LGBT pride celebration.*

Rauch, J. (2004). *Gay marriage: Why it is good for gays, good for straights, and good for America.* New York: Macmillan.

Resource Directory. (1995). *SF Pride Access 1995 official guide 25th annual SF LGBT pride celebration*, 68–79.

Reynolds, R., & Sullivan, G. (2003). *Gay men's sexual stories: Getting it!* Binghamton, NY: Harrington Park Press.

Rich, A. (1980). Compulsory heterosexuality and lesbian existence. *Signs: Journal of Women in Culture and Society*, 5(4), 631–660.

Rofes, E. (2013). *Reviving the tribe: Regenerating gay men's sexuality and culture in the ongoing epidemic.* New York: Routledge.

Rosenberg, S. (2003). Neither forgotten nor fully remembered: Tracing an ambivalent public memory on the 10th anniversary of the Montréal Massacre. *Feminist Theory*, 4(1), 5–27.

Rudy, K. (2001). Radical feminism, lesbian separatism, and queer theory. *Feminist Studies*, *27*(1), 190.

Ryan, L. (2010). Memory, power and resistance: The anatomy of a tripartite relationship. *Memory Studies 4*(2), 154–169.

Scott, D. T. (2011). Contested kicks: Sneakers and gay masculinity, 1964–2008. *Communication and Critical/Cultural Studies*, 8(2), 146–164.

Schudson, M. (1997). Lives, laws, and language: Commemorative versus non-commemorative forms of effective public memory. *Communication Review 2*(1), 3–17.

Schulman, S. (1999, Jan. 19). Man in the hot seat. *Advocate* #776–777.

Segal, L. (1999). *Why feminism: Gender, psychology, politics.* New York: Wiley.

Segesten, A. D., & Wüstenberg, J. (2016). Memory studies: The state of an emergent field. *Memory Studies 9*, 1–16.

Seven Great Minds: Books for the 90s. (1992, Winter). *10 Percent*, 74–75.

Shoemaker, J. (1995, Aug.) Sexism: Lesbians v. gay men. *Lesbian News (21)*, 1, 55–57.

Spivak, G. C. (1999). *Can the subaltern speak?* Cambridge, MA: Harvard University Press.

Sterne, J. (2010). Rearranging the files: On interpretation in media history. *Communication Review*, *13*(1), 75–87.

Tandon, N. (2008). *Feminism: A paradigm shift*. New Delhi, India: Atlantic Publishers & Dist.

Tarrant, S. (2009). *Men and feminism*. New York: Seal Press.

Trailblazers. (2000, Feb. 15). *Advocate*, 28–34.

Ulrich, L. (2007). *Well-behaved women seldom make history*. New York: Knopf.

Valenti, J. (2008). *He's a stud, she's a slut, and 49 other double standards every woman should know.* New York: Seal Press.

Van Doorn, N. (2016). The fabric of our memories: Leather, kinship, and queer material history. *Memory Studies*, *9*(1), 85–98.

Ward, J. (2000). Queer sexism: Rethinking gay men and masculinity. In P. Nardi (Ed.), *Gay masculinities* (pp. 152–175). Thousand Oaks, CA: Sage Publications.

Year in review. (1982, Jan. 21). *The Advocate #335*, 19–21.

Zeisler, A. (2008). *Feminism and pop culture*. New York: Seal Press.

Zelizer, B. (1992). *Covering the body: The Kennedy assassination, the media, and the shaping of collective memory*. Chicago: University of Chicago Press.

2

Networked Social Change: Feminism and LGBTQ Movements in South Carolina, USA

"I see my sexuality as an integral part of my life. It is neither good nor bad. It is not immoral; it is not anti-social; it is not anti-woman. It simply is."
— autobiography of Edward Flud, SC LGBTQ Archives

"Feminist or gay, why are women joining the National Gay Task Force?"
— brochure ca. 1977, archives of South Carolina Chapter of the
National Organization for Women

In the previous chapter, I examined the discourses of these two movements as represented in historiographies of each as well as in LGBTQ independent media. I found that the networks were connected, but weakly. Many gay-male-oriented historiographies explicitly mentioned feminism and feminists, and most feminist-oriented historiographies explicitly mentioned gay men. However, this was a very small number of references within each book, relative to the total number of pages in each book. From the references that did exist, three main types of connections emerged: positive connections of commonality, negative connections of oppositional ideologies, and the cross-pollination of intellectual contributions. However, almost no book exhibited all three themes. In LGBTQ media, similar themes appeared, as well as more nuanced versions of the narratives relating these two groups could be seen unfolding over time. I will now expand upon these stories by turning to a case study of the US state of South Carolina. I move here from the secondary sources of books and magazines to primary research in archives, directly examining the artifacts of women's histories and LGBTQ histories for evidence of their intersections and entanglements.

South Carolina

South Carolina is a state with a current population of approximately 5 million, extending from the Atlantic coast inland to the foothills of the Appalachian Mountains. One of the original colonies before American Independence, it later was the first state to secede from the union at the onset of the US Civil War. It did not ratify the women's suffrage constitutional amendment until 1969. As a conservative and religious state, in South Carolina there has been longstanding cultural pressure against both of these movements, which has encouraged collaboration against common enemies, but also divide-and-conquer sexist and homophobic divisions and oppositions, as expected from the received view described earlier.

South Carolina was chosen as my case study to augment this project for practical, political, and strategic reasons. Logistically, this limits the size of the archives to be examined to something more manageable than the entirety of women's politics in the United States for the past 50 years. As the state in which I currently work and reside, archives and travel funding were more accessible. Politically, this was a choice to intervene in the dominance of the coastal and urban in queer and feminist historiographies by adding examples from a Southern, largely rural state. As Gray (2008) describes, the rural is often positioned as Other to the urban, and attending to rural queer experience and history is one way to queer LGBTQ and social-movement studies dominated by the urban. Personally, as someone who grew up in a border Southern state, Texas, I have long been dedicated to redressing the over-emphasis of urban, coastal areas in LGBTQ history and cultural representations.

Third, as a Southern, conservative, religious state, there has been great cultural pressure against both of these groups here. In 1996, the state legislative committee passed an anti-gay-marriage bill similar to those in Utah, South Dakota, and Idaho, spurred by potential of same-sex marriage in Hawaii. The state constitution was amended with a "marriage amendment" in 2006. Choosing this state forces a challenge to a common theme throughout the historiographic discourses, both implicit and explicit: that straight female homophobia and gay male sexism and misogyny are and have been major obstacles to these groups working together.

South Carolina is the home of late US Senator Strom Thurmond and con-servative Christian Bob Jones University. If sexism and homophobia are major obstacles to feminist women and gay men working together, then, in a place like South Carolina, it should have been extremely difficult for them to do so. But, if they *did* manage to connect at all here, it can be assumed that their connections were broader and deeper in more amenable places, such as New York or Califor-nia. If it could happen here, it must have happened elsewhere, and arguably more so. It has traditionally been difficult to publicly identify as one or the other, even more hard to identify as both. Therefore, any evidence of collaboration would be particularly meaningful. Cultural ideologies of sexism and homophobia should be more ingrained in each group, and they should have been more cautious of provoking sexism and homophobia in others, such as donors, community leaders, and local media, thereby presenting pressure not to align with the other group.

However, I do not approach South Carolina as a bounded entity, but as an actor in a network. In focusing on South Carolina, I do not limit myself to examining only South Carolina-made artifacts and resident persons. I am also interested in how South Carolina individuals and organizations communicated with and about regional, national, and international organizations. Therefore, a newsletter by a chapter of the National Organization of Women (NOW) in Greenville, SC, is meaningful, but so are the national and international publica-tions found in the files of local NOW chapters. They evidence a local organiza-tion's communication networks with other organizations, and are as relevant as the artifacts the local organizations themselves generated. The material presented here is primarily based on archival research in the Louise Pettus Archives and Special Collections, Women's History collections at the Winthrop University, Dacus Library in Rock Hill, South Carolina, and the University of South Caro-lina LGBTQ Collection.

South Carolina and the Received View

There are and have been feminists in South Carolina. Organizations have in-cluded the SC Commission on Women, NOW SC, ERA SC Coalition, Green-ville Feminist Theater, and the SC chapter for the International Women's Year Conference. Other forms of women's organizing and support have taken place within less recognizable organizations, such as ERA support from the SC Home Economics Association, sometimes using more typically Southern politeness and discretion. In a 1977 memo from Barbara W. Moxon, Chairperson of ERA SC to its Steering Committee Members, she advises confidentiality, writing that they "should all keep a low profile about all of the activity we are carrying on." The Greenville Business and Professional Women's Club Records include the minutes of their meeting on March 19, 1974, during which "Irene Thurston, Corresponding Secretary, read items of correspondence from Natelle Hall regarding ERA and convention, both National in Washington and State in Columbia." However, the minutes do not include any details of any discussion and, in the available records of their minutes from meetings held twice a month from January 2, 1973–August 5, 1975, this was the only ERA reference.

Church Women United in SC was a chapter of a self-described movement, not organization. "Citizens in action," they worked trying to make a more just world, largely through migrant aid, transition to peacetime economy, Congressional reform, volunteerism, service, media monitoring (mostly anti-violence, stereotypes of women and minorities, and "sexual depravity," but not anti-porn explicitly), political lobbying and training, and also mission work. In a 1973 memo to SC State Finance Chairwoman from Elizabeth Howell Gripe, Director of Cultivation, Church Women United, NYC, she announces a change from using "chairman" to the "more precise term 'chairwoman'" as a salutation, because "we are trying to recognize also that we are now in a time of transition in the matter of language." The files of SC CWU also contained several flyers and brochures on the ERA and International Women's Year, all supportive. In 1970, the Women's Action Alliance formed as an information clearinghouse for women's organizations, and in March 1975 wrote to 122 national women's groups inviting them to participate in a questionnaire to help develop National Women's Agenda Day on December 2, 1975, during International Women's Year. CWU was one of approximately 70 others who responded, and an agenda for the December meeting was created. A letter of November 17, 1975, to state and local Presidents, Board of Managers, and Chairwomen from Elizabeth Howell Verdesi, Director of Cultivation, and Sister Mary Luke Tobin, Director of Citizen Action, writes that CWU "has traditionally been in the forefront of involvement with women's concerns" and so participated but "was the only religious group on the Working Committee." They expressed "earnest hope that we may enter our third century [as a country] as equal partners, making real the claim of 'liberty and justice for all.'" The national CWU made clear that they will work with other women's groups "on common concerns," but "this does NOT carry the full weight of either approval or endorsement" (emphasis original). SC CWU materials on file included their Citizen Action News Briefs of July 1976, containing a photocopy of an "ERA Update Chart" showing legislative progress from 1975–1977, without comment. In the May 1975, South Carolina Church Woman newsletter article,

"National Board Supports Equal Rights Amendment," the CWU National Board of Managers " 'urgently requested' " legislators support the ERA at the annual board meeting. The article goes on to say that CWU is an open and wide ecumenical movement, and local units can make their own decisions to "act autonomously on social issues," hoping members will travel to throw support behind those in states that haven't ratified. It also notes that, in 1970, the Board of Managers of CWU endorsed the ERA. A note at the end of article states that it was a release from the CWU PR Department, and, since its release, the ERA had been defeated in South Carolina "in an unexpected vote" but "all is not lost."

A 2007 journalism class at the University of South Carolina reported on two more recent organizations. "The Grimke Sisters" is described as a "fairly new" grassroots organization of about 115 volunteers "that reaches out to women, especially minorities," created by Becci Robbins in 2002. Robbins says, "There wasn't a group that was working on women's issues in Columbia." She had been involved with NOW, but it was perceived as "well-off white women," and she wanted to make something more accessible to women of color, and had worked with state lobbying and supporting Planned Parenthood.

LGBTQ organizing and activism has a history in South Carolina as well. According to gay historian Alan Bérubé, the nation's first gay newspaper comes from South Carolina, *Myrtle Beach Bitches*, which was written for gay men in military service during the 1940s. Virago, "a lesbian organization empowering women," published its *Virago Newsletter* in Columbia, the state capital. *The Harris Guide 2001: The Comprehensive Guide to the GLBT Press* also lists *In Unison*, also out of Columbia, described elsewhere as "The Carolinas' Alternative Lifestyle Newsmagazine."

Harriet Hancock, a Columbia attorney, founded the first South Carolina chapter of Parents and Friends of Lesbians and Gays (PFLAG) in 1982, a year after her son came out. 1989, she started gathering signatures of friends and people interested in doing a march. Fears arose of the KKK and possible gunfire. However, "Hancock said the only opposition she really received was from a woman who told her that she shouldn't have used balloons because 'when they deflated, turtles would eat them and die' " (Hammel, 2007, p. 2). The year 1990 saw the first SC Gay & Lesbian Pride March, and formation of the associated South Carolina Gay and Lesbian Pride Movement organization. In 1993, the Gay Lesbian Pride Center (now the Harriet Hancock Center) opened in Columbia. SC Black/Latino Gay Pride began in Columbia in 2006, changing its name thereafter to SC Black Pride. Upstate Pride began in Spartanburg in 2009; Black Pride began in Greenville in 2019.

In *The Big Gay Book: A Man's Survival Guide for the 90's*, editor John Preston lists minimal resource groups and organizations for South Carolina: an AIDS hotline, a bed and breakfast in Charleston, the state ACLU chapter, an AIDS education network, Palmetto Gay and Lesbian Association, and Healing Circle Support Group. In contrast, neighboring states Tennessee and North Carolina had 23 and 21 listings, respectively. Before and since, however, there have been many more groups, largely but not exclusively based in the state capital of Columbia. These have included those mentioned previously, as well as Carolina Black Pride Movement, Lowcountry Gay & Lesbian Alliance, SC Equality Coalition, Human Rights Campaign Carolina (chapter of the national organization combining North Carolina and South Carolina), SC Gay and Lesbian Business Guild, Queer Nation, AFFIRM GLBTQ Youth Center of the Upstate, Alliance for Full Acceptance, Pride of Greenville Choruses, Common Threads HIV charity group, South Carolina Coalition on Human Rights for Sexual Minorities, Lambda Alliance, Metropolitan Community Church (a national LGBTQ-friendly denomination), Dignity (LGBTQ Catholics), Integrity (LGBTQ Episcopalians), SC HIV/AIDS Council, Carolina Rainbow Family Coalition, Central Savannah River Area Rainbow Alliance, US Department of Energy Savannah River Site Gay, Lesbian or Bisexual Employees, College of Charleston Gay/Straight alliance, an SC chapter of the Gay and Lesbian Victory Fund, and Sean's Last Wish, an anti-violence organization. Student groups have included Spectrum at Columbia College, Lambda at Clemson University (later becoming Clemson Gay-Straight Alliance, then Sexuality and Gender Alliance), and the Bisexual Gay Lesbian Straight Alliance at USC, which also had a gay student government president in 2004, Zach Scott. In addition, a number of predominantly gay male leather/Levi/motorcycle clubs and events have existed in the state, such as Swamp Fox, Menamore, Tradesmen, Capital Leathermen, Tarheel Leather Club, The New Tribe, Levi/Leather Brigade, This Thing That We Do, Midlands Power Exchange, Palmetto Adventure, Mr./Mrs. SC Leather & Boy Contest, and a mixed bowling league (Regi, 2007a, 2007b). In 2003, an openly gay man, Marcus Belk, ran for the Democratic nomination for the US Senate election. Although unsuccessful, he was considered a viable candidate during the primary process. In 2007, the University of South Carolina created its GLBTQ Archive.

Commonality and Collaboration

The concept of linking feminist and gay concerns is evidenced among the records of the ERA South Carolina Coalition. *National NOW Times* of December 1977,

lists news items on state gay protections laws, homophobic anti-pornography issues, and progress on federal gay rights legislation. *1977: The Year in Review* from
the National Gay Task Force discusses Anita Bryant and Dade County, and has a
section on President Carter appointing Jean O'Leary to the National Commission
on the Observance of International Women's Year, the only openly homosexual
person on commission, and reports back on 30 states' pro-gay resolutions and
related efforts. "Lesberadas—Houston Lesbians Unite!" from November 1977 reprints an article from *Pointblank Times*, a feminist publication by a self-described
"group of Houston lesbian feminist anarchist gadflies." They discuss planning a
visible action at the Texas International Women's Year Convention, citing as their
first reason the disproportionate violence against gay men: A total 27 in the past
four years having been assaulted or murdered in Houston. They add that they are
prioritizing gay men, rather than lesbians because "lesbians are not as visible, nor
do we make ourselves as vulnerable, as gay men." They also mention a Texas law
against oral sex between people of same sex, and describe their plans and support,
and call for others to join them.

Commonalities also included shared sources of oppression. A photocopy of
an October 4, 1977, article by Lew Scar, medical writer for the *San Diego Union*
newspaper, is reprinted by *The Clarion Call* from National City, California. "Psy-
chiatrist Says: Feminists and Gays 'Emasculate' Family, Nation" describes how

> An eminent psychiatrist blames the women's movement and Gay Liberation for
> what he sees as a decline of the American family and weakening of the nation.
>
> And he says the two movements are achieving that result, not by any kind of
> conspiracy, but by utilizing a common means—emasculation.
>
> "Our land is being flooded by sick people with the coming of each generation,"
> Dr. Harold M. Voth said.

The December 1977, *Phyllis Schlafly Report* story claims that "Houston Proves
Radicals and Lesbians Run IWY." The article, from the influential Christian activist, describes one of the main resolutions passed as "Privileges for homosexuals
and lesbians to teach in the schools, to rent from any landlord, and to have cus-
tody of children," continuing

> Anyone who doubts the total commitment of the IWY Commission to homo-
> sexuals should get a copy of the official 38-page IWY booklet called "A Lesbian
> Guide." On the cover it states proudly: "This booklet was prepared by the

National Gay Task Force and officially approved by the National Commission on the Observance of International Women's Year."

Similarly, the Winter 1977–78 *Voice of Liberty* newsletter from Decatur, Georgia, in its IWY report, decries the sexual preference resolution and describes "a socialist booth with sign 'Down with racism, sexism, and anti-gay bigotry.'" The article is illustrated with photocopies of the logo of NGTF and a sign reading "HOMOSEX-UALS would have equal rights to marriage, adoption of children, employment."

An example of national-local networked connections can be seen in a collection of materials from a South Carolina activist who attended the fifteenth annual Southeastern Conference for Lesbians & Gay Men on March 22–25, 1990, in Raleigh, North Carolina. The conference program evidences feminist collaboration and support with a quarter-page advertisement from NOW, as well as listings for the workshops "Lesbian Rights and NOW" and "Lesbian-Feminism: A Philosophy." Also in the program, the attendee's handwritten notes describe historian Alan Bérubé's talk on *Myrtle Beach Bitches*: "1st gay newspaper in US. During WWII. Was a newsletter to help other gays keep up with where other gays were stationed. 12 or so copies. Writers were arrested and charged with misusing government property, humiliated and dishonorably discharged." This annotated program presents an artifact evidencing how local, regional, and national LGBT networks connected, and then circled back to the local, all while the conference itself provided a switching event into networks of feminist social activism.

Such artifacts demonstrate that the idea of commonalities between gay men and feminist women did penetrate South Carolina organizations. But were they acted upon? At times, yes. In South Carolina, women's and gay organizations did collaborate in the face of shared oppression. In 1975, NOW SC State Advisory Board statement issued a statement on National NOW letterhead protesting the first high-profile case of a gay man's expulsion from military service:

> Whereas discriminatory actions have been perpetrated against homosexuals both male and female in the armed services as indicated by the recent ruling against Sargent Leonard Matlovich and Whereas the National Organization for Women supports our Lesbian sisters. Therefore be it resolved that the South Carolina State Advisory board of the National Organization for Women supports the right of all persons to define their sexual preference without fear of reprisal be it legal, political, economic or social.

An ERA South Carolina newsletter from 1981 writes in its "Legislation" column that

On the federal level, Sen. Paul Laxalt of Nevada has again introduced his so-called "Family Protection Bill." It is heavily supported by the New Right. It is actually an attack on basic constitutional rights and we felt you should know what it is all about. This bill would: ... halt federal protection of the civil rights of those with 'perverse life-styles,' e.g. homosexuality .... You may want to contact Senators Hollings and Thurmond to express your views on this bill.

In 1992, members of SC NOW participated in sit-ins at Cracker Barrel restaurants across the state, protesting their overt discrimination against gays and lesbians. Also at these events were members of the SC chapter of Queer Nation, which had been formed in response to Cracker Barrel. The South Carolina Progressive Network, an activist collective, included organizations for women's reproductive rights, PFLAG, AIDS Services, the South Carolina Coalition against Domestic Violence and Sexual Assault, SC NOW, Tri-County Advocates for Women on Boards and Commissions, and the SCGLPM. In 1993, a stapled packet of "SC NOW Issues" included the national "NOW 100 Day Legislative Action Plan for Women's Civil Rights, Health and Economic Empowerment," which included a "Lesbian and Gay Civil Rights Bill" ("South Carolina Legislative Update," 1993). In a section on "Gay, Lesbian and Bisexual Rights," SC NOW stated their opposition to required disclosure of HIV status, disqualifying homosexual or bisexual persons from the SC National Guard and SC State Guard, prohibition of foster care or adoption by homosexual or bisexual persons, sodomy prohibitions, and the ban on blood donation by gay men.

More recent events include Rev. Patricia Voelker, of MCC Columbia, giving the opening prayer at a 2002 Family Day in Finlay Park, sponsored by the SC Coalition Against Domestic Violence and Sexual Assault, as part of Sexual Assault Awareness Month. *Love American Style: The 8th Annual Human Rights Campaign Carolina Dinner* program from 2003 includes table captains from South and North Carolina. The keynote speaker was former Texas Governor Ann Richards. Although not called a feminist, she is described as having a "career spent opening eyes about the possibilities of women in American public life" (p. 13). An undated flyer described "a town hall meeting on the rights of lesbian, gay, transgender and bisexual people in the workplace," held at the Strom Thurmond Auditorium of the USC Law School in Columbia, its sponsors including gay organizations as well as the SC AFL-CIO and the SC Progressive Network (SCPN). Two long-time gay male activists in the state, Bert Easter and Ed Madden, hosted a preview of the play *Intimate Apparel* by Lynn Nottage, about a single African-American seamstress in 1905 New York City, as a fundraiser for the SC Fund for Southern

Communities, which supports grantees such as SCPN, Carolina Rainbow Family Coalition, environmental, neighborhood, and other groups. An SC Equality Coalition newsletter from 2007 lists a Friends of Planned Parenthood film screening in Charleston on their community calendar.

Conflicts

For a region presumed to be much more suffused with sexism and homophobia, compared to other parts of the country, I found few examples of conflicts between feminist women and gay men. *Myrtle Beach Bitches* had a sexist title, but more by today's standards than its own. I will discuss below more direct conflicts in my focus on the ERA.

Intellectual Contributions

The Sam Nickles Memorial Library is "a quiet space for reading and reflection" housed at the Harriet Hancock Center and "contains hundreds of volumes of books including fiction, non fiction, LGBT oriented literature" (About Sam Nickles, 2018). Currently under reorganization, its available and archived holdings suggest the cross-pollination between feminist women and gay men described in the received view. For example, *Telling the Truth* is a small booklet on radical feminism by Sonia Johnson, who previously ran for US president. "Fifty-two percent of all other oppressed groups are also women," she writes. "The majority of … homosexuals, are women" (1987, p. 7). Rather than creating hierarchy of oppression, she grounds radical feminism and women's oppression as key to resolving others' oppressions.

However, throughout the state women's and LGBTQ archives, there was no feminist or queer theory to be found. In a subsequent chapter's focus groups in the state, however, they will strongly reappear.

Deviations from the Received View

South Carolina also disrupts and complicates the received view. The "liberation moment" is different there. Most historiography positions this moment as one that that occurred simultaneously in the US and Europe in the late 1960s–early 1970s. However, South Carolina breaks this urban-centric view. While the second wave of feminism and civil rights movements did occur in South Carolina then, the gay rights movement that was contemporaneous in major cities was not happening here. The first gay pride parade in South Carolina was held in 1990, almost two decades after the "liberation moment" and, in fact, deep into the re-actionary period of postfeminism, when concerns such as women's equality were misperceived as largely moot. However, during this time we see NOW taking out ads in gay pride brochures and programs, and SC Gay and Lesbian Pride Move-ment (SCGLPM) inviting local NOW speakers and contemplating a keynote invitation to NOW President Patricia Ireland in 1992. Even earlier, clippings files and meeting notes of SC NOW and ERA groups indicate an awareness of the Anita Bryant anti-gay campaign in 1977 as a relevant issue for them, years before any organized gay movement in SC had developed. SCGLPM files even include an example of third-wave or "girlie" feminism, a 2006 flyer for Columbia's "Rad-ical Cheerleaders."

The lesbian switcher and AIDS reunification narratives are complicated here as well. Archival files of organizations such as Palmetto AIDS Life Support Ser-vices, Common Threads, Stop AIDS, and Healing Circle do not evidence a ma-jor presence of women, let alone lesbians, and speak more often of outreach to communities of color than women or lesbians. Most unique, however, is that the leading figure in modern SC LGBT politics has been for decades a heterosexual woman who does not generally identify as a feminist, the previously mentioned Harriett Hancock. Hancock is not an ally or collaborator or coalition member in SC LGBT political history, she is the core of this state's LGBTQ political history.

Additionally, AIDS did not "end" in South Carolina with introduction of combination drug therapies in the mid-1990s. *The State* newspaper in 2003 re-ported that "Southern Discretion Hinders AIDS Fight," a photocopy of which is in the state LGBTQ archives. The article relates that, according to the CDC, the 17-state southern region has more residents living with HIV and AIDS, and is the only part of the country with a significant (9%) increase in infections. The South was estimated to contain 40% of people living with AIDS and 46% of estimated new cases.

I turn now to three specific examples from South Carolina: efforts to ratify the federal ERA, the anti-gay crusade of Christian singer and activist Anita Bry-ant, and events surrounding South Carolina Pride marches over several years.

The Equal Rights Amendment: Collaboration, Opposition, and Competition

The ERA, first introduced to the US Congress in 1921, was a proposed amend-ment to the US Constitution guaranteeing equality between the sexes. It was reintroduced to Congress in 1971 as part of the women's movement of the time.

Although a national effort, the ERA was significant in South Carolina, and the state shouldn't be written off as unimportant in the fight. Senator Strom Thurmond proudly claimed co-authorship of the ERA and supported its ratification. His newsletter, *Strom Thurmond Reports to the People* ran a lead story "EQUAL RIGHTS FOR WOMEN," in which he writes that "The Congress has passed the Equal Rights for Women Amendment. I was pleased to be a co-author of this Amendment" (1972, p. 1).

The ERA was approved by the US Senate in 1972, and then proceeded to move to individual state legislatures, of which 38 were needed to approve it by March 22, 1979 (later extended to June 30, 1982). SC was a significant state because, in the final three years of the extended deadline for ratification, South Carolina was seen by many as having a strong chance to become one of the three remaining states needed. Polls here showed strong support for the ERA, and they had experienced local support in the past. However, some political figures thought homophobia prevented this. In 1978, for example, ERA SC PAC quoted an interview with the mayor of Greenville (home to Bob Jones University), Max Heller, a then-candidate for Congress, that "what has hurt ERA SC is Anita Bryant," referring to the notorious 1977 anti-gay campaign by the Christian singer.

With bipartisan support, the ERA achieved 35 state ratifications but stalled there under a conservative backlash and ultimately did not pass. Senator Thurmond then voted against the extension of its deadline for ratification.

The struggle to pass the ERA dominated the women's movement during this 11-year period, and is repeatedly cited in documents of the time as the top priority of the US women's movement. One way that the movement to pass the ERA connected with gay men was in seeing heteronormative masculinity as structuring patriarchy and women's oppression—the theme of commonality in oppression leading to potential coalition and collaboration.

For example, the Piedmont South Carolina chapter of NOW (1973) listed the "Masculine Mystique"—a play on Betty Friedan's 1963 feminist classic *The Feminine Mystique*—as one of NOW's goals: helping men to see how masculinity limited them, essentially creating consciousness-raising groups for men. A Greenville, SC, NOW chapter newsletter (1974) listed an upcoming discussion, including the topic "What's in the feminist movement for men?" ("Human Liberation: Changing Roles in a Changing Society," 1974). A woman's personal letter to ERA-South Carolina stated:

> We are planning to write some talks for men's groups using some of the magazine articles from the November women's magazines. Then we'll make these

available all over the state. My suggestion is that the steering comm. discuss ways to get invitations to speak before more men's clubs. Also perhaps some men who might be willing to speak. We haven't had much demand for speakers (for men's groups) but part of our educational program should include a real emphasis on this. ("Mabel," 1980, p. 1–2)

Such work logically would also help undo the male homophobia that supported gay male oppression.

Indeed, there was gay support for passing the ERA in South Carolina. Local gay media connected readers to the cause: The *Charleston Alternative* (formerly *Gay Charleston*) listed among its eleven Community Resources "ERA South Carolina Coalition, Charleston chapter. A support network for all individuals who are committed to bringing both women and men to full and equal lives. 766–5250" and "NOW: 871–6114" ("Community Resources," 1982, p. 2). Many position papers and documents in the files of the SC ERA Coalition included gay-supportive materials from state-level and national organizations. The National ERA Campaign Call to Action (NOW, 1979) provided a list of organizations supporting the ERA, which included Gay Pride Conference, Dignity, Integrity, and the National Gay Task Force. The latter three, additionally, were supporting a boycott of states that had yet to ratify the ERA, which included South Carolina. A NOW flyer for the National March for ERA Ratification in Illinois in 1980 included the National Gay Task Force in its list of participating organizations. NOW flyer "A Platform for Tomorrow Built upon the Realities of Today" read, in part:

> To ignore other oppressed groups is to limit our dream of equality. We cannot tolerate in any program sexism, racism, classism, homophobia, ageism, religious bias, or ethnocentrism. … The struggle for Lesbian and Gay Rights must be intensified. We must develop and implement a plan of action that builds a climate for the repeal of oppressive penal codes [sodomy laws] and passage of a national civil rights act for lesbians and gay men. (Smeal, 1980)

Additionally, a "Political Research Office" proposal (Florida NOW, 1977) cited coverage of Florida ERA opponents in two recent issues of the leading national gay news magazine, *The Advocate,* providing evidence of direct awareness of gay press coverage of this women's issue.

The commonality between feminist women and gay men was also seen as existing within a larger coalition of oppressed groups. In a copy of a letter on the letterhead from Herbert H. Fielding & Associates, Legislative and General Public Relations, Charleston, pencil annotations read "January 1978" and "To Black leaders." Attached is an essay, "Notes of the Equal Rights Amendment–Jan. 4, 1978– H.U. Fielding," which paraphrases common campaign language, saying that, "The Equal Rights Amendment is as much a part of the 'total' American struggle for human rights and equality as was the Fourteenth Amendment which prohibited discrimination on account of race, religion or national origin, or the Fifteenth Amendment which provided the right of Black *MEN* to vote" (p. 1). This long essay on the ERA was relevant to and within the context of civil rights, but makes no mention of LGBTQ persons, whose official civil rights movement was in its eighth year. However, stapled to it was a *Washington Star* editorial by Carl T. Rowan, "Why the ERA Can't Be Anti-Family," in which he describes how he did not understand how women could be against the ERA until he saw its opponents' materials at the National Women's Conference in Houston.

> Then I read the advertisement in Houston, placed by the anti-ERA forces, where a little girl says to her mother: "Mommy, can I be a lesbian when I grow up?" Crude and cruel, yes, but it helped enlighten me to the reality that the state-by-state struggle over ERA has never focused on the matter of the right of women to equality; it has always been sidetracked into arguments over some people's sexual hangups, religious passions, political pressures.

Homosexuality became a major argument against the ERA. However, this was not just the homophobic reactions of individuals or groups rejecting the presence of or overtures from lesbians or gay men. It was also a strategic political necessity. During the struggle to pass the ERA, same-sex marriage was raised by ERA opponents as a consequence of the amendment's passage. ERA supporters had to explicitly state that this was not the case (despite widely circulated articles by legal professionals that it might be), but also that they were opposed to same-sex marriage. In other words, it was less the homophobia of individual feminists and more their accommodation of the homophobia of society at large. NOW and other organizations found themselves having to deny that the passage of the ERA would condone homosexuality and legalize same-sex marriages, distancing themselves from LGBTQ persons and groups.

Near the entrance to the South Carolina Women's History archives during one of my visits was a framed diptych of a pro-ERA and an anti-ERA flyer juxtaposed, dated 1973, and supplied by the local League of Women Voters. The anti-ERA flyer featured an image of a skull and crossbones with the headline "WARNING! WARNING! EQUAL RIGHTS AMENDMENT IS DANGEROUS TO WOMEN!!!" The flyer described how the ERA will not help, only hurt, women, taking away current rights they had. Among its four sections specifying and explaining this was:

E.R.A. WILL LEGALIZE HOMOSEXUAL "MARRIAGE"!

All states have laws prohibiting marriage between persons of the same sex. Because these laws clearly discriminate on the basis of the sex of one of the partners, these laws will be overturned by the ERA. "The stringent requirements of the proposed Amendment argue strongly for removal of this stigma by granting marriage licenses to homosexual couples ..." (Yale Law Journal, 1973). Agreeing with this conclusion is constitutional authority Prof. Paul Freund.

And if these couples "marry," will they not be eligible to adopt children, as are normal married couples? After all, denying adoption to couples because "Mommy" is a male, is clearly a discrimination based on sex, and thus would be illegal under E.R.A.! A Minnesota couple, both male, have applied to several adoption agencies for a child; to date their applications have not been refused!

A leader of the national anti-ERA campaign was Phyllis Schlafly. Women who opposed the ERA had a leader in Schlafly, who saw the ERA as "legitimizing the right of homosexual women to raise children," as well as encouraging abortion and a federal day-care system that would brainwash their children. "Nothing I write here will change many minds about lesbians—certainly not the kind of minds harbored by people who were at the women's meeting in Houston shouting that they had come 'to prevent the federal government from promoting perverts.' " Many copies and reprints of her newsletter, *Eagle Forum*, were found in the files of SC ERA. For example, in 1977 Schlafly blasted US President Jimmy Carter for an "extraordinary" meeting with gay activists, the first time they had ever been invited to White House. The news item stated that activists met "with Midge Costanza, President Carter's assistant for public liaison," then went on to say, without explicating the rationale, that "Midge Costanza has also been meeting with pro-ERA leaders in connection with lobbying for the ERA directly from the White House." Two months later, Schlafly wrote, "With this kind of welcome extended to homosexuals, is it any wonder that the [President] Carter administration is lobbying so hard for ERA?" She created an organization, STOP ERA. Its November 1977 newsletter asked, "What's Wrong with the ERA?" and answered that the ERA would permit homosexuals to "marry and adopt children." US Senator Sam Irvin is quoted from the *Congressional Record* saying that "legalization of lesbianism is one of the goals of the National Organization of Women (NOW), as outlined in their platform, 'Revolution—Tomorrow'" to which the article adds, "Their No. One goal in this platform is the ratification of the ERA. The Gay Liberation Movement is another very strong supporter of the ERA" (pgs. 20, 21).

Such attacks put ERA groups on the defensive, including those in South Carolina, where STOP ERA formed a chapter. A letter to SC capital paper *The State,* "Eight Deadly Ills of 'Equal Rights'," warned that the ERA would "require you to acknowledge homosexuality as an acceptable lifestyle." The SC ERA Coalition files include a reprint copy of a *Family Circle* article, "10 Myths about the Equal Rights Amendment," which included "Myth #6 The ERA will invalidate laws banning rape, prostitution, sodomy, adultery and white slavery" (Komisar, 1974). Someone, however, felt the article did not go far enough, and used the open space on second page to type "HOMOSEXUALITY." This was underneath an excerpt of a letter from former US Senator Marlow W. Cook to Ms. Kay Jones of Columbia, Missouri, asserting, "The Amendment will have no direct effect on homosexuality" (1974). Also in the SC ERA records is a NOW Florida brochure from 1977, which reprinted anti-ERA arguments with a typewritten rebuttal:

> None of the 16 states with equal rights amendments in their state constitutions have legalized homosexual marriages. Neither the state nor federal ERA is concerned with the relationship of two persons of the same sex, but rather with laws affecting persons of different sexes. (NOW Florida, 1977, emphasis. orig.)

A photocopy of an article from the SC alternative paper, *Black News,* stated that "E.R.A. will have no impact on abortion laws and would not require states to permit homosexual marriage, two prevalent fears of E.R.A. Opponents" (Sa'adah, 1977, p. 1A, emphasis orig.). SC ERA went so far as to hold a day-long series of talks and panel discussions, which were reprinted as a 50-page booklet, *The Equal Rights Amendment & South Carolina Laws* (Bryan, 1975). The participants assessed that, if the ERA passed, the only significant impact on state legal code would be the need to revise prostitution statues, which then mentioned only women, to specify male prostitution as well (Burnette, 1978, p. 3).

An undated broadsheet from SC ERA stated that the "ERA will neither permit nor forbid same sex marriages. If the law forbids men to marry men; it must also forbid women to marry women." A transcription of an unidentified speech in Aiken, SC, in 1980 wrote:

> One of the big objections to ERA is that it would put a label of approval on homosexual marriages. ERA will have NO direct affect on homosexuality ... it will neither sanction nor condone. It would simply mean that whatever a state's

law may be as to homosexual conduct (whether prohibited or protected), that males may not be treated differently than females and vice versa. (Aiken, ellipsis original, p. 6)

A one-page typed document in the SC ERA Coalition Files stated, "Be alert to smokescreen issues (abortion, homosexuality [sic], federal daycare)." The suggested reply was, " 'That is all very interesting but it has nothing to do with the Equal Rights Amendment' " ("Strategy," n.d.). A press release described survey findings that 40% of Columbia, SC, residents did not even know what the ERA was or thought it referred to racial equality instead of or in addition to women's equality. Attached with the release were reprints of participants' open-ended responses, including "This will just help the homosexuals" (Sociology Research Associates, 1977).

Politicians were aware of such opinions. The Greenville, SC NOW chapter has in its files a letter from SC State Senator Thomas E. Smith Jr. to Ms. Nelda Leon Shore. Smith was a sponsoring member of the ERA proposal, but noted three specific fears he had encountered in discussing the issue: The military draft, imposing equal sexual ratios (affirmative action) in hiring and other areas, and homosexuality, to which he wrote: "I believe that if the law prohibits the marriage of men to men that [sic] it should also prohibit the marriage of women to women; if the law prohibits male homosexuals from teaching, women of the same class should also be excluded" (Smith, n.d., p. 2). The ERA SC Political Action Committee interviewed local candidates and found that, for example, Thom Marett, running for House district #29 from Blacksburg, "expressed concern on several points [regarding the ERA]–homosexual marriage" and said he "couldn't vote against his Baptist beliefs" (ERA SC PAC, 1978).

In 1977, Senator Coleman Poag publicly expressed his support for the ERA, provoking negative responses. A December 16 letter from Oliver E. Willis, of Columbia, to Senator Poag includes a copy of results from a California national polling firm showing that "If the ERA means that homosexuals will be able to get marriage licenses and teach in schools, would you favor or oppose the Equal Rights Amendment? Favor 28% Oppose 66% Not Sure 6%" (1977). Mrs. Ray B. Cromer of Columbia wrote, "Most of the groups howling so loudly for the so called 'equality' of women are Lesbians, misfits, Socialist oriented, left wing groups paid for by the govt. at taxpayers expense." A copy of an anti-ERA letter to President Carter was sent to Poag from Jimmy Wren (1978), Minister at Church of Christ in Lancaster. A letter from Julie Blake of Greenville told Poag that the ERA "advocates that children be raised communally by the state. It also supports abortion, premarital sex, and all forms of sexual perversion" (1987). David Pharr, Minister at Church of Christ in Rock Hill, SC sent a bulletin to his congregation encouraging them to write letters to Poag. In Pharr's own letter, he writes that

> a few results seem certain: … Laws forbidding homosexual marriages and laws preventing homosexuals from positions such as teachers, etc. will be nullified. (It is significant that representatives of homosexuals have been among the most vocal of supporters of the ERA.) (Pharr, 1978)

His congregants echoed these sentiments:

> I feel that the group pushing ERA includes militant feminist, homosexuals and radicals who want to open the door for sexual freedom, gay marriages and threaten tax-exempt churches who do not have female clergy in their pulpits.— Mrs. L. E. Olsen, Rock Hill Jan 17, 1978

> Which groups seem to be pushing the hardest for ERA? It seems to be those that are different such as lesbians and homosexuals. … They want equal rights to be married, adopt, and raise children. … Would you want your child adopted and raised by two lesbians or homosexuals?

> —Arthur C. Whitesell, III Rock Hill 1–28–78

"If ERA Dies" was the title of a column by Chicago writer Joan Beck, reprinted in the *Charlotte Observer* in 1980. It used as a pull quote, "Defeating ERA … won't stop homosexuals from living together." Beck listed anti-ERA myths, and wrote that the recent ERA failure in Illinois and an eventual national failure would not stop progress. Officials who voted against it would suffer electorally.

However, also in the SC ERA Coalition archives, "The Death of ERA" was the headline on a photocopy of an editorial from the *Atlanta Journal Constitution*. It states, "Certainly, supporters of ERA made their share of mistakes. … They took into their tent various freak groups—which gave the No-Way ERA crowd additional ammunition" ("The Death of ERA," 1982, p. 4-A).

After the failure of the ERA, connections between women's and gay movements in SC did resume, but there were also conspicuous absences, particularly immediately after the amendment was defeated. One brochure included an article on coalition-building from *The Wisconsin Women's Network*, incorporating 60 organizations,

> not just women's organizations but also organizations of both women and men with women's issues on their agendas. Among the participating groups are labor

union locals, religious and educational groups, providers of human services, and business-related groups—as well as both the traditional women's organizations and the more activist feminist groups. ("A New Day Beyond ERA," 1982, p. 2)

LGBT groups were conspicuously absent, as they were in the same brochure's list of "Consensus Issues" in its "National Plan of Action," which included battered women, domestic violence, child care, employment, education, poverty, and minority women. A mailing from Columbia NOW PAC gave a scorecard of candidates for election of the Democratic presidential nominee, listing their stances on 12 categories, including non-gender-related ones such as Nuclear Arms and Environment, but nothing about homosexuality, even when other civil-rights categories were included, such as Minority Women (Owen, 1983).

Offering Support: Anita Bryant

In the previously mentioned ERA SC PAC candidate interviews, Max Heller, running for the US House and at the time a popular mayor of Greenville, said he was in favor of the ERA and against extremism, but, "He stated that what has hurt ERA in SC is Anita Bryant" (ERA SC PAC, 1978). Indeed, in the anti-ERA letter-writing campaign to Sen. Poag discussed previously, Mrs. C. M. Wright of Rock Hill wrote, "It seems like the government or something is taking everything over. I wish we had someone with back-bone enough to try and stop some of it. Mr Poag you just might could be that person. Anita Bryant took a stand and I haven't seen anyone with courage like her" (1978).

American popular singer Anita Bryant moved into political activism with her 1977 "Save the Children" campaign, which overturned a Dade County, Florida ordinance that had prohibited discrimination on the basis of sexual orientation. The campaign received national media attention and support from Christian activists, helping forge the template for future "culture wars" that would harness wedge issues, especially sexuality, by American conservative politicians and activists, continuing to the present day. "Save Our Children," unlike the efforts of Phyllis Schlafly described previously, was not an anti-feminist or anti-ERA effort, even though it took place during the efforts to ratify the ERA. However, whereas the specter of homosexual marriage divided women's and gay social movements, the women's movement offered support for LGBT persons under attack by Bryant. SC NOW records include a flyer from Save Our Children, comprised of a collage of headlines about homosexual pedophilia and child abuse. A "Dade County Alert" (1977) presented a two-sided flyer of excerpts from national media coverage of Bryant's campaign. The flyer asked for contributions and support statements to fight Bryant. NOW Alert from, in part, the NOW Task Force on Sexuality & Lesbianism, to NOW Leadership List, urged NOW to support fighting the Dade County referendum, provided addresses for local contributions, and asked for media monitoring and responses (Whitlock & Scott, 1977).

In 1978, the National Women's Conference was held in Houston, Texas, and delegates there voted to approve "The Resolution on Sexual Preference," which stated that

> Congress, state and local legislators should enact legislation to eliminate discrimination on the basis of sexual and affectional preference in areas including, but not limited to, employment, housing, public accommodations, credit, public facilities, government funding, and the military. State legislators should reform their penal codes or repeal state laws that restrict private sexual behavior between consenting adults. State legislatures should enact legislation that would prohibit consideration of sexual or affectional orientation as a factor in any judicial determination of child custody or visitation rights. Rather, child custody cases should be evaluated solely on the merits of which party is the better parent, without regard to that person's sexual and affectional orientation.

The newsletter of the *National Gay Task Force* ran a front-page story, "National Women's Conference Supports Sexual Preference," describing the voting. NGTF provided "We Are Everywhere" balloons for supportive attendees. When the three-part motion was introduced, the "crowd roared its support." Speakers in support included

> NGTF board member Charlotte Bunch, NOW president Ellie Smeal, former NGTF board co-chairperson Betty Powell, Patricia Benevides of Seattle, Jeanne Cordova of Lesbian Tide in Los Angeles and—to the surprise of just about everyone—Betty Friedan, who reversed her anti-gay position and urged delegates to join her in support of the resolution. ... "We have all made mistakes and we have all learned," Friedan said. "I now see that there is nothing in the ERA to protect homosexuals. We must help women who are lesbians in their own civil rights." (Women's Caucus of NGTF, 1978, p. 1)

The Greenville NOW newsletter wrote a scathing book review of *The Anita Bryant Story* by Anita Bryant. The review was given significant placing: it took up 2.33 of 15 interior pages of content, making it a full 15% of the publication, the longest single article, even longer than an update on the ERA. The author wrote

I resented the fact that Bryant always referred to gays in her book as militant homosexuals. She does not seem to recognize them as human beings capable of living and loving the same as your "normal" heterosexual human being.

In her book, she constantly refers to gays as "he" and "him". One of the few references she made to women was when she discussed the women's movement, she said there were a large number of women with lesbian tendencies as leaders of the movement. (Tillis, 1978, p. 5)

The reviewer goes on to point out the connections between homophobia and sexism: "If she worries about her son being assaulted by a male homosexual teacher, who [sic] not worry about her daughter being assaulted by a male heterosexual teacher?" (p. 15). The review concludes:

A great deal of anger, hurt, and frustration has been directed toward Anita Bryant by the gay community–justly so–But I think as feminists we should stop and take a look at what has happened to Bryant as a woman. She is being used– used by her pastor! Who would have paid any attention to Miami and the gay rights bill, if it had been led by Brother Bill, her pastor, or Bob Greene, her husband? (p. 15).

A National Gay Task Force membership solicitation letter to conference delegates from March, 1978, from Jean O'Leary (co-executive director of the conference) and Gloria Steinem reflected fondly on the passing the sexual preference motion. "Unfortunately, however, the arbiters of public morality, under the inspiration of Anita Bryant and others, continue to threaten the rights of gay citizens" (O'Leary and Steinem, 1978). The letter went on to mention attacks on lesbian parenting and three metropolitan gay-rights ordinances that were being put to public referendums soon that they did not want to see overturned, as had happened in Dade County. Women's organizations had come to the support of an attack primarily on gay men, and were looking to prevent more in the future.

A Switching Event: SC Pride Marches, 1990–2007

Efforts to pass the ERA and stop anti-gay campaigns, such as Anita Bryant, show the complicated and contradictory trends in communication networks among feminist women and gay men's social movements. Aware of and in contact with each other, these networks also extended to local and national networks of each, even in as conservative a state as South Carolina in the 1970s and early 1980s. I turn now to an ongoing event, SC Pride March, and present examples of how it has operated as a network switcher—not a person, in Castells' sense, but an event that served to connect communication power between networks.

South Carolina's first statewide LGBT Pride March was held in 1990 in the state capital of Columbia. Just three years later, in 1992, they were able to convince a state legislator to speak at the event: Gilda Cobb-Hunter of Orangeburg, "a strong advocate of women's rights" who "fought long and hard for passage of the marital rape bill" (C.B.B., 1992, p. 1). According to reports, another speaker, "Kyira Korrigan, past president of USC's Bisexual, Lesbian and Gay Association, challenged the marchers to fight oppression by the patriarchal establishment in all its forms–racism, sexism, homophobia and discrimination against any group" (C.B.B., 1992, p. 1).

The event organizers, SC Gay Lesbian Pride Movement (SCGLPM) frequently connected members to feminist concerns. Their newsletter of March 1994 announced an upcoming Pro-Choice Rally organized by NOW (SCGLPM, 1994). Mitzi Smeltzer, a NOW speaker, was listed in the program schedule for the 1995 GLPM Rally, and Bluestocking Books was listed as one of GLPM "buddies." The next year, the renamed SC Gay and Lesbian Pride March and Festival and expanded to a three-day event, and there were four main "rally speakers," including celebrity Chastity Bono. A separate Speakers' Forum included NOW. In 1996, SCGLPM Board meeting listed NOW among other planned groups with speakers for the upcoming Pride event, and their LGBT Center Activity Report listed a NOW chapter as one of the "new groups being organized for the Center" (SCGLPM, 1996, p. 4).

In May of that year, however, the County Council of Greenville, SC, issued a public condemnation of homosexuality as "incompatible with community values." In response, the Tour DuPont dropped the county from its bicycle race, the Olympics shrouded its torch when it came through the county on its way to Atlanta, and the planned Special Olympics events left town. Furthermore, the following spring, Pride moved from Columbia to Greenville in response. Although not without some organizational difficulties, this tactic of re-locating Pride in response to local acts of homophobia proved successful enough that it would be repeated the following year, although this time in a situation that explicitly linked women and gay men (Caroliniana Finding Aid, 2012; Robbins, 1997; Sack, 1998; Wyman, 1997).

In 1997, a statewide hate crimes legislation was proposed, Senate Bill 37, authored by Sen. Darrell Jackson, which included language that specifically protected gays, lesbians, and women. However, SC State Attorney General Charlie Condon declined to support the bill and wrote his own hate crimes bill that focused on race and did not include language about gays, lesbians, and women.

Condon said, "I have no intention of allowing radical fringe groups to dictate the priorities of my office. ... A bill we designed to bring attention to vicious crimes of racial hate is now being used by gay-rights advocates and feminists to bring attention to their various grievances against society" (quoted in Associated Press, 1997, p. 1). He withdrew his bill after the state Senate subcommittee heard testimony on gay bashing and other legislators wanted to add gay language to his bill (Associated Press, 1997, p. 1).

Community media repeated Condit's language here and elsewhere linking gays and feminists as fringe groups (Snell, 1997; Watts, 1997). A widely quoted press release from SC GLPM stated, "By exempting us from 'Hate Crime' protections, the Attorney General says it's okay to attack women and gay people. It is clear that Mr. Condon is positioning himself for future political ambitions at our expense" (Snell, 1997, p. 1). In addition to the "fringe" umbrella, another interesting linkage between women and gay men appears in handwritten notes in a folder of materials from the Columbia chapter of PFLAG labeled "Hate Crimes File," which lists among "myths that exist" the idea that "gay men want to be women" (Hancock, 1998). This note speaks to the thought processes that link sexism and homophobia, which the proposed Hate Crimes legislation was seeking to prevent in South Carolina.

Also in 1997, Myrtle Beach City Council member and soon-to-be mayor Mark McBride spoke out again the planned opening of a gay nightclub downtown. "'We don't want this garbage on the Boulevard,' McBride said, making note of transvestites and people in 'dog collars and chains'" (quoted in NGTF, 1997, pp. 3–4). By late November of that year, PRIDE '98 announced their selection of Myrtle Beach as location for the festival the following Spring. "Many have speculated that this statement was the catalyst that drove GLPM to select Myrtle Beach as the site for the '98 festival. But PRIDE '98 organizers say plans were already in progress before McBride's remarks" (NGTF, 1997). However, other sources confirmed that Myrtle Beach was chosen in response to McBride's comments (Caroliniana Finding Aid, 2012; "McBride comments cemented choice," 1997).

In 1998, Myrtle Beach hosted SC Pride, with much controversy leading up to it from powerful business interests and Christian groups. For example, the city's largest real estate developer overrode a venue's contract for a performance by gay disco group Village People. The event continued, nevertheless, and the *Official Pride Guide* listed among the speakers that day Candy Kern, NOW Board Member and State Development Chair for SC NOW. After these two exceptions, SC Pride returned to Columbia (although Upstate Pride began occurring in Spartanburg in 2009).

SC Pride 2005 featured support from a third-wave/girlie feminist performance troupe, Columbia's Radical Cheerleaders ("We're here! We cheer! We're reBELLEious!!!!") who also appeared at a Roe v. Wade rally and other events. In 2007, NOW took out an advertisement in the SC *Pride Guide*, proclaiming, "South Carolina Chapters of National Organization for Women are proud to be a SC Pride Supporter for 18 years" (2007, p. 16).

During this period, SC Pride events offered opportunities for networks of feminist women and gay men to connect in mutual support, but also when connected by oppressive forces. Despite the optimistic vision of future collaboration in NOW advertisement quoted above, a trend was already in progress in Columbia, and which I witnessed firsthand at Upstate Pride over the years. This was the transformation of LGBTQ Pride events from political rallies and protest marches into largely de-politicized, "family-friendly," entertainment festivals. This unintended, potentially negative side effect of the success of both social movements, however, goes beyond the scope of this book.

Having presented original research on how networks of feminist women and gay men interacted in South Carolina, I proceed next to examining the two groups' representations of each other in scholarly theory and cinematic narratives.

References

Unless otherwise indicated, all primary materials are from the Winthrop University Dacus Library Louise Pettus Archives & Special Collections or the University of South Carolina Caroliniana LGBTQ Collection and South Carolina Pride Movement materials.

A new day beyond ERA. (1982). Brochure.

About Sam Nickles. (2018). Harriet Hancock LGBT Center. Retrieved from https://harriethancockcenter.org/sam-nickles-lending-library

Aiken. (1980, Sept. 2). Text of speech.

Associated Press. (1997, March 28). *The Front Page*, 1.

Bryan, M. (Ed.). (1975). *The equal rights amendment & South Carolina laws*. SC Coalition for the ERA.

Burnette, M. M. (1978). The Equal Rights Amendment and South Carolina law. Updated and revised from research by M. Carrington Salley in 1975.

C.B.B. (1992, July). Third successful march for S.C. *Virago: A Lesbian Organization*, *7*, 7, 1.

Castells, M. (2009). *Communication power*. Oxford, UK: Oxford University Press.

Community Resources. (1982, Nov.). *Charleston Alternative*, *1*, 1.

Dade County alert. (ca. 1977). Flyer.

"The Death of ERA." (1982, Jan. 22). *Atlanta Journal Constitution*, 4-A.

ERA SC PAC. (1978). Reporting forms for congressional candidate interviews.

Gray, M. L. (2008). *Out in the country: Youth, media, and queer visibility in rural America.* New York: NYU Press.

Hamel, M. (2007). Parents, family and friends of lesbians and gays. Student work from Ernest L Wiggins journalism class at University of South Carolina. USC LGBTQ archives.

Hancock, H. (1998). Meeting or possibly presentation notes on a sheet of yellow legal paper. PFLAG Columbia. Author and date inferred from context.

Human liberation: Changing roles in a changing society. (1974a, Feb. 7). *NOW News, 1.*

Human liberation: Changing roles in a changing society. (1974b). Greenville NOW chapter newsletter.

Jervis, L., & Zeisler, A. (2006). *BITCHfest: Ten years of cultural criticism from the pages of Bitch magazine.* New York: Macmillan.

Johnson, S. (1987). *Telling the truth.* Berkeley, CA: The Crossing Press.

Komisar, L. (1974, May). 10 myths about the Equal Rights Amendment. Reprint copy of article from *Family Circle* magazine, no page numbers visible.

LGBT Finding Aid. (2012). University of South Carolina Library Caroliniana collection.

Mabel. (1980, Jan. 21) Letter to Jean Crouch, Chair, ERA-South Carolina.

McBride comments cemented choice. (1997, Nov. 16). *The Sun News*, p. A1.

National ERA Campaign Call to Action. (1979). NOW.

NGTF. (1997, Dec. 12). Myrtle Beach Pride. Email. Retrieved from. http://www.qrd.org/qrd/usa/south_carolina/myrtle.beach.controversy.over.pride.festival-12.12.97

NOW advertisement. (1990). (Advertisement in Pride program). South Carolina Lesbian and Gay Pride Movement, p. 17.

NOW advertisement. (2007). *SC pride guide.* South Carolina Gay and Lesbian Pride Movement, p. 16.

NOW News. (1973, Oct.). Piedmont, SC NOW. Vol 2.

O'Leary, J,. & Steinem, G. (1978). Letter to Delegates. National Gay Task Force.

Owen, F. (1983, Nov. 13). *Columbia NOW PAC.* Mailing.

Pharr, D. (1978). Correspondance. Winthrop University Dacus Archives.

Political Research Office proposal. (1977). Florida NOW.

Robbins, B. (1997, May). A city divided: Greenville stages morality play. *Point: South Carolina's independent newsmonthly.* Retrieved from http://www.scpronet.com/point/9705/p04.html

Sa'adah, G. G. (1977, Dec. 3). S.C. sends 22 delegates to Women's Conference." *Black News*, 1, 36, 1A.

Sack, K. (1998, July 7). "Gay rights movement meets big resistance in S. Carolina." *New York Times.* Retrieved April 30, 2020 from https://www.nytimes.com/1998/07/07/us/gay-rights-movement-meets-big-resistance-in-s-carolina.html

SCGLPM. (no date, but postmark of March 15, 1994). 1994 pro-choice rally. *Community News* section, p. 2.

SCGLPM. (1996a, Mar. 17). Board meeting minutes.

SCGLPM. (1996b, Oct. 20–Nov. 17). LGBT Center Activity Report, p. 4.

Smeal, E. (1980). NOW flyer.

Smith, Thomas E. (n.d.) Letter to Ms. Nelda Leon Shore, Greenville NOW.

Snell, T. (1997, Mar. 25). GLPM criticizes Condon's antics with hate crimes. Press release.

Sociology Research Associates. (1977, Mar. 2). Columbia Survey on Equal Rights Amendment.

"South Carolina Legislative Update." (1993, June 10). *SC NOW Issues.*

"Strategy." (n.d.).Flyer.

Tillis, C. (1978, Jan.–Feb.). Such trash: *The Anita Bryant Story. Greenville NOW Newsletter, 1,* 1, 5, 14–15.

Watts, T. (1997, Apr.). *Unison,* page unknown.

Whitlock, K., & Scott, A. (1977, May 13.) "NOW Alert."

Women's Caucus of NGTF. (1978, Jan.) It's time. *NGTF Newsletter,* 5, 1.

Wren, J. (1976). Correspondance. Winthrop University Dacus Archives.

Wyman, S. (1997, April 18). Rallies to shift attention back to debate over homosexuality. *The Greenville News,* 1D, 4, 14.

3

Representing Each Other: Gays in *The Second Wave*/Lesbians in AIDS Cinema

Feminist women and gay men, as this book explores, have common vectors or sources of oppression and discrimination that would suggest the utility of their collaboration and coalition. As shown in the first chapter, a discourse analysis of nonfiction books on the histories of the women's and LGBTQ equality movements finds frequent, if limited, discussions of each other, however. Across the works examined, common themes emerged of commonality, opposition, and intellectual contributions. Broad and complex, these themes appeared as well in my case study of these two social movements in the state of South Carolina. From archival materials found there, unique contours and expressions of the particulars of these social movements could be found. Perhaps most importantly, for a region of the United States often neglected in research on women's and LGBTQ movements, this research showed that there were histories of each in the Southeastern US. Moreover, a perspective of communicative networked power allowed us to conceive of these movements as attempts to reprogram social networks, at times connected by switchers—individuals or organizations that connect networks—or what I called switching events, such as the campaign for the Equal Rights Amendment and LGBTQ Pride parades in South Carolina. Networks, however, are neutral structures, and the communicative power that flows through them can have various intents and ends. Indeed, in South Carolina we saw how themes of commonality, opposition, and intellectual contributions also appeared there.

Having established this baseline of historiographic narratives, and augmented them with specific details from original research in South Carolina, I turn now from cumulative analyses of artifactual evidence to more detailed exploration of key texts and representations. My methodological process has been one of exploring avenues opened and new questions asked. I began by exploring what has been said in historiographic discourses, then examined LGBTQ alternative media as an alternate historical record. Having established a received view from these, I wanted to switch to a region they often overlooked: the southeastern US. I also wanted to move from a cumulative approach to a case-study one, in order to enrich the received view with particularity and nuance, and disrupt the generalization and progress narrative suggested by the received view. However, all the approaches of the previous two chapters involved my interpretations and analyses of primary and secondary artifacts and media.

In this chapter, I aim to continue my queer methodology by now focusing on examples of how each group has represented the other. This extends the respective presences or absences in previous chapters to a more discursive notion of how they envisioned or constituted one another. Rather than the stable connections of networks, here I examine gay men as a subject of feminist women, and vice versa. Furthermore, I expand into two new sites of investigation, academic theory and popular culture, in order to increase the locations examined thus far. This was intended to further destabilize my research topics by foregrounding the notion that, for example, a gay man is not a stable thing that joins a march or is recorded in a document. It is also an idea in the mind of feminist women. On one hand, these expansions of my search were chosen to broaden my inquiry with the addition of two seemingly disparate arenas of social and cultural life. However, I argue that they were also intimately linked: The academy is not a direct pipeline to popular culture, but it can influence as well as presciently identify social changes reflected in popular culture. Moreover, popular culture, particularly in the tradition of cultural studies within which I operate, is often a topic of academic study, valued for its significance as, not only a window into a particular time, place, and culture, but also as a location where cultural meanings are made, contested, maintained, and re-made.

For example, the film *Top Gun*, upon its release in 1986, was seen as a paragon of Reagan-era masculinity. Film scholar Susan Jeffords (1994) described the action movies of the 1980s as demonstrating a shift from the conflicted male anti-heroes of 1970s American popular cinema to a "hard-bodied" masculinity of patriotism and virile aggression, reflecting the changing ideologies of the time. While *Top Gun* stars Tom Cruise, Anthony Edwards, and Val Kilmer were not quite the same degree of bodybuilder-athletes as Arnold Schwarzenegger, Sylvester Stallone, or Chuck Norris, their roles as elite US Naval pilots fit in well with the American representations of masculinity in popular films of the time. All were, as well, adamantly heterosexual. As a skinny, gay theatre student in a suburban high school at the time, I found such representations and the ideologies they represented oppressive and distasteful, and avoided them like the plague. (In fact, I was already conscious of struggling to avoid the developing plague of AIDS.)

Enter the academy. British writer Mark Simpson (1994), a gay male scholar and cultural critic, published an essay in his book *Male Impersonators*, which was addressed on the bookjacket copy as, "Why is *Top Gun* such a flamingly 'gay' movie?" Simpson foregrounded the over-the-top homosexual subtext of the film, including its now-infamous final line, "You can ride my tail any time." More than a frisson of homosociality, the film could be read as an explicit text of latent or closeted homosexuality. The witty and insightful essay was seen as provocative by many.

The same year, *Top-Gun*-As-Gay-Love-Story was the punchline of the American romantic comedy film, *Sleep with Me*. Celebrity film director Quentin Tarantino made a cameo appearance in a party scene to deliver a fast-talking exposition of how *Top Gun* was gay. Since then, the film has become recognized as a gay icon (Simpson, 2016), suggesting the entanglements between academic theory and entertainment. Indeed, when covering this material with my current students, the idea of a hyper-masculine film having a gay subtext—and not simply because of the gay rumors surrounding one of its stars—is taken as, not shocking, but an understandable example of the complexities of sexuality, gender, and representation.

As Stuart Hall (1985) reminds us, representations are ideological practices. Whether through popular narratives or intellectual essays, representations of social groups are part of the cultural practices of creating shared beliefs about who those groups are. Such constitution of identity categories takes place in complex, multi-faceted, and competing practices to form, maintain, and disrupt the dominant ideologies of a particular time and place.

In this chapter, I explore representations of gay men created by feminist women, and representations of feminist women created by gay men. I begin by searching for representations in a classic collection of feminist scholarship, *The Second Wave: A Reader of Feminist Theory*, edited by Linda Nicholson (1997). I then repeat the process, but within popular culture, searching for lesbians in predominantly gay male films about AIDS: *Chocolate Babies*, *The Hours*, *How to*

Survive a Plague, and *The Normal Heart*. As I will discuss further, these categories of "gay," "man," "lesbian," "woman," and "feminist" are all quite slippery, with multiple variations and complexities. This is in line, however, with this project's queer methodology of treating social identities as unstable and dynamic from the onset. While themes of commonality, opposition, and intellectual contributions will reappear, this chapter also presents a critical consideration of absences and an argument for opportunities lost, as well as further questioning about the themes found so far.

Furthermore, in this chapter I directly engage with the figure of the lesbian. As I have suggested previously, within the context of LGBTQ movements, lesbians have been often conflated with feminist women, at times in an almost synecdoche type of fashion. But lesbians are not all feminists, nor are all feminists lesbians. Moreover, the presumption that lesbians are the switchers between the women's movement and the LGBTQ movement erases the heterosexual, bisexual, asexual, and pansexual women in gay activism, as well as the gay men involved in feminism. As I will discuss, second-wave feminist theory did address gay men variously, but lesbianism was a much more contentious and common topic, often treated as the only form of non-normative sexuality that was of relevance, or simply conflated with homosexuality in general. With the onset of the AIDS epidemic, lesbians were often described as heroic allies of gay men. Therefore, I look for them in gay cinema, describing four examples: one of general absence, one of caregiving, one of political coalition, and one of breaking out of the caregiver role.

Searching for Gays in *The Second Wave*

Edited by Linda Nicholson, *The Second Wave: A Reader of Feminist Theory* is a highly regarded authoritative collection of essential second-wave feminist theorizing. Although it presents problems by oversimplifying the multiple movements and subsets of feminism, the "wave model" remains a useful heuristic. Generally, the "first wave" is associated with the women's suffrage movement. The "second wave" covers the explosion of multiple, wide-ranging schools of feminist thought peaking in the 1960s and 1970s. The radical, revolutionary, and liberationist strains of second-wave feminism (e.g., perceived bra burning) provided the raw material for negative stereotypes and misrepresentations in popular and cultural backlash to this era. The "third wave" represents the subsequent three decades of decentering Western, white women as the subject and leaders of feminism, a re-embrace of traditional feminine dress and behaviors, celebrations of sexuality as empowering rather than oppressive, and a concurrent "postfeminist" culture that rejected feminism as achieved and therefore unnecessary, with equality valued but the identity of "a feminist" rejected—a contrafactual and contradictory cultural logic, which feminists examined extensively in popular culture artifacts such as *Sex and The City* and *Bridget Jones' Diary*. Still a subject of debate, if one persists with the "waves model," the fourth wave incorporates more global perspectives, broadened understandings of sexual and gender variance, an embrace of networked communication technologies, and "feminism" becoming popular again, albeit with a rise in popular misogyny. Moreover, fourth-wave feminism is also associated with an increased emphasis on diversity and intersectional perspectives that potentially challenge the lesbian conflation I discuss in this chapter.

The Second Wave contains 23 different essays, all classic and impactful, at a total of 414 pages. It remains one of the best collections for capturing the major issues and debates during this period of the women's movement in the US, considered at times very closely aligned other social movements, such as LGBTQ, race, youth, anti-war, anti-capitalist, and other movements for social change aligned in a liberationist ethos. This was one of my introductory textbooks when studying feminist theory in graduate school, and I chose it here to re-approach, in a systematic way; my initial encounter with it was a feminist-identified gay man. Would I find myself here? What follows is an analysis of every mention of gay men in the book.

Allies, Implicitly or Explicitly Stated

Unlike the materials described in previous and subsequent chapters, there were no explicitly anti-gay or explicitly oppositional representations in the essays in *The Second Wave*. As ample evidence has suggested, this does not imply a lack of homophobia and misandry among second-wave feminists; it does show that, by 1997, those views were not reflected in this representation of the second wave.

Instead, the potential for collaboration and coalition is expressed by several depictions of gay men as potential allies, although these moments are not extensive and range from explicit references to more implicit suggestions.

Patricia Hill Collins (1997), in "Defining Black Feminist Thought," references a perspective that defines feminists "as individuals who have undergone some type of political transformation theoretically achievable by anyone" (p. 242). Although not the focus of her essay, this acknowledgment signals a potential open door for gay men to be feminists.

Some authors describe the dismantling or rearranging of social systems of biological sex, gender, and sexuality as benefitting women's liberation. Editor Linda Nicholson (1997), paraphrasing the chapter from Monique Wittig, writes that "the refusal to become or remain heterosexual always entails the refusal to be a man or woman" (p. 262). In "The Woman Identified Woman" manifesto, the Radicalesbians collective (1997) argued that, "In a society in which men do not oppress women, and sexual expression is allowed to follow feelings, the categories of homosexuality and heterosexuality would disappear" (p. 154). Shulamith Firestone (1997) writes in "The Dialectic of Sex"

> The end goal of feminist revolution must be, unlike that of the first feminist movement, not just the elimination of male *privilege* but of the sex *distinction* itself: genital differences between human beings would no longer matter culturally. (A reversion to an unobstructed *pansexuality*– Freud's "polymorphous perversity"–would probably supersede hetero/homo/bi-sexuality.) (p. 24–25, emphasis original)

Although more essentialist gay thinkers might disagree, from this perspective, men who love and/or have sex with other men would be beneficiaries of feminist revolution and, arguably, contribute to it by participating in destabilizing male privilege (as partially predicated on heterosexual relations) and sex distinctions (as also based on heterosexual dualisms).

In "The Traffic in Women," Gayle Rubin (1997) makes an inclusive gesture toward lesbians but also, and perhaps more so, gay men, in challenging the hetero-centrism of marxist feminists, noting that, "A sex/gender system involves more than the 'relations of procreation,' reproduction in the biological sense" (p. 33). Similarly engaging marxist feminism, Michelle Barrett (1997) in "Capitalism and Women's Liberation," argues for more understanding of neglected areas of sexuality, masculinity, and femininity (p. 124), which would ostensibly include benefits for and contributions from gay men. However, she also states that the basis for feminism changing the relations between women and men will be an "autonomous women's liberation movement" (p. 129)—not a coalition with other movements—but "the strategy must involve political engagement with men rather than a policy of absolute separatism" (p. 129).

Linda Alcoff (1997) presents a curious expression in "Cultural Feminism Versus Poststructuralism." In describing identity politics, she writes that

> For example, assimilated Jews who have chosen to become Jewish-identified as a political tactic against anti-Semitism are practicing identity politics. It may

seem that members of more easily identifiable groups do not have this luxury, but I think that just as Jewish people can choose to assert their Jewishness, so black men, women of all races, and other members of more immediately recognizable oppressed groups can practice identity politics by choosing their identity as a member of one or more groups as their political point of departure. (p. 348)

Although not specifically mentioning gay men, the tactic and broader identity politics she describes have certainly been adopted by some activist gay men, and the parallel to Jews in being less immediately recognizable than other oppressed groups seems obvious. And yet, a nagging question remains: Why not mention sexual or gender minorities here?

The most explicit reference to commonality between feminist women, gay men, and others comes in the collection's final chapter. Uma Narayan (1997), in "Contesting Cultures," addresses the rhetoric of "family values" used by the US Christian right, in its ascendancy in American politics during the 1980s, to stigmatize any deviation from traditional gender roles and nuclear families as anti-American.

> Totalizing and dangerous views of "culture" and "nationhood" can be found in current attempts to portray "Christian values" or particular constructions of "family values" as constitutive of "American culture" and "the American way of life." …[Such attempts] function to variously stigmatize the predicaments and choices of single mothers, women on welfare, gays and lesbians, immigrants, and members of the "underclass" as "un-American." (p. 406)

Here we see feminist issues explicitly woven together with other oppressed groups in their oppression by a common enemy.

Homosexuality Is (Primarily) Lesbianism

However, references to gay men in *The Second Wave* are rare. Overall, they have a minimal presence. Homosexuality is frequently a topic of extended discussion, but this is in terms of lesbianism, the relationships between lesbianism and feminism having been an issue of major debate during the second wave. Were lesbians, particularly lesbian separatists, the ultimate embodiment of feminism, due to their independence from men? Was lesbian homosexuality a threat to the broader cultural acceptance of women's rights? What insights could lesbians offer in terms of gender, sexuality, pornography, BD/SM, transgender persons, or other issues at play?

These debates are well documented elsewhere. What is notable in critically reading *The Second Wave*, however, is how often homosexuality is solely a discussion of lesbianism and its implications for feminism (e.g., Irigaray, 1997; Hill Collins, 1997). Nancy Chodorow (1997) discusses "heterosexual erotic orientation" (p. 182) and "heterosexual relationships" in and "around the psychodynamics of the family" (p. 183). Her specification of "heterosexual" indicates awareness of the exceptions, amending other psychoanalytic feminist theories based on a generalized, universal understanding of family dynamics and erotic development. Universal heterosexual theories that do not somehow account for other sexualities only serve to further pathologize them. However, she also seems somewhat dismissive when she writes

> Most women are heterosexual. This heterosexual preference and taboo against homosexuality, in addition to objective economic dependence on men, make the option of primary sexual bonds with other women unlikely–though more prevalent in recent years. (p. 189)

Again, the subject of non-hetero sexuality is reduced to lesbianism. Lesbianism's increased prevalence is asserted, but couldn't this be instead an increased visibility due to the advances of a concurrent LGBTQ rights movement?

Radicalesbians (1997) move to articulate an interesting distinction between gay men and lesbians in "The Woman Identified Woman," which asserts that "lesbianism is also different from male homosexuality, and serves a different function in the society" (p. 154). True, this is an important perspective, one that to this day has been perhaps under-investigated (let alone in comparison to bisexual and other persons). However, the authors do not go on to explain exactly how they are different. They assert that

> "Dyke" is a different kind of put-down from "faggot," although both imply you were not playing your socially assigned sex role. .... [and] are not therefore a "real woman" or a "real man." The grudging admiration felt for the tomboy, and the queasiness felt around the sissy boy point to the same thing: the contempt in which women—or those who play a female role—are held. (p. 154)

This assertion of difference within common oppression is fairly unique. Both gay men and women suffer from abuse for deviating from heteronormative sexuality, which is taken as failure in living up to their biological sex's true standard. However, in terms of gender performances, the argument suggests, they are valued differently, as the tomboy rejects and the sissy boy embraces femininity, the source of misogynistic contempt. Interestingly, while drawing attention to homophobia and misogyny as separate cultural forces of oppression, this is a rare suggestion that, from at least one perspective, gay men had it worse.

It also suggests certain conflations of gender identity, performance, sex, and sexuality. A sissy boy or tomboy could be heterosexual or asexual. Their gendering could be conscious performances or descriptive perceptions by others. They could be in stages of transitioning, or expressing fluidity. These are, of course, more contemporary perspectives, but it suggests prior linkages: gay men at times seen as necessarily associated with femininity. The role, place, or expression of femininity within feminism remains contentious, as will be seen in my subsequent chapter involving more recent focus groups. Arguably, as Halberstam's exploration into female masculinity (1998) was a disruption of and refusal toward dominant conceptions of masculinity, perhaps male femininity, in the figure of the gay man, presented a potential disruption of or refusal toward dominant conceptions of sex and gender among many feminist theorists during the second wave.

"No Gay": Conspicuous Absences

The same chapter by Radicalesbians (1997) moves from its insightful, albeit brief, comparison between lesbian and gay men, to focusing on lesbians only:

> For a lesbian is not considered a "real woman." And yes, in popular thinking, there is really only one essential difference between a lesbian and other women: that of sexual orientation—which is to say, when you strip off all the packaging, you must finally realize that the essence of being a "woman" is to get fucked by men. (p. 154)

Having followed the previously quoted section, this seems to suggest a continued discussion of gay men, if unmentioned. For, the obvious question arises, who else gets fucked by men? Does this make gay men realizations of the essence of being a woman? Or at least a gay male who has anal sex and does get penetrated (and who might not necessarily be a 'sissy boy' at all.) What might sound like a snark here is actually a very significant issue. The debate over what defines a woman, from biology to social construction to language, was a widespread question of feminist theorizing before, during, and after the second wave. This suggestion that a sexual role defines woman-ness is what I consider a conspicuous absence of gay men. They have been already mentioned or alluded to in the text, and would be a logical counterpoint or question to raise in the argument, but that doesn't happen. As I will describe later with regards to the chapter by Catharine MacKinnon, and its citations of Andrea Dworkin, hindsight makes clear these opportunities are lost when gay men are conspicuously absent from feminist theorizing.

In "The Unhappy Marriage of Marxism and Feminism," Heidi Hartman (1997) defines patriarchy as "a set of social relations between men, which … establish or create interdependence among men that enables them to dominate women" (p. 101). As a gay male feminist, I know that I am part of patriarchy, and yet also part of who it dominates, which is not reflected in Hartman's definition of patriarchy (admittedly, one of many). Hartman goes on to list 1960s social movements that raised new questions for marxists: "the civil rights movement, the student free speech movement, the antiwar movement, the women's movement, the environmental movement, and the increased militancy of professional and white-collar groups all raised new questions for marxists" (p. 113). No LGBTQ is mentioned, and that social movement did not spring fully formed from the Stonewall Inn in June 1969. Earlier riots had occurred on the West Coast. In the 1950s, homophile groups had peacefully lobbied for LGBTQ acceptance, and many members had marxist backgrounds or familiarities. And yet, Hartman argues that

> A struggle to establish socialism must be a struggle in which groups with different interests form an alliance. Women should not trust men to liberate them after the revolution, in part, because there is no reason to think they would know how; in part, because there is no necessity for them to do so. (p. 113)

My copy of *The Second Wave* was previously used. I enjoyed, when reading it, having a delayed conversation with the previous owner's marginalia. On this page of Hartman's essay (p. 113), they had drawn arrows to each of the quotes I've used above. The arrows originated from a circle drawn in the upper right margin, colored yellow with highlighter, within which was written: "No gay."

"A Brief History of Gender Inequality at the Supreme Court" is part of Wendy W. Williams' (1997) contribution, "The Equality Crisis: Some Reflections on Culture, Courts, and Feminism." Originally appearing in *Women's Rights Law Reporter* in 1982, the article reviews significant sex-related court cases, statutory rape laws, sexual crimes, and similar legislative issues. However, the article doesn't mention Doe v. Commonwealth (1976), in which the US Supreme Court upheld Virginia's sodomy law or the State of Iowa case which struck down infidelity that state's sodomy law. Often applied to heterosexual non-procreative sex, sodomy laws seem a relevant dimension of legislation involving equality and gender. But the article does not mention these cases or other decisions handed down in the years immediately before the article's publication, such as People v. Onofre and Commonwealth v. Bonadia.

Nancy C. M. Hartsock (1997) theorizes the epistemology of a feminist standpoint, but no gay male standpoint or even simply a sexual-minority standpoint. Monique Wittig (1997) argues that "Lesbian is the only concept I know of which is beyond categories of sex (Woman and man), because the designated subject (Lesbian) is *not* a woman, either economically, or politically, or ideologically" (p. 270). Is a gay man not a man? Is a gay man a woman? These questions are not asked, and the implications of their answers are not insignificant. Absences are difficult to analyze. In these examples, are the missing gays the result of a blanket heterosexuality? Were they considered inconvenient or irrelevant outliers?

The Queer Case of Judith Butler

A notable exception, or perhaps more accurately a queer inversion, in *The Second Wave* is Judith Butler's (1997) "Imitation and Gender Insubordination." In presenting her theory of gender performativity, Butler discusses homosexuality at length, including male homosexuality, as individuals, subcultural practices, and theoretical illustrations—but feminism is only mentioned in two source citations. Editor Nicholson, in introducing Butler, articulates more explicitly the connection between Butler's theory and feminism:

> In acting *as* a woman we seek, unsuccessfully, to portray ourselves as possessing such a unitary gender. The same can be said for acting *as* a gay or lesbian. To act "as a lesbian" always goes beyond the simple injunction to act as one already is; rather, it involves the demand to performatively enact some stipulated idea of what a gay or lesbian "really is." (p. 263)

The questioning of categories and their creation has long been central to feminism, from "Ain't I a Woman" to "A Woman Is Made Not Born." Butler represents one of several feminist scholars bringing the post-structural theorizing of the discursive constitution of subjects and subject positions to this project, challenging feminisms based on an essential female subject. Butler not only uses explicitly gay male examples; she challenges another feminist writer for her representation of gay men. "The parodic or imitative effect of gay identities," she writes "works neither to copy nor to emulate heterosexuality, but rather, to expose heterosexuality as an incessant and *panicked* [sic] imitation of its own naturalized idealization" (p. 308, emphasis original). Butler here answers the invitation for gay men or rectifies their absences in the examples previously discussed. "If it were not for the notion of the homosexual *as* copy, there be no construct of heterosexuality *as* origin," (p. 307, emphasis original) she writes, emphasizing again the necessary destabilization heterosexuality. Yet, she criticizes fellow feminist Kaja Silverman's inquiries into male homosexuality as oversimplified and conforming easily "to the regulatory requirements of diagnostic epistemic regimes" (p. 311).

As a gay male feminist, this essay is the only one where I find myself significantly represented. However, although mentioning gay men several times and drawing upon them as examples, Butler is primarily doing so in the service of theorizing about the nature of gender-making activities. She does not discuss feminist women and gay men in terms of more applied coalition and collaboration.

Opportunities Lost

I conclude my critical reading of *The Second Wave* with what I argue is the cumulative effect of these reductions, absences, and questions unanswered: opportunities lost. The intents of the authors are not at stake for me here—clarity of argument, homophobia, misandry, essentialist ontologies, convenience, ignorance, etc. What resonates with me most as a gay male reader of *The Second Wave* is a sense of what could have been. Again, while it is unfair to critique older theorizing on the basis of new or more advanced understandings of gender, biological sex, and sexuality, we see in these writings opportunities in which thinking about those issues in open debate, working with and talking to politicized gay men to interrogate these issues could have brought that more informed understandings sooner.

In examining issues of identity, subjectivity, sex, sexual representation, pornography, sex, and gender; useful perspectives, counter-examples, and insights could have come from gay men, bisexual men, asexual persons, transmen and transwomen, and intersexed persons. Even the frequently discussed lesbians could have been engaged with more to inform discussions and advance theorizing. If you are trying to create broad, generalized theories about oppression based on sex, sexuality, and gender, the case studies of sexuality without women or without men would seem to cry out for analysis. Moreover, if you're trying to theorize the role of women in sexuality, you can't just conflate gay men with women. How does patriarchy structure relationships without women? And yet, of course, gay men can be completely sexist and patriarchal as well. I am not unfairly criticizing these authors from a perspective of hindsight. I am, more accurately, mourning the opportunities lost, wondering what advances could have been made in both theory and practice had gay men, bisexuals, transpersons, and others been involved more explicitly in second-wave feminist thought.

The most egregious example in *The Second Wave* is Catherine A. MacKinnon's (1997) "Sexuality." The feminist scholar who was my graduate school advisor, Sarah Banet-Weiser, said when introducing this reading, "You may disagree with MacKinnon 100%, but you have to admire her intellect." I do. Others have critiqued her argument elsewhere. My reading here is to try to suggest how this intellect, grappling mightily with the urgent issue of male sexual violence, could have taken different directions had gay men and others been more significantly included in the analysis.

The importance of MacKinnon's argument that feminists must interrogate sexuality cannot be understated. "To suggest that the sexual might be continuous with something other than sex itself—something like politics—is seldom done," she writes, describing that it "is treated as Detumescent, even by feminists" (p. 160). And yet, would an LGBTQ perspective at this time really not have seen sexuality as continuous with politics?

More significantly, her move, drawing on and developed with Andrea Dworkin—not included in *The Second Wave* but cited heavily in "Sexuality"—to fold all sexual acts within male sexuality as a mode of female oppression, if not the primary mode, is more than a little problematic. MacKinnon argues that "male dominance is sexual" (p. 158) and that

> Male power takes the social form of what men as a gender want sexually, which centers on power itself, as socially defined. ... Masculinity is having it; femininity is not having it. [Masculinity precedes male as femininity precedes female, and male sexual desire defines both.] Specifically, "woman" is defined by what male desire requires for arousal and satisfaction and is socially tautologous with "female sexuality" and "the female sex." ... The ruling norms of sexual attraction and expression are fused with gender identity formation and affirmation, such that sexuality equals heterosexuality equals the sexuality of (male) dominant and (female) submission. (p. 161)

She accuses "Kinsey and his followers" of pathologizing any female disinterest in sex with men and trivializing rape and child sexual abuse, without acknowledging Kinsey's work on the unexpected preponderance of homosexuality (p. 162). Her conception of sex is resolutely heterosexual and penetrative: "If we knew the boundaries were phony, existed only to get eroticize the targeted transgressible, would penetrating them feel less sexy?" (p. 162).

No, "sexuality as such still centers on what would otherwise be considered a reproductive act, on intercourse: penetration of the erect penis into the vagina (or appropriate substitute orifices), followed by thrusting to male ejaculation"

(p. 162–163). This implies that homosexual sex is somehow an inferior copy, a weak substitute—an argument opposite to that of Butler. MacKinnon's model does not merely reinscribe dominant heteronormativity, it insists upon it. "What is called sexuality is the dynamic of control by which male dominance—in forms that range from intimate to institutional, from a look to a rape—eroticizes and thus defines man and woman, gender identity, and sexual pleasure" (p. 165). This implies that gay sex, lesbian sex, and, indeed, any sex act is based on patriarchal power roles and literal and figurative penetration. Someone is always "the man" and someone is always "the woman." This heteronormative conception fails to account for non-penetrative sex and sex in which roles of active and passive, or dominant and submissive, are switched or flip-flopped during a sexual encounter. Moreover, what of triads or group sexual encounters?

In their effort to define and legislate pornography as violence against women, she and Dworkin dismiss gay male pornography and sexuality as simply mirroring the power hierarchies of patriarchy. Citing Dworkin's book *Pornography: Men Possessing Women,* MacKinnon writes, "Through pornography, among other practices, gender inequality becomes both sexually and socially real. Pornography 'reveals that male pleasure is inextricably tied to victimization, hurting, exploiting'" (p. 167). Rape is "the defining paradigm of sexuality," to avoid which "boys choose manhood and homophobia" (p. 167). The reference here to homophobia as part of patriarchy and heterosexual male dominance is intriguing, but not developed further in the essay. Instead, homosexuality is dismissed:

> Nor is homosexuality without stake in this gendered sexual system. Putting to one side the obviously gendered content of expressly adopted roles, clothing, and sexual mimicry, to the extent the gender of a sexual object is crucial to arousal, the structure of social power which stands behind and defines gender is hardly irrelevant, even if it is rearranged. Some have argued that lesbian sexuality—meaning here simply women having sex with women, not with men—solves the problem of gender by eliminating men from women's voluntary sexual encounters. Yet women's sexuality remains constructed under conditions of male supremacy; women remain socially defined as women in relation to men; the definition of women as men's interiors remains sexual even if not heterosexual, whether men are present at the time or not. To the extent gay men choose men because they are men, masculinity is affirmed as well as undermined. It may also be that sexuality is so gender marked that it carries dominance and submission with it, whatever the gender of its participants. (p. 169)

MacKinnon treats certain sexual practices—top/bottom, butch/femme, role-play—as definitive of all homosexuality, when, instead, they are elements of some same-sex sexuality, but far from definitive. Moreover, numerous heterosexual, bisexual, and pansexual persons participate in the erotics of exaggerated gender roles and performances. MacKinnon, however, refutes sexual diversity in practices and representations.

> Pornography's multiple variations on and departures from the male dominant/ female submissive sexual/gender theme are not exceptions to these gender regularities. They affirm them. The capacity of gender reversals (dominatrixes) and inversions (homosexuality) to stimulate sexual excitement is derived precisely from their mimicry or parody or negation or reversal of the standard arrangement. This affirms rather than undermines or qualifies the standard sexual arrangement as the standard sexual arrangement, the Definition of sex, the Standard from which sexuality as such inheres. (p. 170)

MacKinnon views sexuality as a hopelessly closed system, dismissing non-normative genders, sexualities, and sexual practices as exceptions that prove the rule. Personally, this is more than a bit insulting. This is reinforced in the notes to the article, where MacKinnon quotes Dworkin:

> In practice, fucking is an act of possession–simultaneously an act of ownership, taking, force, it is conquering; it expresses in intimacy power over and against, body to body, person to being. 'The sex act' means penile intromission followed by penile thrusting, or fucking. The woman is acted upon, the man acts and through action expresses sexual power, the power of masculinity. Fucking requires that the male act on one who has less power and this valuation is so deep, so completely implicit in the act, that the one who is fucked is stigmatized as feminine during the sex act even when not anatomically female. In the male system, sex is the penis, the penis is sexual power, its use in fucking is manhood. Page 23. (p. 178–179, note number 38, taken from Dworkin's *Pornography*)

This one specific reference to same-sex sexuality is relegated to a footnote, and also seems to exclude sexualities of power bottoms, femme tops, butch bottoms, flips, and switches. Such variance would have been well known to Dworkin, as a member of the SM community who gave interviews to gay publications. Therefore, it seems unlikely MacKinnon was unaware, but, rather, insistent on a theory of universalized, dominance-based, male sexuality that saturates all other expressions of sexuality.

I cannot help but wonder, if LGBTQ persons, members of fetish and BD/SM communities, sex workers, and producers of pornography had been engaged with, how could we benefit today in our understandings of sexual violence, patriarchy, and women's oppression? And what of the mutual benefits of gay men and feminist women understanding each other better through communicating about their practices? Imagine, for example, a gay male feminist defense of bathhouses as consciousness-raising groups, in which gay men broke class barriers, expressed frustration with prescribed social roles, formed alliances, and challenged patriarchy, albeit in more physical than verbal forms of communication. Rather than a convenient dismissal, how much richer could MacKinnon (and Dworkin's) theorizing have been with engagement with gay male feminists? What opportunities were lost by our absence here? Their arguments were a foundation for enacting Canadian legislation against pornography, yet this would prove a relatively futile strategy with mass adoption of the Internet in the mid-1990s.

The second-wave debates over sexuality and pornography were also seen by some as creating the anti-pleasure stereotype that was deployed in backlash against feminism and deployed in postfeminism's "taking feminism into account" (McRobbie, 2009). In particular, the perceived erotophobia and homophobia of second-wave feminist debates around sexuality, BD/SM, sexwork, and pornography were seen by some as driving young lesbians away from feminism and into more primary identification with gay men.

And then there was AIDS.

Searching for Lesbians in AIDS Cinema

Every history is a story. In this section, I turn to cinematic narratives about the AIDS epidemic to see what stories are told there about lesbians during the crisis. As noted previously, lesbians and gay men are often said to have overcome sexism, hostility, stereotypes, and competition to work together, collaborating in the coalition of groups combatting the AIDS epidemic.

This is where the stories of gay men and lesbians begin to intersect with my own life stories. I recall being told this by older gay men at the time: "Lesbians and gays hated each other until AIDs came along" and "The only good thing about AIDS was that it brought lesbians and gays back together." In fact, a common joke at the time was that, if AIDS was God's retribution, lesbians must be the chosen people, given that they were the lowest-risk group. And this suggests the true admiration and appreciation we had for the altruism of lesbians in AIDS activism, although there was also a counterargument warning against a sense of false security among lesbians. At one time, dentals dams became as ubiquitous as condoms in the bar bowls and safe-sex kits distributed by STOP AIDS Chicago, a group with which my partner at the time worked. Thin rectangles of latex designed to prevent oral-to-vaginal HIV transmission among lesbians, there were attempts to get gay men to use them for rimming as well. Lesbians were, once, the most unthreatened queers in the epidemic, and yet, a presumption of safety was something no one wanted to risk in those days. Safe sex, ironically, also provided a discourse about sexual pleasure. I remember watching a comic performance at a nightclub in which a lesbian activist demonstrated on a banana how to apply a condom. With feminist debates around pornography, BD/SM, and sexuality still in progress, promoting safe sex circumvented those debates with a discourse founded in an ideology of sexuality as good, necessary, and a source of pleasure. Urging people to practice safe sex implied without stating that people should be having and enjoying all kinds of sex.

Thus, here I turn to an intersection of these two switching moments: AIDS and queer art. AIDS fueled homophobia and erotophobia, providing justification for the religious right and their political affiliates during the Reagan-Bush administrations to launch attacks on artists representing sexuality, especially queer sexuality. Therefore, queer art about AIDS should be a rich place to look for gay male representations of feminist women, particularly the feminist lesbians involved in AIDS activism.

A word on categorizations here: As I have described, I use terms here, such as "gay" and "woman," with the acknowledgment that these are discursive constructs, contingent on time, place, cultural context, and other factors for their multiple meanings and associations. I acknowledge the dynamism of such concepts even while, as a researcher, I deploy a form of what postcolonial feminist scholar Spivak (1990) calls "strategic essentialism" in the process of this inquiry. I will treat certain subjects as if they were historic and stable. Moreover, I intentionally enact the methodological sin of presentism is projecting contemporary concepts into the past in my reading and interpretation of materials. As discussed in the chapter on historiographic discourse, the public memory of feminist women and gay men is nascent, and this project aims to add to and shape that formation of public memory. I operate from such a position of dynamic entanglement between past and present, rather than asserting a false neutrality. I am telling a series of stories here, and stories about stories, which does not exclude rigor and integrity from my analyses. Indeed, it adds to them. I reject the concept of myself as an objective scribe accurately representing the past. As described in the earlier discussion of queer methodology, this project draws upon multiple methods, but also multiple ways of knowing. My subjectivity is, in this sense, an added layer of data: an investigation into the social movements of feminist women and gay men, diffracted through the crystal of a middle-aged, white, cisgender, gay male feminist. In both feminist and queer activism and scholarship, personal experience has been elevated as a tool to counteract the erasure and oppression of dominant knowledges and ways of knowing.

Therefore, instead of seeking evidentiary "proof" of lesbian feminists in AIDS cinema (e.g., interviewing screenwriters, directors, and documentary subjects), I am seeking how they are narrativized. This means that I am open to working with the ambiguity of narratives and with marking figures as lesbian or feminist by my terms. This is not an assertion that they themselves (even if fictional) actually identified as such at that time and place. They are lesbian figures within these narratives.

To begin with, I identified 198 films dealing to a significant degree with AIDS, distributed during the years 1985–2018. (See *List of Films* at end of this chapter.) This list was compiled from publicly available user-created lists, such as those on Wikipedia and the Internet Movie Database, augmented with a few from my own memory. My intent was not to define AIDS cinema, but to document how others have identified and remembered AIDS cinema. Therefore, I did not question and remove titles from other lists that I thought may not meet my personal definition of an AIDS film. I approached the list created here as a small part of the ongoing act of building public memory, compiling and consolidating lists others have created. In this sense, I was also acting as a member of the network of persons interested in the topic, drawing on and connecting their efforts. Next, I examined the plot synopses, comments, and advertising materials to ascertain general storyline information. This was in order to identify common themes, which are discussed below.

Common Themes

In contrast to the historical narrative, lesbians and feminists were not prominent across AIDS cinema. There were no films along the lines of *"Women Die Faster!" The Story of Women and AIDS* or *Healing the Divide: Lesbians, ACT UP and AIDS*, imaginary titles of films which could have told the story of coalition and collaboration between women, lesbians, and gay men during the AIDS crisis.

Instead, women in AIDS cinema fell roughly into three categories: non-Western documentary subjects, Western narrative protagonists with AIDS, and caregivers to persons with AIDS.

Women and girls in developing countries, who have AIDS, appeared as the subjects of documentaries, such as *AIDS: The Woman's Story* (USA, 2004), which documents women with AIDS in Kenya, Brazil, and Thailand. Others included *Seeds of Hope: HIV/AIDS in Ethiopia* (USA, 2004), *Tapestries of Hope* (USA, 2009), *We Are Together* (UK, 2006), *The Orphans of Nkandla* (country unknown, 2005), and *The Blood of Yingzhou District* (USA, 2006).

Western women also appeared in AIDS films, but more often as the protagonists of fictional narratives or dramatizations, and often were heterosexual. Two main sub-themes emerged here: Women with AIDS and women as caregivers (sometimes both). Stories of women with AIDS included *A Mother's Prayer* (USA, 1995), in which a widow struggles to accept her AIDS diagnosis and plan for her son's care after her presumed-to-be-inevitable death. The road-trip film *Boys on the Side* (USA, 1995), stars Mary-Louise Parker as a heterosexual woman with AIDS joined by a lesbian, played by Whoopi Goldberg, and a woman escaping an abusive boyfriend, played by Drew Barrymore. The death from AIDS of lesbian model Gia Carangi is dramatized in two biographical films: *Gia* (USA, 1998), starring Angelina Jolie, and the short film *The Self-Destruction of Gia* (USA, 2003). In *Tyler Perry's Temptation: Confessions of a Marriage Counselor* (USA, 2013), a professional matchmaker, played by singer-actress Brandy (Norwood), reveals herself to have been infected with HIV from a friend's abusive boyfriend. Some films also combined a woman with AIDS with her taking on an activist/educator role. For example, Molly Ringwald starred in the made-for-television film, *Something to Live for: The Alison Gertz Story* (USA, 1992), in which a woman with AIDS takes on the role of educating the public about AIDS and preventing it.

In the second theme, in both documentaries and fictional narratives, women appeared as caregivers of persons with AIDS, often family, educators, or healthcare professionals. The first major US film to deal with AIDS, the made-for-television film *An Early Frost* (1985), features Gena Rowlands and Sydney Walsh, as the mother and sister, respectively, of a man recently diagnosed. Judith Light stars as the mother of the teen AIDS poster child in *The Ryan White Story* (USA, 1989). Gay playwright Terence McNally's *Andre's Mother* was filmed for the US television series *American Playhouse* in 1990, telling the story of the mother, grandmother, and lover of a man who had just died of AIDS. The documentaries *DiAna's Hair Ego* (USA, 1991) and *DiAna's Hair Ego Remix* (USA, 2017) focus on a hairdresser in the US South, DiAna DiAna, who converted her salon into an

AIDS information center. The docudrama *And the Band Played On* (USA, 1993), based on the 1987 nonfiction bestseller by journalist Randy Shilts, featured Lily Tomlin as Dr. Selma Dritz, a physician and epidemiologist. In the 2006 Canadian documentary *Sari's Mother*, the mother of a 10-year-old boy with AIDS struggles to find care for him during wartime.

These films exhibited a great deal of variety in their depictions of women within the context of AIDS. However, lesbians were rare. Moreover, women were often generalized as persons with AIDS, caregivers, educators, or individual activists. Searching for organized groups of feminist/lesbians, rushing to join the fight of AIDS activism, I turn now to four specific films to examine their differing treatments of the lesbians during AIDS.

Four Stories

Of the original list of films identified, 123 were described in their sources as produced or co-produced in the United States. To select films to analyze more closely, I chose to eliminate non-US films, given that the focus of this project has been feminist women and gay men in the United States. I then wanted to focus on "gay male films," in order to find examples how gay men in particular were representing lesbians within the context of AIDS narratives. My criteria here was that the films should have some combination of gay production (e.g., source material, screenwriters, directors), gay male content (e.g., protagonists, subject matter), and/or marketing to gay audiences (e.g., posters, LGBTQ film festivals).

Finally, I chose four films as having some type of significant lesbian presence and also representing a mix of fiction and documentary. I also wanted to include examples of films created both concurrent with peak years of the AIDS crisis and more recent films looking back or historicizing it. In addition, I looked for a mix of mainstream and independent productions. The resulting four films were:

- *Chocolate Babies*, 1997, an independent fictional narrative,
- *The Normal Heart*, 2004, a mainstream fictional narrative based on a 1985 autobiographical play,
- *How to Survive a Plague*, 2012, an independent documentary, and
- *The Hours*, 2002, a mainstream fictional narrative based on a 1998 novel.

I do not claim these four films to be representative of AIDS cinema, as I reject the notion of a generalized type of "AIDS movie." They are instead insightful examples of stories told about the AIDS crisis, which, to varying degrees and in interesting ways, depict the roles of lesbians and feminists.

Common Oppression, Coalition Politics: Chocolate Babies

> Who here is HIV positive? C'mon don't disappoint me. Well, I've got news for you. We are all HIV positive. You and you and you and you and your brothers and your sisters and mothers and all your chilluns. AIDS is number one on the charts as the number one killer of Black women. I am Jamela, an HIV positive. Positively danger-ous when I'm pissed, so don't try it.—Jamela

Each major character in Stephen Winter's *Chocolate Babies* (USA, 1997) has a brief scene delivering a spoken-word performance at a queer club. In hers, Jamela, a member of the titular "gang of self-proclaimed raging, atheist, meat-eating, HIV-positive, colored terrorists" not only asserts her HIV-positive status, but does so in the manner of a network switcher. She reaches out to connect members of the audience with her HIV-positive network, to reprogram networks of queer persons and persons of color to see themselves as part of the network of those with and impacted by HIV. She is actively attempting to build coalition, to collaborate with other social movements and activism. Is she, then, the heroic subject of the lesbian-in-AIDS-activism narrative? Maybe. Not really. Well, sort of.

As I will argue, director/writer Winter uses a strategic ambiguity in his depic-tion of Jamela. While there are many details to suggest she is lesbian or bisexual, this is never explicitly stated, unusual in a film in which so many persons are so frequently stating their identity politics. What Jamela definitely is, however, is a feminist woman of color, one involved at the deepest levels in a radical queer collective working on AIDS activism. Her possibility as lesbian, bisexual, or het-erosexual, I suggest, makes her a figure of potential, of optimistic depiction of collaboration and coalition. Yet, she also represents a fatigued-too-soon caution-ary tale about exactly such optimism, presenting a dimension of cynicism and regretful failure of coalition that is striking in a film full of such youthful energy and activism.

Winner of the Best Picture Award at the South by Southwest Film Festival, *Chocolate Babies* was critically praised as it played the festival circuit. It maintains today a following among queer artists and academics. However, it is likely the least widely distributed or recognized film of the four examined here. An inde-pendent production, it was written and produced during the mid-1990s, before combination drug therapies had begun to have a significant impact on AIDS treatment. The crisis was in full terminal swing, with no signs of abating. The film is suffused with feelings of pointed resolve and insistent humor, dynamic and joyous, qualitatively distinct from the trajectory of many AIDS films that depict a journey from bafflement and rage to resignation and tragedy.

The film concerns a group of five activist friends: Max (Claude E. Sloan), a gay African-American man; his sister, Jamela (Suzanne Gregg Ferguson), a single mother; Larva (Dudley Findlay Jr.), a promiscuous, loud, and large gender-nonconforming gay man; Lady Marmalade (Michael Lynch), a singer, unapologetic drug addict, and heterosexual transwoman; and Sam (Jon Kit Lee), a recently radicalized Filipino man, who is dating Max. The radio news calls them "gay terrorists ... alternately described by their victims as 'ugly black women,' 'overdressed homos,' or 'freaks." This " 'gay gang' "—whom the mayor reported refers to as " 'this bunch of colored fags' "—are gaining attention for civil disobedience demonstrations and performances around issues such as affordable housing access and a closeted city councilman who supports policies hurtful to women and children of color. Their militancy is rising over the regional government's work developing "AIDS acquisition files," a comprehensive list of all HIV-positive persons in the tri-state area.

Jamela makes the film's first move. The opening shot of the film introduces the gang standing resolute and united on a sidewalk in front of brownstones, staring straight ahead at camera, with Jamela and Lady Marmalade in front of the three men. Jamela takes the first step forward as the group confronts the closeted African-American city councilman who had blocked healthcare legislation for African-American and Latino children. Cheering, Jamela rubs fake blood on the councilman's face, and Larva shouts, "We are Black faggots with a political agenda. We your worst nightmare!" From this first sequence, Jamela is clearly an equal, if not driving, part of collective, but her sexual orientation is not specified. Is she a "faggot"? Perhaps, as in her spoken-word piece, we all are.

There are suggestions Jamela could be lesbian or bisexual. Everyone else in the group is queer, and they are collectively referred to as "gay," "fags," and "faggots." No mention is made of her having relationships with men. During a party scene, there are women clearly marked as lesbians in the crowd, boyish ones with tousled hair and baseball caps, and a woman of size with masculine, close-cropped hair. Jamela dances with her arm around her, then later next to one of the ball-cap lesbians. Jamela has a baby, but the child spends the film staying with her aunt, not a parent or lover of Jamela. When Larva proclaims his sexual preference for "light-skinnded men," Jamela accuses him of being "colorstruck," questioning his potential internal racism for not being attracted to Black men. Ostensibly, she could be read as the "overly politically correct" lesbian stereotype, but has also exhibited good humor and support for the group throughout the film. She smirks at Larva explicitly describing a sexual escapade, and then laughs at Larva's double entendre about the "World *Trade* Center."

Jamela is central to the gang, if not its driving force. Jamela participates in their demos and debates strategy. She is fully with the gang as they take the stage at the nightclub, collectively warning the audience about the AIDS list. Max has charm and charisma, but she seems to be the group's conscience. In one of the gang's rooftop planning meetings, Larva is arguing with group, and Jamela questions his commitment: "Answer the fucking question: Are you in or out? Use your brain; it's not hard." Lady Marmalade assures the group that she is in, but doesn't want to go to jail if arrested at a demonstration or action. Jamela proclaims, "She's out!" Lady Marmalade, however, insists she is in, and has been longer than Jamela, calling her a "high-yellow Cleopatra Jones." Jamela, in turn, accuses her of being high on drugs at that moment. She calls her an addict, questioning her ability to contribute to the gang. Lady Marmalade replies, "I *am* an addict. So are a lot a people. We all got issues, Miss Shaniqua, and you can't lay them all out on me. I am an addict, baby, but I am not the problem."

In scenes such as these, Jamela is shown as fully participating in the group, in debating its very nature and constitution. She is the group; she does not come to or join the group, as the historic lesbian AIDS narrative suggests. She helps develop strategies and tactics, and is the sharpest mind in the collective: Sam is naive, Max is drunk, Lady Marmalade is high and drunk, and Larva is self-centered and hedonistic. Jamela holds her own and is not afraid to stand up to the others. She is perceptive, correctly suspecting that Sam is up to something in councilman's office.

Jamela is definitely a feminist. She and Larva debate whether abortion rights are a relevant issue for the group:

Larva: I'm sorry, I thought we were a self-proclaimed queer terrorist group dedicated to queer terrorism.
Jamela: We are!
Larva: So why should I expend energy in some abortion clinic dealing with tired fish Pollyannas who want to kill their kids?
Jamela: No, but, you see, I have the right to control my body.
Larva: So control your body by not fucking!

They debate intersections between abortion, rape, AIDS, and victim-blaming until Jamela accuses Larva, "Divide and conquer. That's how it always falls. *You* are why every revolution has failed!" Here, we see the conflict between a feminist woman dealing with gay male misogyny ("tired fish") and sexism (reducing reproductive rights to a matter of sexual self-control, and this from the group's most vocal advocate of promiscuity). First, Jamela experiences the conflicts that have disrupted collaboration and coalition between gay men and feminist women. Then, she calls it out for what it is. She acknowledges the moment of conflict and connects it to other efforts at revolutionary social change, which all have failed due to broken coalition.

In contrast to other films I will discuss, she is not an addition to the group or peripheral; she is an essential part of it. In contrast to the lesbians-join-gays narrative, she was always already there. She is not a woman driven to AIDS activism because of losing someone or out of a sense of political solidarity; she is and always has been friends and family with these people, part of a community long under siege from racism, sexism, homophobia, and then AIDS. She is not an addition.

This, I argue, is the importance of her ambiguous lesbian potential. It foregrounds her community identity and prevents it from being overwritten by the lesbian-gay reunification narrative. She aligns with the lesbian gay narrative, however, in the sense that she has the potential to be read as lesbian support. However, she does not do so with explicitness that would have erased heterosexual women from the story: as people with AIDS, as mothers, as activists. Jamela reminds Max that being HIV-positive is different for women: "If I get cancer," she says, trailing off, "If it moves into my cervix." As she told the audience at the club, "AIDS is number one on the charts as the number one killer of Black women." Women, not just lesbians. Winter avoids what, I argue, is one of the problems of the lesbian-gay reunification narrative: the erasure of heterosexual and bisexual women. The chant at the ACT UP demonstration for national healthcare in Chicago, as I recall, was "AIDS is a disaster! Women die faster!"—not "Lesbians die faster!"

Jamela leaves the gang over her brother's self-destructive drinking, but returns when he is shot during an attempt to return the kidnapped councilman. With Sam's mother tending to Max's wound, Jamela rests her cheek on her screaming brother's chest, crying but singing loudly to comfort him as they remove the bullet. She and Sam's mother here suggest the caregiver theme of women in AIDS mentioned previously, but, in *Chocolate Babies*, it is a moment, not the defining theme. Jamela instead presents a potential lesbian, but also open to being read as all women impacted by AIDS and involved in activism. The familiar narratives of commonality, collaboration, coalition, and conflict are all presented but, instead of a lesbian coming to the AIDS movement, she is and has been an integral part of it and related concerns. Her experience as a woman of color offers a broader perspective than that of the lesbian who helps out the politicized white gays, or an individualized narrative decontextualized from politics, both of which I will now discuss in other films.

"Tell Me You Can Use Me for Something" — The Normal Heart

The Normal Heart was first produced as a play in 1985, also the year of the first major AIDS films. Playwright Larry Kramer was already an established gay novelist (*Faggots*) and outspoken voice in New York gay politics. Produced off-Broadway, it tells a thinly fictionalized account of Kramer's experiences in the onset of the AIDS epidemic, focusing on the formation of a gay men's health activist group. The play was revived in 2004 and eventually made it to Broadway in 2011, winning three Tony Awards. The 2014 film, then, represents a narrative both contemporaneous with the early years of the AIDS crisis and retrospective in telling one history of it.

The film version was released on cable network HBO after decades of rumors of cinematic adaptations, involving efforts from even the likes of Barbra Streisand. Kramer wrote the screenplay for this 132-minute film, with Ryan Murphy directing. Murphy, whose projects have dealt with the murder of Gianni Versace, the queer ballroom scene, the feud between Joan Crawford and Bette Davis, as well as numerous gay storylines in other projects, has no contemporary when it comes to visible, out, gay male directors and producers at this point in time. In addition, the film's cast included several of a new generation of successfully out gay male actors: Jim Parsons, Matt Bomer, B.D. Wong, Jonathan Groff, and Denis O'Hare.

The film presents the first days, then years, of the epidemic in NYC, with gay men organizing in face of indifference and hatred to share information, lobby officials, and provide care. Before the virus has even been identified, and while friends, lovers, and colleagues are sick and dying around them, Kramer's character, Ned Weeks investigates the new sickness and fights apathy and hostility within the gay community. Many in the gay community in New York are presented as apolitical, others are closeted, and for others their politics are centered in promiscuity and sexual liberation. "Gay politics" in New York is depicted as fractious, contentious, and ineffective. In his living room, Weeks co-founds a community organization, Gay Men's Health Crisis (GMHC). As the epidemic advances, and the President Reagan still hasn't said the word "AIDS" in a public speech, Ned moves toward a strategy of threatening civil disobedience. He is fired by the Board of GMHC. However, the credits sequence of the film hints at what many viewers know: Kramer would go on from that defeat to start the more militant and arguably effective AIDS Coalition to Unleash Power, or ACT UP.

Ned is positioned as an outspoken but unwilling hero who dares to speak what people do not want to hear, and he acknowledges the risk that spreading the word about AIDS in the media could further stigmatize and pathologize gay men. However, he recognizes the danger, before most others, as warranting such attention. He faces homophobia from his straight doctor brother and resistance from his community, but nevertheless forms a group of persons who address the health crisis with humor and camaraderie. He fights the perception that AIDS is a deserved retribution upon deviants or a natural extension of people who were already "sick."

In other words, *The Normal Heart* is Ned's story. It is the story of an important person at an important time in the history of AIDS, but still primarily the story of one man.

Ned, however, has a prominent female counterpart in the heterosexual woman, Dr. Emma Brookner, played by megastar Julia Roberts and based on the actual American AIDS doctor and researcher Linda Laubenstein. *The Normal Heart* has her as a strong female character from almost the beginning. With the whirring motor loud in the sound mix and a close-up of the wheelchair controls, Brookner's disability is foregrounded from very onset, suggesting the source of her empathy for persons with a new, stigmatized disease. It is revealed later that she nearly died from polio as a child, and was in an iron lung. "Polio was a virus, too," she tells Ned. "Nobody gets polio anymore."

As one of the first doctors treating AIDS, despite the homophobic and ignorant practices of hospitals, caregivers, and funding sources, she fits the caregiver pattern of women in AIDS cinema. She is also an activist and educator within her realm, acting in parallel with Ned's directness, bravery, and honesty. She claims to be taking care of more people with this disease than anyone in the world as she fights for research funding. She describes herself as an unwilling leader, much like Ned. She outs a closeted lead doctor on a national research funding panel—something she says she had promised never to do—who is denying her funding. Like Ned, she has become more militantly politicized. She warns the NIH funding panel, "Women have been discovered to have it in Africa, where it is clearly transmitted heterosexually!"

Although not asserting specifically feminist positions or issues, her role as a leading woman in medicine at the time and her social activism qualify her in my book. However, unlike Jamela in *Chocolate Babies*, she has no suggestions of lesbianism, bisexuality, or potential sexual queerness. Although she fits some patterns of women in AIDS cinema, where are the lesbians in *The Normal Heart*?

One rainy afternoon, while quipping and dropping double entendres, several members of GMHC are moving into their new offices in a two-story house. Arriving at the door is a zaftig woman in a frumpy denim vest. Played by Danielle Ferland, who was in her late 40s at time of filming, she is in marked contrast to mostly younger, stylish, and handsome male characters.

"Hi," she says, "My name is Estelle. And, my best friend, Harvey, died last night." As somber piano music starts, she continues, "We went everywhere together, you know? Like Broadway, the Rockettes, and ice skating. He was a beautiful skater." She gets choked up, her voice breaking, but continues:

> I'm a klutz, but he didn't care. We had so much fun. Dammit, I want to do something! Even though, all my lesbian friends say, what have you guys ever done for us? But I don't care. This is for Harvey. Please, tell me you can use me for something.

She breaks down, crying, and is hugged by Tommy (Jim Parsons), who says he needs a hotline director. "Can you do that?" "I don't know how." "I don't either," he tells her. "We'll figure this out together."

The scene dramatizes the narrative of lesbians joining AIDS activism. Estelle has been politicized by grief over Harvey's death, and is overcoming the animosity held by other lesbians. She is not motivated by an inherent sense of political coalition or shared oppression. Moreover, she is not shown bringing her own politics, perspectives, or experiences to the cause. The scene suggests that gay men had to show lesbians what to do, that they did not bring their own unique organizing and political skills. The lesbian here has to be literally trained and put to work by gay men, who were figuring it out themselves, but still in charge and leading the way. It suggests lesbians came out of individual grief, not a collective, inherent sense of LGBTQ solidarity.

As the scene unfolds, a television news crew arrives, surprising the men. Ned soon arrives with two magazines featuring AIDS on the cover, and proudly announces he had invited the news crew in order to out the closeted president of the organization, Bruce (Taylor Kitsch). "You can be gay 24/7, Ned," Bruce pleads, "but I can't!" Ned replies with mixed anger and sorrow, "When I look at you, I worry we're not going to win." Estelle stands by watching.

At the end of the scene, Estelle is introduced to the group. Bruce says "Welcome," and the opening notes of Roxy Music's "More Than This" swells on the soundtrack. Ned and his boyfriend drive to a beach house.

The somewhat pitiful lesbian is welcomed into GMHC, and asks to be told what to do. She doesn't have to fight for a share of leadership, get her voice in, or deal with sexism. It is a sympathetic and positive, but somewhat patronizing view, and definitely oversimplified. However, the "politicized by grief" or "made sympathetic by grief" narrative aligns her with the broader theme of women in AIDS movies who are friends and family of men with AIDS.

We next see Estelle working hard at a phone bank with approximately 10 other people, including possibly one other lesbian: another forty-something, white woman in a sweater-vest, with short brunette hair and a button-down shirt. She has no dialogue.

Estelle shouts out, "Tommy, I think I got us maybe four qualified social workers to volunteer. They're all lesbians!" To which Tommy replies, "Thank god for the lesbians."

The scene expands the individual narrative of Estelle's arrival into a broader story of women, specifically lesbians, joining the fight against AIDS. However, in GMHC, they are working for gay men, not equally developing strategy or making decisions. There is no discussion of women with AIDS. And, social workers are still caregivers. They even cook! One of the men announces to their sick friend, "Estelle made you some stuffed cabbage for later!" in a later scene in which she is not present. Nor was Estelle present as a character in the original play upon which the film is based.

Ultimately, Estelle and the Other Lesbian (revealed in the credits as Carol) fall in with the other many forces against which Ned battles. When he is fired by the Board of GMHC, Estelle remains silent and deadpan while a hateful, accusatory letter is read aloud to Ned. The scene seems to suggest that most of the room agrees with the Board's condemnation and firing of Ned, and she seems part of this agreement: frowning, hands clasped in front of her. Carol is glimpsed from behind. The group regathers in Ned's office as he packs his things, including Estelle and Carol, who both remain stoic. Ned delivers a speech about great gay men in history, from Alexander the Great to Alan Turing, saying, "That's how I want to be remembered, as one of the ones who helped win the war." He does not mention any great lesbians.

Indeed, lesbians in *The Normal Heart* do help, but are ultimately among the many who fail to support Ned in his sense of urgency and strategy of civil disobedience. In its Ned-against-the-world narrative, the film squarely places lesbians within "the world." They are sympathetic by virtue of their gay friends (suggesting that some lesbians and gay men were friends, despite earlier conflicts) and perhaps stereotypically inherent feminine caregivers (social workers). However, in a story so full of explicit explaining of political strategy and tactics, the political alignment between gay men and lesbians, let alone all women, facing common sources of oppression, is never suggested. In the film's penultimate scene, we glimpse a few lesbian couples at an LGBTQ dance during Yale's Gay Week that Ned attends. Paul Simon croons "The Only Living Boy in New York" as Ned cries, watching young couples.

Unnamed Dykes in the Crowd: How to Survive a Plague

Alternating with the closing title cards of *The Normal Heart* are shots of a man's hands gathering Rolodex cards, alluding to Weeks (Kramer) going on to start ACT UP. The impactful AIDS activist group is widely cited as the crucible in which lesbians and gay men came together. I turn now to a retrospective documentary film about ACT UP, *How to Survive a Plague*. Released in 2012 and nominated for an Academy Award for Best Documentary Feature, it was directed by a gay male journalist who had covered AIDS for many years, David France, and is dedicated to his partner, Doug Gould, who died of AIDS-related pneumonia in 1992. It is thus a gay male film in its production and also in its content. While including several women, it largely focuses on Robert Rafsky, a Harvard-educated, New York public relations professional who became a spokesperson for and central figure in ACT UP. His work with AIDS and death from it frame the film. He is the only person to feature significant personal details, with several sections of home movies of him, his daughter, and ex-wife.

However, there are several women in the film as it covers the years 1987–1995. Iris Long, identified as a "Retired Chemist," is described by Larry Kramer in his contemporary interview as "this housewife" who "just showed up one day" and offered to help them with understanding medical science and drug trials. Identified as not gay, she fits within the caregiver theme, much like Dr. Emma Brookner in *The Normal Heart*. She goes on to take a lead role in ACT UP's Treatment + Data Committee, which would later spin off into the Treatment Activist Group (TAG). Heterosexual civil rights activist Mathilde Krim is interviewed for her work with the American Foundation for AIDS Research (AmFAR), which grew out of the AIDS Medical Foundation she established in 1983. As a physician, researcher, and ally, she fits as well within the caregiving theme. Similarly, heterosexual woman Susan Ellenberg, PhD, is interviewed and identified as "Chief Biostatistician, Division of AIDS" with the National Institutes of Health.

What of lesbians? They are there, but you wouldn't know it from the film. As one of the interviewees notes in an essay reflecting on the film, "The movie focuses on three HIV-positive men to tell the larger story of the early years of AIDS treatment activism" (Franke-Ruta, 2013, paragraph 11). This interviewee, Garance

Franke-Ruta, is a lesbian (Franke-Ruta, 2016). Now a prominent United States political writer and editor, she is identified in the film merely as "Teenager." She is shown in archival footage and a contemporary interview, speaking in particular about her work with the Treatment + Data Committee. Also featured in the film is Ann Northrop, identified as a "Former Network News Producer," seen in the beginning of the film speaking at a New York City Hall demonstration. She reappears throughout the film in archival footage and a contemporary interview. Although not identified as such, her feminist credentials include working on the WCBS-TV program *Woman* and writing for *Ms.* magazine. Similarly, her identity as a lesbian is not explicitly stated, although she left CBS in 1987 to educate on AIDS and homosexuality for New York City's Hetrick-Martin Institute for Lesbian and Gay Youth, wrote for LGBTQ publications, and was the only openly homosexual member of the New York delegation to the Democratic National Convention in 1992. Dr. Barbara Starrett, "AIDS Physician," is interviewed, but her lesbianism is not mentioned, nor is her co-founding the Women's Health Collective at St. Marks Clinic, which later became the Community Health Project with the Gay Men's Health Project.

I was only able to identify these women as lesbian through research independent of the film.

Unlike *The Normal Heart*, in *How to Survive a Plague* there is no explicit moment of lesbians joining the movement. The Women's Caucus of ACT UP is not mentioned, nor are similar groups such as The Lesbian AIDS Project of the GMHC in New York. Stories such as this, from a 1999 *New York Times* article, are not part of this film's story:

> Coming out was once the predominant topic for [lesbian support] groups like this one, All the Queens Women, which gathers each month at Borough Hall in Queens. But the issues for these women have evolved. No longer battling for a voice in the feminist movement, no longer consumed only with their gay brothers dying of AIDS, lesbians have turned their attention to their own health. (Thompson, 1999, ¶3)

I cannot speculate on the intention of the filmmakers here, but in examining representations of lesbians in AIDS cinema, *How to Survive a Plague* presents them in two ways, both unnamed. As I have described, the major female subjects of the film are not named as lesbians through their own words or others' descriptions. In a similar but opposite fashion, women who appear to be lesbians are often seen in crowd scenes of archival footage, but unnamed. In judging appearances, I am admittedly relying on my own personal experiences with and memories of activist lesbians in the late 1980s and early 1990s: leather jackets, hair spiky or in a mold-ed pompadour, round glasses, and other looks. Peering at the film's crowd scenes, ACT UP meetings, public actions and "zaps," and news footage, they appear of-ten, if not making up the majority of the crowd. There are three women outside New York City Hall, arms linked, chanting "Health care is a right!" Women are shown being arrested. Women are seen boarding buses to leave Bethesda after having interrupted Dr. Ellen Cooper, FDA Regulator for AIDS Drugs, at a meet-ing. Women are protesting the Catholic Church's position against contraceptives at St. Patrick's Cathedral. There is a red-haired woman smoking in an ACT UP shirt at the 1989 Sixth International Conference on AIDS in San Francisco. There is the woman wearing glasses with Franke-Ruta at a drug company demonstration in 1990. Women are scattered throughout a demonstration in winter, 1991. In 1994, four women of color are at an ACT UP meeting, and there is a white wom-an with short hair on stage. All look to me similar to lesbians at the time, based on my memories but also the many LGBTQ newspapers, magazines, and books from the period I reviewed over the more recent years of working on this project.

Finally, another type of woman is seen throughout the film in archival footage of events more than meetings. These are older women, conservatively dressed, who often have gray hair. Were these, perhaps, older lesbians? Or friends, family and caregivers, or persons with AIDS? Or another story yet to be told?

The women who look lesbian and the lesbian women not identified as such in *How to Survive a Plague* provide evidence of lesbian participation in ACT UP. However, they do not tell a story of coalition—which is the 'C' in ACT UP, re-call—as they are unnamed and, therefore, disconnected. We see them and hear lesbians in the film, but we do not see or hear the story of lesbians and AIDS ac-tivism. The film performs a strange, contradictory movement. On the one hand, it makes an effort to document the involvement of women at the highest levels of organizing: facilitating meetings, delivering media training, taking votes, debat-ing strategies, and being beaten by a policeman's billy club. On the other hand, the film's lack of speaking collectively about "women" or "lesbians" erases the col-lective narrative of groups working together. It is the reverse of *The Normal Heart*. Women here have voices, agency, and screen time, but no one says, "Thank God for the lesbians."

Lesbians are, however, mentioned as sharing the common oppression of homophobic violence and discrimination with gay men. In 1987, ACT UP is shown at St. Vincent's Hospital in Greenwich Village to protest treatment of queer patients. An African-American man demands, "You will not beat up on faggots, and you will not beat up on lesbians in a hospital in our community!"

A white, lesbian-appearing woman talks about two gay women who were beaten up there.

The film makes a feminist statement, or allusion at least, in noting the latest instance of the Western medical establishment's sexist history of treating the male body as universal, particularly in medical scientific research, thereby neglecting women's unique differences. In a 1989 demonstration, an unnamed woman interviews a man identified as Jim Jensen. With a bandage on his throat, he is walking while attached to a rolling IV bag, wearing a denim jacket over what looks to be a hospital gown. He explains that he is observing and participating in the demonstration at the National Institutes of Health facility because he is actually enrolled in a clinical trial there for combination-drug therapy to fight HIV (the "cocktail" that would eventually prove effective, and whose fast-tracked FDA approval the film credits to ACT UP's pressure and research). The interviewer asks him, "Are there any women in your trial?" "No," he replies, "there aren't any women at all." "People of color?" she asks. He thinks a moment, then replies, "Uh, no there are not." She asks him, "Why do you think that is?" He scoffs and says, "Just the beginning of the problem." The particular impacts of HIV/AIDS on women and people of color, the focus of *Chocolate Babies*, here receives a somewhat cynical nod, but is at least acknowledged.

How to Survive a Plague tells a very specific story: A group of people within ACT UP, and only ACT UP in New York City. The other ACT UP chapters around the world, and the accomplishments they made, are never acknowledged. Lesbian women, and feminist women, while not explicitly addressed, at least can be seen and heard. They are participants but, without bringing to the film awareness of the role of AIDS in bringing together gay men and lesbian women, one would not learn that story from the film. It offers evidence, but only if you are looking for it.

A Party Is Being Thrown: Breaking out of Caregiving in The Hours

> Straight guys are jerks. Gay guys are jerks. Straight women are jerks. That leaves lesbians. They're up in their ivory tower somewhere laughing their heads off at the rest of us. I shoulda been a dyke!—Nick, *Parting Glances*

Parting Glances, the only completed film by gay director Bill Sherwood, who died of AIDS, is widely considered the first, and one of the best, US films about AIDS. Shot in 1984 and released in 1986, it tells the story of a gay male couple in their 20s living in New York City. One is caring for his ex-lover, Nick (played by a then-unknown Steve Buscemi), who is dying of AIDS, and comes to a party thrown by the couple's gal-pal, Joan (Kathy Kinney).

Sixteen years later, in 2002, a woman throwing a party for her gay friend would be a central component of another AIDS film, the winner of the Academy Award for Best Picture, *The Hours*. The film is based on gay author Michael Cunningham's novel of the same name, which won the 1999 Pulitzer Prize for Fiction and the 1999 PEN/Faulkner Award for Fiction. It is directed by Stephan Daltry, who is married to a woman but describes himself as a gay man. It weaves together three storylines in three eras: Virginia Woolf (Nicole Kidman) writing her book *Mrs. Dalloway*, about a woman throwing a party; a suicidal 1950s housewife and mother (Julianne Moore) reading the same novel as she prepares a family celebration of her husband's birthday; and a bisexual woman preparing a party for her ex-lover, a bisexual man dying of AIDS, who has won a prestigious literary award, and whose nickname for her is "Mrs. Dalloway" (Meryl Streep).

AIDS, here, is not the sole focus of the film, but one component of a meditation on creativity, depression, suicide, and women's changing roles in Western culture. Indeed, one of the top critical reviews of the film on Google Play is titled, "Enough of this tired femiNAZI junk" (Nakhai, 2013).

The modern sequence, set in New York City, is credited as taking place in 2001. However, the condition of the man dying of AIDS, Robert (Ed Harris), suggests more the mid-1990s at least, before combination therapy was widely available to treat AIDS. This would align as well with the time Cunningham was likely writing the novel upon which the film is based. This film, then, can be seen as a bookend to the early years of the crisis during which *Parting Glances* was made, and is depicted in *The Normal Heart* and parts of *How to Survive a Plague*. It is occurring about the same time as the events in *Chocolate Babies* as well. However, now the party-throwing gal-pal of *Parting Glances* has her own story and, in this story, she confronts and breaks free from the limitations of her role as caregiver.

Far from unnamed, the sexuality of Clarissa (Streep) is our introduction to the character. Her female partner of 10 years, Sally (Allison Janney) begins the story walking home in the early morning light to join a sleeping Clarissa in bed. Clarissa, who works as a book editor, begins her day of preparation for the party they are throwing for Robert, a male friend and, we will discover, former lover, who has just won "the most prestigious" poetry prize. She splurges at the florist then lets herself into Robert's loft, where she throws open the curtains to find him clearly in the late stages of AIDS. He is very gaunt and haggard, somewhat confused, hearing voices, and his bony body extrudes from his bathrobe. He asks her jokingly, "Have I died?"

It is established that she is a loving but strict caregiver, and has been doing so for years. She enforces his doctor's orders, makes sure he eats and takes his pills. She encourages him to have a good attitude and be excited about the party tonight. As they visit, Clarissa seems a bit avoidant or in denial. Robert accuses her of using him to avoid looking at her own life. She, indeed, avoids the subject and encourages him again to come to the party. She promises to come back that afternoon to help him get dressed, but, upon leaving the loft, we see her nearly rush into the elevator out of breath, falling back against its interior wall, shaken.

Clarissa is breaking down. As we will discover, this is due to her role as caregiver. She has been living through caring for Robert as opposed to her own life. Being an AIDS caregiver has been her life. But her story here is about breaking out of that role.

We see Clarissa fighting back tears while preparing for the party and, ostensibly, this could merely be merely grief over Robert's condition and anticipation of losing him. But, it speaks to something larger when she asks herself, "Why is everything wrong?" A famous literary figure, Lewis (Jeff Daniels), shows up early, and turns out to be the male lover for whom Robert left Clarissa. However, he has been absent at least since Robert's diagnosis, living on the opposite coast. Robert got the love, but Clarissa got to be the caregiver. As she delicately separates egg whites from yolks, she tells Lewis, "I seem to be unravelling." She breaks down, crying. "Don't go," she pleads. "Explain to me why this is happening."

Lewis tells her he "felt free for first time in years" after leaving Richard, suggesting her own trapped state, but she changes the subject: "Tell me about San Francisco."

As the narratives crisscross, we learn that the woman in the 1950s sequence is Robert's mother, who considered suicide, but decided instead to abandon her family after the birth of her second child. This betrayal by the ultimate female caregiver, a mother, fuels Robert's rage and is rewritten as suicide in his "difficult" novel. Clarissa is, then, his replacement mother, but trapped in the role, just as his mother was. There is no explicit indication that Robert's mother is lesbian or bisexual, although no explicit reason is given for her unhappiness, and it is a plausible one.

When Clarissa arrives to get Robert ready for the party, he is in an elevated state, claiming to have mixed his medications, and excitedly tearing down his curtains and opening windows. He pleads for Clarissa to let go of him, and to let him go. They reminisce tenderly while he sits in an open window. "I love you," he tells her. "I don't think two people could've been happier than we've been." He then throws himself out the window to his death.

Cleaning up the canceled party with her lover and daughter, Robert's estranged mother arrives, and they discuss their life choices:

> He had me die in the novel, but I know why he did that.
> You left Richard when he was a child.
> I left both my children. I abandoned them. They say it's the worst thing a mother can do. You have a daughter.
> Yes, but I never met Julia's father.
> But you so wanted a child. You're a lucky woman. There are times when you don't belong, and you think that you're going to kill yourself.

She tells Clarissa about leaving her husband and children, instead of killing herself:

> It would be wonderful to say you regretted it. It would be easy, but what does it mean? What does it mean to regret when you have no choice? It's what you can bear. There it is. No one's going to forgive me. It was death. I chose life.

As Clarissa ends her day, she holds her lover's face and kisses her passionately, suggesting a renewed embrace of consciously living her own life, of recognizing and appreciating the moments of which it is comprised.

The politics of the movie are wholly individualized. There is no mention of women's rights, feminism, ACT UP, or any organized political activism in *The Hours*. Its narratives, however, point explicitly to larger social issues, such as metal health, creative freedom, and, most overtly, a feminist perspective on constrictive social roles of gender and sexuality. It depicts the classic feminist concept that the surrounding sexist society can drive a sane woman mad. This is the same sexist, homophobic society that lets a bisexual man die of AIDS. The film has sympathy for those who choose death as a desperate form of agency, but presents a moral of choosing life instead, even if it means choosing your life over those of the people who love you and whom you love. Letting those ties dictate your life can make you crazy, suicidal, or at least unhappy, and this tension between living for your own happiness and living for or through others is at the core of this caregiver's story. In this gay male AIDS film, we have an explicitly bisexual woman, not simply a lesbian, who is struggling to move past her role as an AIDS caregiver and the strain under which it has put her, as part of her feminist journey of self-actualization.

Conclusion

None of these films tell the story of lesbians overcoming past animosities and rushing to the support of gay men in the face of the AIDS epidemic. Indeed, it appears no film has yet made that its central story. I look forward to it. I also hope that it attempts to communicate the complexity of relations between feminist women and gay men that is suggested by these four films: equal collaborators in coalitions despite the frustration (and futility?) of coalitions; altruistic organizational partners, leaders, and participants of varying types, and caregivers who struggle with the toll of caregiving.

As with gay men in *The Second Wave* collection of feminist theory, this chapter has been framed as a search. AIDS films seemed a likely connection between gay men and feminist women, based on the historic evidence. Yet, again, the process of searching has been rewarding and frustrating. The connection is there, it can be found, but it is limited, imperfect, unnamed, and requires effort to seek out and interpret. This project is about documenting complexity and multiplicity. The stories that have been told—in written histories, archival artifacts, academic theory, and cinematic representations—are imperfect and unfinished. Rather than answers, they provide indicators of work to be done.

In the next chapter, I turn from artifacts and evidence to letting gay men and feminist women speak for themselves, about themselves and each other, and among themselves behind closed doors.

References

Alcoff, L. (1997). Cultural feminism versus poststructuralism. In L. Nicholson (Ed.), *The second wave: A reader in feminist theory* (pp. 330–355). New York: Psychology Press.

Barrett, M. (1997). Capitalism and women's liberation. In L. Nicholson (Ed.), *The second wave: A reader in feminist theory* (pp. 123–130). New York: Psychology Press.

Butler, J. (1997). Imitation and gender insubordination. In L. Nicholson (Ed.), *The second wave: A reader in feminist theory* (pp. 300–316). New York: Psychology Press.

Chodorow, N. (1997). The psychodynamics of the family. In L. Nicholson (Ed.), *The second wave: A reader in feminist theory* (pp. 181–197). New York: Psychology Press.

Collins, P. H. (1997). Defining Black feminist thought. In L. Nicholson (Ed.), *The second wave: A reader in feminist theory* (pp. 241–259). New York: Psychology Press..

Firestone, S. (1997). The dialectic of sex. In L. Nicholson (Ed.), *The second wave: A reader in feminist theory* (pp. 19–25). New York: Psychology Press.

Franke-Ruta, G. (2013).The plague years in film and memory. *The Atlantic*, Feb. 24. Retrieved from https://www.theatlantic.com/entertainment/archive/2013/02/the-plague-years-in-film-and-memory/273449/

Franke-Ruta, G. (2016). My search for a lesbian Donald Trump supporter. *Huffington Post*, Sept. 8. Retrieved from https://www.huffingtonpost.ca/entry/lesbian-donald-trump-supporter_n_5 7b37995e4b04ff883992340

Hall, S. (1985). Signification, representation, ideology: Althusser and the post-structuralist debates. *Critical Studies in Media Communication, 2*(2), 91–114.

Hartman, H. (1997). The unhappy marriage of marxism and feminism. In L. Nicholson (Ed.), *The second wave: A reader in feminist theory* (pp. 97–122). New York: Psychology Press.

Hartsock, N. C. M. (1997). In L. Nicholson (Ed.), *The second wave: A reader in feminist theory* (pp. 216–240). New York: Psychology Press.

Irigaray, L. (1997). The sex which is not one. In L. Nicholson (Ed.), *The second wave: A reader in feminist theory* (pp. 323–329). New York: Psychology Press.

Jeffords, S. (1994). *Hard bodies: Hollywood masculinity in the Reagan era*. New Brunswick, NJ: Rutgers University Press.

MacKinnon, C. A. (1997). Sexuality. In L. Nicholson (Ed.), *The second wave: A reader in feminist theory* (pp. 158–180). New York: Psychology Press.

McRobbie, A. (2009). *The aftermath of feminism: Gender, culture and social change*. Thousand Oaks, CA: Sage.

Nakhai, A. (2013, Dec. 15). Enough of this tired femiNAZI junk. Google Play. Retrieved April 15, 2020 from https://play.google.com/store/movies/details/The_Hours?id=vF0gPdSeSoI&hl=en_US

Narayan, U. (1997). Contesting cultures. In L. Nicholson (Ed.), *The second wave: A reader in feminist theory* (pp. 396–414). New York: Psychology Press.

Nicholson, L. (Ed.). (1997). *The second wave: A reader in feminist theory*. New York: Psychology Press.

Radicalesbians. (1997). The woman identified woman. In L. Nicholson (Ed.), *The second wave: A reader in feminist theory* (pp. 153–157). New York: Psychology Press.

Rubin, G. (1997). The traffic in women: Notes on the political economy of sex. In L. Nicholson (Ed.), *The second wave: A reader in feminist theory* (pp. 27–62). New York: Psychology Press.

Simpson, M. (1994). *Male impersonators: Men performing masculinity*. New York: Routledge.

Simpson, M. (2016). How did *Top Gun* become so gay? *The Telegraph*, May 12. Retrieved from https://www.telegraph.co.uk/men/thinking-man/how-did-top-gun-become-so-gay/

Spivak, G. C. (1990). *The Post-colonial critic: Interviews, strategies, dialogues*. New York: Routledge.

Thompson, G. (1999). New clinics let lesbian patients be themselves. *New York Times*, March 3. Retrieved from https://www.nytimes.com/1999/03/30/nyregion/new-clinics-let-lesbian-patients-be-themselves-effort-help-group-that-often.html

Williams, W. W. (1997). The equality crisis: Some reflections on culture, courts, and feminism. In L. Nicholson (Ed.), *The second wave: A reader in feminist theory* (pp. 71–92). New York: Psychology Press.

Wittig, M. (1997). One is not born a woman. In L. Nicholson (Ed.), *The second wave: A reader in feminist theory* (pp. 265–270). New York: Psychology Press.

4

Talking Amongst Ourselves: Gay Men and Feminist Women (Before Trump)

We're both fighting the man.

—KRISTIN, focus group participant

This project has asked, what have been the communications between, about, and among feminist women and gay men in their respective social movements? I have thus far explored historiographic discourses, archival evidence, and representations in feminist theory and gay male AIDS films. Themes of commonality, competition, and mutual influence have recurred, although no singular, definitive narrative has emerged. Furthermore, this topic has not been found to be the focus of any single, sustained investigation or story. Desiring to hear directly from participants in these movements, as well as to learn how or if they were networking, I organized a series of focus groups to gather information from them. Additionally, these focus groups were intended to extend this investigation into the present.

My approach to using multiple methods in this project has been intended to triangulate from various sources of information, providing, not a single take on the topic, but varying ones, which can be compared for similarities and differences. In this chapter, I will highlight that difference by relying as much as possible on the voices of my participants. My intention in the method and research design is to turn it over to them. In the earlier chapter on historiographic discourses, I quoted Chandra Talpede Mohanty's call for "excavating subjugated knowledges and histories" (2005, p. 175). Here, my research design aimed to do so more explicitly. As longstanding subjects of neglect, oppression, and bias, both feminist women and gay men have not been in positions of power to tell and preserve their own stories and histories to the degree of dominant social groups, particularly those in institutions of education and research. While there has been great improvement in recent decades, I do not presume that official records and existing scholarship, or even feminist and LGBTQ media and representations, are sufficient sources. Therefore, in this chapter I sought to elicit the direct voices of gay men and feminist women involved in struggles for equality. Moreover, this was a continued effort at disrupting hierarchies of knowledge production by de-centering my authoritarian position as researcher. Instead of claiming and interpreting artifacts as evidence of feminist women and gay men in struggles for equality, I sought out persons who self-identified that way, gathered them for semi-structured conversations, and analyzed the themes that arose. In this analysis, I aimed to see how they compared to themes I had previously identified, but also what new themes and ideas they presented. This was to not only increase the queer diffraction discussed previously, but to also give my research participants opportunities to speak for themselves.

Therefore, in the presentation of this information, I have chosen to employ a different style, that of foregrounded transcription. I limit my commentary to brief sections so that the participants can speak more for themselves. I have cleaned up the transcripts in removing pauses, conversational transitions ("you know," "like," "I think," etc.), stuttering, repetitions, and moderator prods or clarifications, and then grouped excerpts in themes. I played the role of instigator in organizing these groups and forcing the juxtaposition of feminist women and gay men in their conversations. This was my "agential cut," as described in a previous chapter (Barad, 2007). This means that, while I acknowledge the boundary-making choices of my research, I do not assert that my structuring choices represent actual, distinct separations. I approach my subjects as, not separate things, but as entangled, ongoing processes of becoming and re-becoming. For example, in dividing the groups into essentializing categories of "gay men" and "feminist women," I do not assert that these are distinct or stable categories. As you will see, some participants resisted the categorizations. Instead, I acknowledge it as an action on my part to engage and deploy these categorical concepts for the purposes of instigation and investigation of their mutual entanglements.

I initially tested focus group questions and structure in a pilot group comprised of six graduate students, all cisgender women, and moderated by a graduate student who was a heterosexual, cisgender woman. Working with her, we refined our moderators' guides and began recruiting participants for our formal focus groups: two segregated groups each of feminist women and gay men were planned for a total of four groups. The groups met in spring. One group of gay men and one group of feminist women were recruited in the area of Charleston, South Carolina and held at a focus group facility there. Located along the coast, Charleston is the largest city in South Carolina and an island of more liberal politics in a decidedly conservative state. Two parallel groups were held in a conference room at a large research university in the Upstate, the northern part of the state, considered a very conservative area and one of the most conservative student populations in the country. I led both men's groups as a self-identified gay cisgender man, and my research assistant led the women's groups as a self-identified feminist and cisgender heterosexual woman.

"Feminist" as a term still held many negative associations. Therefore, as a recruiting strategy, we sought out cisgender and transgender women of any sexual orientation, and we asked them, how familiar do you consider yourself with the social movements for female equality, such as women's rights or feminism? How involved have you been now or in the past with the social movements for female equality, such as women's rights or feminism? Respondents who indicated "average," "a lot," or "extremely" to either question were invited to participate. We recruited cisgender or transgender men who identified as homosexual, bisexual, or pansexual. They were asked similar questions: How familiar do you consider yourself with the social movements for sexual minority equality, such as gay rights or LGBT rights? How involved have you been now or in the past with the social movements for sexual minority equality, such as gay rights or LGBTQ rights? Similar responses of "average," "a lot," or "extremely" were invited to participate. Participants were provided a modest stipend, beverages, and snacks as compensation. The demographic details of the group are provided below. Throughout, all names and identifying details have been omitted or changed. Only one person was excused from the groups, a heterosexual man who had passed through the screening process that limited the men's groups to gay, bisexual, or pansexual men.

Gay men met in two groups. The Charleston group consisted of eight participants, who all self-identified as white non-Hispanic, gay, cisgender men: Evan, 21; Steven, 42; Mitch, 66; Andy, 72; Ken, 49; Travis, 47; Dan, 60; and Erik, 22. Eight men met in the Upstate, seven of whom identified as gay, and one, Sam, as bisexual. All self-identified as white non-Hispanic, cisgender men: Scott, 22; Reggie, 23; Benjamin, 19; Nate, 20; Paul, 21; Sam, 21; Curt, 21; and Justin, 19.

Feminist women met in two groups. The Charleston group consisted of 10 participants, nine of whom self-identified as heterosexual and one, Nell, as lesbian. Seven identified as white non-Hispanic, two as African-American (Alice and Reanne), and one as Hispanic (Luisa). All identified as cisgender women: Polly, 54; Alice, 41; Liz, 41; Barbara, 70; Reanne, 53; Tina, 34; Nell, 61; Stephanie, 29; Luisa, 33; and Amy, 38. Nine women met in the Upstate, eight of whom identified as cisgender women and one (Pat) as a transgender woman. Gina, Kennedy, and Jane identified as bisexual. Kristin identified as pansexual. Pat and Iris identified as lesbian. Christie, Carol, and Lois identified as heterosexual. All identified as white Non-Hispanic: Gina, 31; Christie, 22; Carol, 49; Pat, 24; Iris, 21; Kennedy, 28; Lois, 19; Jane, 22; and Kristin, 21.

The focus groups were audio- and video-recorded with the participants' consent. My research assistant and I took turns moderating groups and taking notes on groups as they occurred. After each group, she and I conversed and mutually reflected upon the discussions. The group conversations were then transcribed by the research facility and two additional graduate students. I then analyzed the transcripts for dominant and insightful themes, described below. While the content of the Charleston and university meetings did vary, there was enough commonality among the feminist women and gay men to suggest these themes were significant.

However, time moves quickly. What I describe here were conversations that took place in 2012, and were transcribed and initially analyzed shortly thereafter. As this project advanced, I re-examined them in 2019. What I had initially considered a snapshot of the contemporary moment had rapidly become historicized. Rather than offer this as disconnected and decontextualized, I present it here with some annotation and additional analysis from the present. Here, and in the remainder of the book, I proceed from the perspective of entangled past and present. Rather than a mini-presentism of imposing current understandings on seven years ago, what I mean by this is my current point in time provides an additional layer of analysis, a crystalline refraction. In my queer methodology, the past is not a fixed moment of truth, but always a subject of interpretation, the meaningfulness of which dynamically engages with the present. As Michel de Certeau (1988) reminds us, "the past is the fiction of the present" (p. 17). In building toward my conclusion, in this chapter and the next, I foreground that perspective. In line with this, the sum of my interpretation and analysis here is primarily that of editor and arranger, presenting the conversational themes of each group that were dominant and/or particularly relevant to the larger inquiry of this project.

The Lesbian Switcher

At every stage of this project, from research findings to casual conversations, the perception of lesbians as the "switchers" between networks of feminist women and gay men has been persistent. As I have discussed previously, this perspective erases the contributions of heterosexual and other non-lesbian women, not to mention gay male feminists. Moreover, while not to detract from the contributions of lesbians to both social movements, it places upon them an undue double burden as beholden to both. The dominance of the lesbian-switcher perception, to such a degree that I would argue it is the dominant view, performs an ideological move of separating the two movements. By focusing on lesbians as the only link or overlap between the two movements, it occludes the much larger systemic issues that unite them, such as patriarchy, misogyny, and sexism, as well as specific social issues that touch them both, such as healthcare or violence.

ANDY: From my experience, it's very difficult for men and women organizations to work together. ... Well, it seems to me that if you get a group of lesbians together they get things done, if you get a group of gay men together they get things done. Boy, you get them together and it just falls apart.

DAN: I've seen that many times .... You get lesbians and gay men together, and it's just, "I want it this way," but if you've got just gay men working on it, they all seem to agree. Or if you've got lesbians, they do too. And it's like, you're kind of fighting on what this one wants and what that one wants. I've seen that many times.

MODERATOR: So, what if it's a mixed group of women? What if it's a group of gay men and a group of women that are straight, maybe there's some lesbians in there, but it's mixed? ...

DAN: Well, I think it could depend on their attitudes, too. Cause some women don't like gay men and some women do, so I mean, it's just attitudes. If they've got a good attitude it shouldn't be a problem.

Here, gay men showed a persistence of the lesbian switcher perception. Despite many questions and reminders by the moderator regarding gay men and women in general, inclusive of lesbians and heterosexuals, when asked about feminists, several participants frequently answered in terms of lesbians.

SCOTT: I thought lesbians are always angry.

JUSTIN: There is kind of a stereotype too that a lot of lesbians and gay men don't get along very well. ... I don't think it's a good stereotype at all. 'Cause I don't have a problem with any lesbians, but I don't know. I don't exactly know where it even came from or why, is that a common stereotype?[1]

MITCH: I think, between gay men and lesbians, there often times is tension, and I think because it's a question of defining roles. In maybe the broadest possible sense, we're trying to get in touch with our feminine side, not just be the macho basketball player, watch sports, guzzle beer, and lesbians are trying to assert that women can do anything, and, if you don't believe it, they'll beat the shit out of you. And, I think there is a lot more tension between gay men and gay women …. Gay men and straight women get along famously, we understand straight women.

The women's groups also fell back on this phenomenon. The first thing Nell said at the start of her group was, "I would like to see closing the gap between gay men and lesbians." Although she was a lesbian herself, it was another example of how quickly a discussion about feminist women, when juxtaposed or put into intersection with that of gay men, became a conversation about lesbians.

NELL: Anytime it's gay rights. I'm going to be very actively involved. I've been out and have a lot of experience. I've been out for forty-two years now. I don't hide it anywhere. I will not. I've been fired. I have a lot of experience with it, and yeah, I will support and do whatever I can with … well, anyways, the first pride movement I started here, in Charleston, and so, that was … it's three years now, so yeah, I'm pretty active. I stay in touch with all the gay men, the groups. We constantly stay in touch, and I also run a group for lesbians. There's over 600 of us.

As Nell indicates, however, there were actual lesbian switchers. Other women questioned the categorizations imposed upon the conversation.

KENNEDY: I'm having a hard time figuring out … where do gay women fit in this? … Like, where do they fall in when we're talking about gay men and women?
IRIS: Or transsexual, transgender men …
GINA: The feminists, like the bad feminist stereotype … is the lesbian dyke stereotype. … It's the aggressive man-eater who's throwing her bra in the fire and resisting patriarchy and shearing her hair off, and moving to North Hampton and banning all male … things.

One of the questions around lesbians, and the lesbians-as-negative-feminist-stereotype, that arose was, Do they experience less homophobia, and therefore more social approval, and possibly then more political potential? In this discussion, notice how "lesbian" suggests both same-sex-loving women and a stereotype for any strong woman, from feminists to Hillary Clinton:

LOIS: Well, it could be because of, I mean, for me, the stereotypes I see is that gay men are seen as being more feminine, and so oh, that's not cool. Lesbian women are seen as being more masculine. … I guess if the majority of people like women better, that they'll be like, "Gay men are feminine. They're okay, but lesbian women are masculine, that's weird. We don't want them on our turf." When I say that I'm speaking from the male perspective …

KRISTIN: I feel like any minority group is preferable to men than to women. So, we get a Black president before we get a female president. Black men had the right to vote before women had the right to vote. I feel like we're going to have a gay man president before we're going to have a woman president.

LOIS: Yeah, like you're insinuating kind of this patriarchy … even crosses the threshold into homosexual males.

KRISTIN: I feel like men universally prefer dudes over women, no matter what is up with the dude.

JANE: I really don't think I agree though.

KRISTIN: Really?

JANE: Yeah, how many hate crimes about where …

KRISTIN: I didn't mean to minimalize what they even go through, because I know that they're also afraid for their physical safety a lot of the time, but …

PAT: I feel like there's a lot more women in higher offices than there are outwardly presenting gay men.

JANE: You have to be straight-acting to be …. I mean, you can say that about women too, but …

LOIS: We say that, but there's no woman president. They've kind of plateaued. It's just … to say what you were saying, who knows? Maybe a gay man could pass females to the role of presidency. … Barack Obama, that was a big deal because he reached the pinnacle, he was the president. … We don't know who's going to win that race between gay men and a woman to presidency.

JANE: But, I find that a little weird as a litmus test.

KRISTIN: It is strange, and not necessarily a good litmus test. I just remember when Hillary Clinton, the way she was presented was so. … People just had such angry reactions to her, even other women. But imagine her running against some kind of gay guy … a guy that's not like a stereotype, but happens to be gay.

PAT: Right.

KRISTIN: I feel like people can forget about him being gay enough to vote for him.

Allies with Commonalities

Overall, both groups exhibited the theme previously seen of gay men and feminist women having certain shared experiences and character traits, enabling them to work together.

STEPHANIE: Oh, we work great with gay men. Women work great with gay men.

CAROL: I don't think that we can assume that gay men are necessarily progressive. … Look at all the closeted gay Republican senators. … Not the most progressive bunch, and they are gay men.

LIZ: I think they'd be first likely to support any political things concerning like women's rights. I think maybe in that sense, but, I don't think you can assume that there'd be, on an emotional level, a connection there between them supporting us and us supporting them. Politically, most would obviously lean ... towards a more liberal sense where they support each other's political rights.

ANDY: [Gay men and women working together is] easier than gay men/straight men, gay women and straight women.

While taking care not to generalize all gay men as progressive, many participants did speak of their and others' identities in essential, almost universal terms.

REGGIE: My favorite thing [about being gay] would probably be having genuine platonic relationships with women.

JUSTIN: I have a more open mind from being gay. If I had been straight, and the way I was raised, I would have probably been more close-minded. I can also relate and communicate with women.

SAM: Being bisexual, I'm able to see different sides of all the issues affecting straight men, gay men, girls, and I'm easily able to talk to my roommate and help her out with some problems if she has them, or a friend of mine, or people, since you say, I literally look at different sides of just about every issue.

MITCH: My observation is that gay men and straight women get along, famously, for a very obvious reason. We're not trying to get in their pants. They finally have men that they can talk to, I find that constantly with my female students for example, especially. I used to teach in Bumfuck, Missouri, and I was like the only man over the age of 12 that they that they could talk to as an equal as opposed to just, trying to make time with them.

Mitch here suggests a sexual competition that other gay men would address. Note, also, his specifying of straight women suggests gay-lesbian conflicts, in contrast to the lesbian switcher theme. In a more inclusive spirit, Jane asserted that "A straight man can be a feminist. Anyone can be a feminist."

The commonality of shared cultural interests had appeared in previous research, such as certain forms of art and music, and reappeared with regards to a more contemporary form of popular culture.

GINA: This is why so much of manga has been helpful ... to the gay rights lately. ... Yaoi is Japanese graphic novels. ... that are focused on male-male relationships, and there are a lot of very popular Japanese ones that have been increasing, and also same-sex couples on anime. ... The whole sub-genre within manga that is becoming increasingly popular is helping.

JANE: In just the last couple years, I've also seen a lot of gay couples in web comics, because I've gotten like 16 that I check every day because I'm that much of a dork, but there's one in particular which is called *Yet Another Fantasy Gamer Comic*. ... There's a gay couple that's shown in bed together very frequently, and ... it's not ... I hate this word. It's not dirty. It's not revealing. It's just two young men who are frequently shown in bed together.

Common Sources of Oppression

Less positive shared experiences, however, were discussed more often.

NATE: Gender-based perceptions control both violence against women and their own oppression, as well as oppression of gay people. If you realize that or feel that way then you can stand up for both issues.

JUSTIN: I was talking to [a friend], and he mentioned that, just like because we want to have sex with another man, that somehow makes us less of a male and therefore, we aren't treated as equally. I definitely agree with that.

BRENT: I would feel more comfortable going in [to a women's group] as a gay man than a straight one. I feel they would feel I was a bit more interested in their cause than I they would for a straight man. ... In a dark way, because both groups are oppressed by the same sort of person, straight male. Gay men and women.

ERIK: I've heard some friends saying that a lot of the fear that the past society has had against gay people stems from a fear of women or stems from the oppression of women. They tend to associate gay people as acting more like women, and therefore giving up the privileges that society gives them for being male. ... Maybe some gay men act more feminine than others do, but I think men are men regardless.

PAT: A lot of homophobia is motivated by misogyny ... because women are supposed to be subject to men, and when you're gay ... a man should never be subject to another man. I think a lot of that is misogynistic.

KRISTIN: I read this thing on Facebook that said that homophobia is the fear that men are going to do to you what you have been doing to women.

However, some noted this was a potential for being allies, but not necessarily one that had been entirely achieved.

AMY: Remember that discrimination is discrimination, and we tend to forget that because we think of how we're discriminated against, and then we don't think about the fact that we're just doing it to someone else. We talk about how it's different somehow, and I think that until we can do that, we'll all have a hard time working together.

PAT: I would like to see is a change in what we consider to be normative, so less hetero-normativity, less cisnormativity, less patriarchy, those sorts of things.

CAROL: I want to be able to use words like feminism or transgender or sexuality or abortion at a Board of Trustees meeting and not be told that I should never use those words in that place.

TIM: Discrimination of color, age, sex, gender, all that stuff, it's just covered up, just equally felt....

MITCH: Yeah, it's really just the fact that we're all facing the same enemy, which is discrimination and stupidity. ... In theory, feminist groups or women's groups should work well with gay groups, because they're both fighting the status quo. ... If you look at the Black civil rights movement of '50s and '60s, there were lots of white folks involved. ... The reality is that women and men suffer from the same base of discrimination, which is a totally traditional, out-of-reality concept of masculinity. The man should be the center of the universe, the man should dominate the wife and the family, that real men drive trucks and drink beer and shoot guns, all these damn stereotypes. The core of women's separatism is the fact that they're just tired of men trying to dominate. Screw 'em. We don't need 'em. We suffer from the same problem. We don't fit that super stereotype, and we both suffer from the same source of discrimination. ... I'll bet you money that a good number of the men who are involved in [women's rights] activities are gay men. They understand discrimination and they understand the problems related. ... I think a lot do, I don't think most do.

Note how Mitch equivocates: "I think a lot do, I don't think most do." Often participants would assert a characteristic about gay men or feminism, or their relationships, only to, upon reflection, proffer a more moderate claim.

PAT: In our culture, one of the major facets of heterosexual masculinity is some sort of dominance over women, and gay men lack that. They have nothing to prove. ... They have more of a propensity to fight for women's rights and respect the dignity of women. ... One of my roommates is a gay male, and he feels very passionately about women's issues. When Rush Limbaugh went on his tirade about Sandra Fluke,[2] he was irate about that. ... He doesn't necessarily have a vested interest in women in terms of an attraction there, but he still has the respect. ... He has an objective perspective. ... Unfortunately, we wish we could say, "Hey, gay men are marginalized. Women are marginalized. People that are marginalized should come together," and unfortunately that doesn't happen.

TINA: It's the same with women [as with gay men]. ... People are looking positively, "Well look, women are allowed to do this and that, and we get respect for this and that, so who cares if we can't do that and that." But there's always going to be some women that are going to be like, "Hey wait, this sucks." Same with gay men. If gay men want to go into fashion or if someone who seems gay or is queer or whatever wants to go into those areas, yeah, but good luck if they try to branch out. It's the same thing with women. It's kind of a glass ceiling thing for gay men.

Both Are Stereotyped

In the recent years before the focus groups, media representations of LGBTQ persons had greatly increased, and were largely positive, from hit television shows such as *Ellen* and *Will and Grace*, to films that differed as much as *Philadelphia* and *Hedwig and the Angry Inch*. Increasingly, celebrities in visual media, music, politics, and sports had come out. Yet, despite such rising visibility and positive representation in culture, feminist women and gay men both described shared experiences of being stereotyped.

CURT: A lot of people think that all gay males have this feminine persona about them.

JUSTIN: People have preconceived ideas about who I am when I tell them I'm gay or react negatively. An example of that would be, just Wednesday night, I went to a dialogue and before the dialogue actually started someone asked me what brought me there, and I told them that I had heard about it through the GSA, and he asked me what it was, and I told him Gay-Straight Alliance, and, after that, he just nodded his head and left the room.

NATE: With straight men, there's the expectation that when you become married, you become settled or civilized, and with gay men that never happens, so it's more seen as being juvenile throughout life.

GINA: I have to work at getting [students, particularly men] to respect me as an authority figure and as a figure of knowledge. There's always the first few days of class where it's trying to get them to recognize that I have authority, basically because I have breasts. ... If I'm talking about gender issues or women's issues, I'm suddenly a sexist, and a feminist. The bad connotations have got layered into that just because I'm trying to get them to discuss power and authority.

BARBARA: One of the biggest insults I've ever gotten [came from a person who] meant it as a compliment. He was a friend of mine. He said, "You think like a man." What does that mean?

TINA: Men have no idea what it's like to be a teacher and be a woman. You have to fight so much harder for authority. ... People are like, "You're a woman. You're thin. There's no way you can lift stuff."

LIZ: I enjoy being feminine and the femininity. I love dressing up. I love wearing lipstick, fixing my hair, wearing five-inch high heels, but also, sometimes doing that, you get different looks from some people. ... They discredit you, thinking that there's some bimbo walking down the street, so you have to prove yourself. ...

CHRISTIE: I really take pride in my sense of empathy. I feel like, as a woman, it's socially acceptable to be very empathetic. Which, I guess you could say is a bad thing. Maybe it's not so good that men can't participate in that same way. ... I take pride in being really intelligent. ... I feel that as a woman, ... if I'm doing well in class and getting good grades and that kind of thing, it's not as acceptable ... not as attractive maybe to people. Maybe it's the dumb blondes who get the good rap.

Stereotyping was even a problem among gay men and their allies.

ERIK: I get frustrated when people within the gay community have their own ideas of what it means to be gay and what you're supposed to act like or look like and then when I'm judged for being different even though I have the same key trait as them.

SAM: My roommate is like, "I don't want you to be a regular guy, I want you to be a funny gay guy."

PAUL: The stereotype of promiscuity. ... I think that a lot of gay media would really push promiscuity. But it's also a stereotype from people outside the gay community.

KRISTIN: I just wish that every university, or even high school, had a required women's studies class so that I wouldn't have to explain when I tell people that I'm feminist or when they say, like, "Oh, you're a feminist," they think that I'm saying that I hate all men.

Indeed, at the time of the focus groups, the word "feminism" was only beginning to emerge from negative, backlash stereotypes into the more popular form it has today. One woman said, "It seems like maybe [women have] been a little bit brainwashed and told, if you speak out, there's all these horrible labels, like if you're a feminist or then everyone hates you." As an instructor, when teaching feminist theory and gender studies, as well as LGBTQ history, I still found students in the mode of what Susan Douglas (1995) described as "I'm not a feminist, but ...." While they supported ideals of equality between the sexes, students were reluctant to embrace a feminist identity.

ANDY: ["Feminist" is] a word I love, but it has a bad connotation, uppity. ... I'm speaking that in positive rather than, they're up, they're in your face.

NATE: [Feminists are stereotypes as women who] would have an abortion even if they weren't pregnant.

At this time, LGBTQ rights, however, seemed to be rapidly becoming acceptable and desired social policy, among even my more conservative students.

Violence

KRISTIN: I have to worry about rape constantly, since no woman really has any sort of total physical security. I think most women that I know have been raped at some point.

Participants noted physical violence as a threat to themselves and others.

NATE: We don't focus enough on crimes against women. That's a critical part of our culture, a lot of world cultures. That's inherently tied to our oppression as gay people. ... When you declare yourself as not being necessarily male or female, in essence being straight or gay, that's why.

SCOTT: But the US is very low on power distance, which means in comparison to other countries we do not have a higher level of masculinity over women. For example, Mexico is really high. In other words, women are submissive to their husbands, and they do what they tell them to. ... We've made better strides in that category than other countries.

NATE: Sociologically that looks at the power structure, not the actual infrastructures of society. We have improved that. But the actual actions of people, I think there's still violence against women.

SCOTT: There's definitely still violence, but as far as improving it, I think the US has improved much quicker than many other countries.

TINA: If you want to change anything, any idea, any problem, media is going to be the number one. People are receiving these messages daily. It's all around us. If you wanted to change the perception of women and ideas, talk to the TV networks and the magazines and the billboards, the people who own all that. It's the only way.

NELL: If it's covered. How do you know it's happening if it's not going to be covered by the media? Gay bashing, ... men, women, ... now bullying is becoming a focus. That's changing, thank God, but there's a lot that goes on that just will never get covered.

Gender

Although some of the gay men did discuss gendered stereotypes as commonly oppressing women and gay men, it was a more extended and substantive conversation in the women's groups. In contrast to, for example, the more fixed notions of gender and sexuality described in the previous chapter on second-wave feminist theory, young persons in particular in the focus groups had embraced more dynamic notions of gender and sexuality, such as gender fluid, nonbinary, and pansexual.

JANE: I keep thinking [that feminine interests] are not valued as much as interests for a masculine male, like listening to Taylor Swift and playing dress up.

LOIS: The education of younger kids ... raising the next generation of people ... we need to seriously instill this. ... The whole gender dichotomy, it just can't be there if we want to see real changes. ... Kids' books that are .... blatantly like, "We are all human." ... We can all be alike. We can all, just break down those barriers completely. It seems like it would be such a caricature to have a children's book that says, "These kids are best friends. ... One's Black. One is white. This one's gay. This one's straight, but look, they're friends." But, that can make a difference.

PAT: [In the past,] people seriously thought you had to be cured if you were gay, or you could never live a happy life. ...

KENNEDY: But at least it's not in the DSM [*Diagnostic and Statistical Manual of Mental Disorders*, the authoritative diagnostic manual published by the American Psychiatric Association]. Taking [homosexuality out of there] made a big difference.

PAT: According to the current version of the DSM, I'm crazy [for being transgendered]. ... The DSM still has a long way to go.

CAROL: The minute they depathologized homosexuality in the DSM, gender identity disorder became a pathology ... So, it wasn't gay men as long as they were masculine enough ... and could operate in society. It was feminine gay boys ... that became the problem.

KRISTIN: I would honestly rather be a woman than a gay man today because women in general probably have ... more privileges than a gay man would, and especially in South Carolina, but, if I was betting, I would bet that we'd have a gay man president before we have a woman president.

CAROL: I don't think it's about gay men versus women. It's about straight masculine presentation. Look at Hillary. Hillary's cleavage and her cankles were the focus when she was running for the presidential nomination, but that latest meme that shows her ... in her aircraft carrier, and she's like, "On it." I'm taking that photo and putting it big in my office. I love that picture of Hillary Clinton. It's such a ... re-imaging of her. Of course, it's an incredibly masculine Hillary Clinton. It's a Hillary Clinton who is going to be more manly than most men in the Congress right now. In a certain way, as long as she's now straight-male presenting, she's not a threat. She's somebody we all love.

KRISTIN: Watch how they vilify her four years from now, though.

CAROL: We'll see.

KRISTIN: With that persona, they're going to be-

CAROL: But a gay man, for example, who is incredibly straight-presenting and masculine-presenting, no problem. I don't know that it's gay men versus feminists so much as it is how close can you cozy up to the straight masculine persona.

JANE: It's presence of non-normative sexuality where white, straight, male, Anglo-Saxon, Protestant, not-standing-up-because-it's-too-close-to-dancing sexuality that's considered the norm.

CAROL: Thinking about ... your claim "It's hard for me to gain authority in the classroom." I have never had problem gaining authority in a classroom. Why? Because I come much closer probably than either one of you to a straight-male-assertive kind of teaching ... and dressing, and everything else, and so I don't think it's about women having a problem gaining credibility in the classroom. It's feminine women having problems gaining credibility in a classroom.

Gender was seen by some as a key to better collaboration and coalition:

PAT: I think that we need to put the femininity back in feminism.

CAROL: No.

PAT: Well, I think that ... the second wave ... okay, maybe I-

CAROL: No, go ahead. I'm just joking with you.

PAT: -came across the wrong way. I don't know. I'm not an expert on the topic of women, but I feel like, based on [my] limited knowledge, second-wave feminists said, "Let's gain respect by being more masculine or just erasing gender differences entirely. Let's all just be people and not have any differences at all." Thus, essentially making women and men more alike. ... I think that hurts both of the groups we're talking about today. This is particularly true in people ... on the male to female spectrum. I gave a seminar here on campus on Wednesday, and I talked a little bit about this idea of transmisogyny, and it really shows up there because, if you ever see any kind of documentary portrayal of this, it's always ... focused on transwomen and their expressions of femininity and the trappings of femininity—the makeup, and the hair, and the clothes. ... It's all about sexuality and attracting men, appealing to men, and there was a day when transwomen could not even get permission to transition unless their therapist thought that they could be attractive to men after their transition. The devaluation of femininity harms everybody, and that's what I mean when I say we need to put femininity back in feminism. It's not to make people more feminine, but just to say, "Hey, however you choose to express your gender."... Femininity doesn't mean weak. It doesn't mean passive. ... It doesn't mean sexual or anything like that necessarily, so, I really do think that's the issue here. It's not so much male versus female, it's masculine versus feminine.

JANE: I like being girly. I like doing girly stuff. ... That's one of the reasons I struggle with identifying as a feminist because ... I want it to be okay for me to be girly. ... The traditional image of feminists, like we were talking about earlier, is the—I hate using this word—the dyke image. I want people to know that's not how it is. There's people out there like that, great. They're awesome, but there's also people who are cisgender and ... it's okay to be cisgender. Being cisgender doesn't mean ... that you hate people who are not cisgendered. ...

CAROL: It's complicated. It's fun to have options, to sometimes be girly, but not have to be girly. ... This was my, "No, I don't want the feminine back in feminism." If what "the feminine" means is pink or .... very girly self-presentations because ... you see women with really girly presentations [and they] just don't always make it real far. Plus, women need to be more assertive. Does that mean they need to be assertive in the same way as men? No, but they need to be able to be assertive without having the b-word flung at them ... and the same thing with gay men.

It was somewhat surprising, and disheartening, to see second-wave feminism, discussed at length in a previous chapter, still suffering from such backlash, negative stereotypes. Even among the women in the 2012 focus groups, a generalized notion of second-wave feminism as being anti-feminine, rather than critiquing the oppressive aspects of dominant ideals of femininity, persisted. However, it was encouraging to see the discussion of gender explicitly link feminist women and gay men.

CAROL: I want to dismantle those [gender] boundaries a bit more so that there's room for a Michele Bachmann style, minus her air head. There's no room for that ever, and a Hillary style. ... I want women to have more options. ... I want gay men to have more options, but I don't need every gay dude on TV to flame, right? There need to be options for straight-presenting gay men. There need to be options for gay-presenting straight men.

JANE: There needs to not be categories like this.

GINA: Both the feminists and notions of queerness are resisting the heteronormative. Those modes of resistance, there's a certain logic to which they become a counterpoint, and so they become a struggle against two opposites, which is why transgender people and bisexual people have particular problems within the gay community, because they don't fit the "We are against those people." They're this extra group. [I'm] trying to consider both women's issues and gay rights as this continued opening of options: You can be a guy, and you can be a feminist, and you can be a feminine-acting guy and still be straight, if you want.

Conflicts with Each Other

Oppositional themes were present in the discussions as well. These ranged from blanket indifference to mutual stereotyping, and also presented a focus again on lesbians.

Indifference

Both sets of groups described moments of indifference to the other's issues.

TINA: Charleston is a liberal pocket in a conservative state. College of Charleston ... has a reputation that there's a lot of feminist movement, and they're a lot more supporting of gay rights. ... If you go to feminist [events], there's all kinds of homosexual men. They definitely support and are interested in whenever there's a feminist movement, but I don't feel like, if there were a thing for just gay men, there would be a bunch of women that would go to support gay men, whereas they're more supportive of feminists.

However, more common was perceived gay male indifference to women's issues. Curt, who described himself as "oblivious" to women's issues, said, "I don't really know what feminism is." Two women suggested that the causes of such indifference could range from women's issues simply not being on the agenda to a broader tendency for gay men to be apolitical.

IRIS: A lot of my experience has been with gay men because I'm a leader of [my university's] Gay-Straight Alliance. We don't really talk about feminist issues. We mainly talk about the issues in the LGBT community, but we are open to having ... partnerships with feminist groups and all sorts of other people. I don't know how gay people feel about feminists, but I have no problem with gay men.

CHRISTIE: Gay people seem to feel separate from any sort of political things. They're not really in a group with feminists on it. I remember trying to get people to sign up to volunteer for the Democratic party, and no one was really interested because they know that all politicians, even Barack Obama, are just going to ignore them largely.

Several men did mention awareness of women's issues, such as contraception, health care, and reproductive rights, although none discussed collaborating with women on these issues. Indeed, one man's comment suggested the perspective that those issues were not relevant to gay men. Andy said, "I think that the lesbian community has done a far better job [organizing around abortion] than the straight community has." He seemed to presume that no gay men had been involved in organizing around the issue.

ANDY: If a lesbian friend had an issue that they would feel strongly about, and they wanted my support, I would do it. But to actively volunteer to be part of that [women's] movement, I don't think I would.

KEN: We stick to our own.

ANDY: Unless an issue affected me personally. ...

KEN: Certain groups stick with their own people. People find common ground. That's why you see the women over here and the men over here. They gravitate to that.

DAN: If I was to get involved with women's group to help them to work on a certain issue, and they wouldn't care about any of my issues, then why should I care about theirs? I like to hear from them, at least a little bit, they feel about what I'm going through, too.

ANDY: We're selfish. We only work for us.

This was suggested as well in this exchange between two women.

KRISTIN: My gay male friends are just as oblivious to what's going on with women politically or in any other way as other guys are.

GINA: Unless you're an open-minded, more educated gay male, you're not really going to be more aware of women's rights.

Although focusing on difference—which shouldn't necessarily preclude collaboration—Erik made an observation suggesting underlying misogyny.

ERIK: A lot of the gay people that I've met and known don't really like to be associated with women's rights because we're not women. Some gay people get offended being always associated with lesbians and transgender and bisexuals because it really is different. You may fight for the same rights, but it's different. I don't necessarily feel that way, but I definitely have heard that opinion.

"We're not women" could be taken as a statement of fact, but also as a form of sexist dis-identification for gay men: "We're not *women*."

Stereotyping Each Other

Actual and perceived sexism, racism, and other forms of negative stereotyping appeared as sources of conflict during both sets of groups.

REGGIE: I'm guilty of this, having the lesbian-stick-in-the-mud stereotype. ... Where you know that your gay-guy friends will be the ones that are down for going out and having fun, and your lesbian friends just want to sit at home and make a family, and be a cute little couple together. It's a terrible stereotype to have, and so you try not to do that, and, yet, I still have that perception at times.

LIZ: We're all constantly stereotyping each other. When we speak of somebody, it's a white woman, or it's a Black woman, or it's a gay man. ... Why don't we just say, "Well, the lady I was sitting beside tonight in the gray."...

LUISA: Color's still going to be there. However, I'll be the first one to stereotype, not [always] in a negative way. ... There's stereotypes for a reason. I'm not saying everybody fits in them, or it's right, but ... for my own personal thing, the Puerto Rican stereotype, I've seen 90 percent of the people fit into it, and 10 percent that didn't.

KEN: I think [feminist women perceive gay men as] being weak, and not taking full advantage of being born a man.

NELL: It's very different from gay women and gay men. Very, very different. Men have that privilege going on that women have not had, and so there's a difference there. Gay men don't deal with women, unless they're straight. ... "Period, what's that?!" Unless they have sisters or something. Straight men are more aware.

TRAVIS: [Women tell gay men], and I've heard this before, "You're so into yourselves, you're so narcissistic."

At times, negative stereotyping was clearly demonstrated, specifically around the second-wave backlash image of feminists.

DAN: When I hear feminist, the first thing I think of is a woman that doesn't need a man for anything. Except for personal reasons, but as far as professional, they can fix cars, they can do anything themselves, they don't need a man to do anything....

CURT: Feminist, they hate men, sometimes. Not hate them, but ... they don't need them, so, if you're any type of male, you're part of the oppression.

BENJAMIN: Just over the top, that's what I think of when I think of feminist.

JUSTIN: I'd say stereotypical [attributes] like bra burning, letting their armpit hair grow, or hair all over their body. More masculine.

SAM: Or just like, "Hey, that's a great dress you have." Next thing, sexual harassment lawsuit!

PAUL: Over-sensitivity. … Feeling they need to be more dominant, assertive, exaggerated assertiveness.

EVAN: I always think of feminist extremes, like super rights-activist.

One form of stereotyping was in the perceived differences in gendered styles of leadership, which created logistical problems with collaborating.

MITCH: My experience is that, much more than men, women gravitate towards a consensus. They want everybody to feel good about the decision, where a man will just take a fucking vote and then say, "Yeah, we've talked about it enough, let's just take the vote." That has probably been my most frustrating thing in my life, dealing with feminists, especially the lesbians, is just you die of old age waiting for someone to decide something because you're waiting for a consensus.

Mitch's complaint about consensus suggests a failure in communication between gay men and feminist women. He was aware of consensus as an organizational tool, but was either unaware or did not mention its roots in feminist organizating. The insistence on consensus—notably a tool utilized in ACT UP and evidenced in the films discussed previously—was intended to resist hierarchy and ensure equal participation of all voices. A better understanding of how consensus resists heteronormative, masculinist organizing and preserves minority participation could generate greater patience among gay men with its practice. Indeed, among some gay groups, such as Radical Faeries, consensus is practiced for exactly these reasons. Note also how personal experience is used to validate the stereotypes, even when suggesting that they "possibly" may be only stereotypes.

TRAVIS: In organizations I've been involved in, and also in professional work situations, where it could possibly be a stereotype, but it definitely, in combination with experience that I've had, but to me, men in general, be they gay or straight, tend to want to get something done, wrapped up, decided upon, voted upon, and completed. Women have tended to be, at least in experiences I've had to work with, tend to be a little bit more bogged down in the process, and bogged down in affective, more bogged down in the feeling, the emotions that the process creates, and really trying to get all of them to agree as a group of women before they move forward. The experience that I've had working in organizations and professionally with jobs is that men just want to get it done, "Let's get it wrapped up, make a decision." …

ANDY: Well, my experience has been that women take longer, but they get it done. I mean, get a group of lesbians and they have a project, it'll get done.

Andy again referred specifically to lesbians, rather than feminist women in general. This tendency was apparent when the men's groups talked about inherent differences between gay men and lesbians.

ANDY: How do the young straight and gay, lesbian and straight people, get along at the university?

ERIK: I wouldn't say they get along all that well. ... Or at least, not that they don't get along, but they don't work together. One, we have the gay, bi, transgendered, lesbian alliance at our school, and whenever I would ask people if they were going to meetings, or if they're involved at all, the gay men would all say, "No, it's just a bunch of lesbians." I'd be like, "Oh." I didn't realize that that was a reason not to go or whatever. I don't know. I found it surprising. ... At work, there is a lesbian woman that works there, and, I didn't ask her about it, but I remember overhearing her saying, "Yeah, gays and lesbians don't really get along that much."

SCOTT: One of the things we thought of [at our university] was the lavender graduation [an LGBTQ-specific graduation ceremony]. The reason we decided not to do it is because, not only is it separating ourselves out, it's still at the same time grouping us all together, like everybody at this table, where we're constantly grouped together as LGBTQ and, quite honestly, the only thing that we all have in common is that we're different. We shouldn't be grouped together as "you're the same as a lesbian because you're gay." The only thing we have in common is the fact that we're different, so we decided against the lavender graduation.

Despite sometimes exhibiting generalizations and stereotypes, throughout the men's conversations a frequent topic was resistance to generalization. The participants frequently pointed out the idiosyncrasies of their experiences and opinions, and described the importance of how other contexts, such as country, region, age, social groups, and others, could shape things differently. The women's groups pointed this out as well. Barbara said, "It's not universal. It's not all gay men are oppressed by society. ... There is a lot of oppression in segments in society, and some gay people experience it more than others." The women also had more extended discussions on racial differences, driven by the African-American and Puerto Rican women participating.

The Gay Best Friend. Several gay men resented a stereotype that was not specifically associated with feminists, but with women in general: the "gay best friend" (GBF). Moreover, this recently popularized image was a positive stereotype. However, they saw it as a feminization and reduction of them, which was an obstacle to working with women.

CURT: Women have the whole preconceived notion of the gay best friend. I don't really know why, ... but women a lot of times will feel more comfortable around gay males. Probably because there's no way they're going to get hit on or something like that. ... I think it's nice that they can have somebody that they feel comfortable with and able to talk to. ... But, I don't think it's fair to be like, all gay males will agree with women, and all women will agree with gay males. You still have like gay Republicans and gay Democrats, that's two different spectrums.

SAM: My roommate ... she's a straight girl. She's said several times ... she's always wanted to have a flamboyantly gay roommate. She really wishes that I was. I just say, "That sucks."

NATE: It's not necessarily a negative stereotype unless it's not true. It just creates a really awkward phase of actually getting to know somebody, because a lot of females do that to me. I'm like, "No, I go hiking, I sleep in hammocks, I don't do random flamboyant things. We're not going to get along if this is how you treat me all the time."

SCOTT: We've all had a "fag hag" conversation, or probably have had a fag hag to some extent. I don't think that it's a negative thing if they want to be friends with gay people. They can be friends with gay people. As long as they respect your values and who you are, then, if you genuinely want to be friends with me, that's fine. I'm still going to call you a fag hag.

JUSTIN: With another group of gay men, we have talked about how women expect us to know a lot about fashion and stuff like that. That kind of irks us. The stereotypical gay best friend isn't as true as a lot of women want to think it is.

NATE: Girls be like, "I think my boyfriend's gay." "Is he?" "I don't know."

SAM: I'll sit and talk about it to gay men, but I'll talk to a lot of my straight female friends about it, too. After I've gotten to know them or we're really close. ... You can talk to female friends about it, too, not just gay men.

Resentment of the GBF stereotype suggested perhaps the broader cultural de-valuation of femininity, whether in cisgender women, transwomen, or gay men. Although here a negative, it nevertheless evidenced a conceptual linkage with potential to be challenged, reworked, or otherwise re-approached as a source of collaborative efforts.

In Competition with Each Other

Another conflictual theme was that of competition between their social movements, expressed along several dimensions, such as for public opinion:

KRISTIN: We're competitors. Universally, people don't like the feminist girl, but they do kind of like the gay guy. He's kind of precious. One is cuter than the other.

JANE: I don't think you can say either stereotype is terribly positive.

KRISTIN: Yeah, but people have patronizing tendencies for the gay guy, but at least they don't hate them and think of *Daria* [an animated comedy about a sardonic young woman].

Others described political competition more specifically.

BRENT: At the political level, one group or the other might feel that they're taking the attention off their issue. … Personally, I've seen a lot more gay issues than general women issues.

BARBARA: I think there has always been some amount of competition between movements. The women's movement came along. There was a lot of resentment with civil rights activists that, "We haven't finished our fight, and here you are taking all the-"

LUISA: Spotlight.

BARBARA: "-the attention and the thunder," and there's some feeling in the gay community that "our oppression is worse than your oppression." … "Why, you don't have it so bad. Look what happened with us." There is some competition. We ought to acknowledge it. It doesn't mean we can't help each other. It doesn't mean that … the roots are exactly the same. They have to do with respect for human beings and opportunities for human beings.

REANNE: Barbara, are you saying that it's difficult for both movements to be on the soapbox at the same time, or-?

BARBARA: It's possible, but there are some feelings that … "I want to help you move you out of the way because-"

LIZ: They want the attention.

BARBARA: I want to be heard.

AMY: It's the attention, and then, in the South, it's also the money, the grants. … You have to fight for your organization to get that money, so if you're helping another organization, you're taking away from your own organization. I've seen that a lot here in South Carolina, but also men, in my experience, the gay men that worked in the feminist movement, have acknowledged their position of power that they receive. The men who don't help out don't acknowledge that they have that position of power that comes with just being male.

STEPHANIE: If you're saying that women support the gay men more than you see the gay men supporting the lesbian women, I think it goes back to women being more compassionate and caring about others around them.

Competition between the movements was not simply in the sense of an abstract notion of limited social willingness to accept them, but also the concrete issues of funding support and media visibility (the "spotlight" or "soapbox"). However, competition was also described as a conflict on a personal, individual level.

NATE: Your female friends worry about you trying to turn their crushes gay. I don't know if anyone has ever went to a club with a female, and they're just like, "Don't try to seduce those guys." I'm always like, "I wasn't going to anyway." ... You go to a gay club expecting to see real hot guys, and then see you a woman seducing a guy. You're going to get really pissed off at her. Most gay guys would. That happened kind of in one of those when I was with some friends, and we had a whole group of girls who wanted to go clubbing and we walked in and all the guys turned around and were like what are the girls doing in our club, you're wasting floor space.

MOD: Both sort of invading our personal space, but would you also say they're a degree of competition?

NATE: They are if there are bisexual guys there that night.

The conflict, then, had dimensions of both individual competition for partners and also social competition for space.

KRISTIN: It's really strange that the gay movement is really moving forward, albeit slowly, while the women's movement has just sort of gone backwards. It's like we're losing.

JANE: "Oh no, the gays are fighting back, on to the women!" I'm sorry, that was really terrible.

KRISTIN: It's like, "Okay, we're not going to bother the gay guys for a minute because they're kind of winning. ... Let's go over to women, mess with them."

Although not explicitly a zero-sum model of competition, women did compare the progress of the two movements.

LIZ: The gay family definitely has a harder life than the women do, because we're still accepted because of our sexuality. ... We like the opposite sex. That's accepted. ... We're still accepted to have our families, raise our families, and still live normally. We may argue and bitch and complain because ... we get paid the same exact ten percent less or whatever, but the gay community has so much more they're fighting for. ... They've got a longer way to go than women.

On a more productive note, one woman suggested that expanding and diversifying the definitions of identity categories could alleviate competition.

JANE: Part of the problem is definition in the gay community. My experience with community action in the gay community has, first of all, "Oh, you're bisexual and not a lesbian? Go away." There's a certain extent to which the attempt to redefine homosexuality is, let's just use this painfully broad term for a moment, as something other than, "I am a man. I like men. I like anal sex. I am physically male and gender-present as male, and this is my in-group." Trying to make that in-group definition to overcome the ... pathologization ... has kind of obscured the ability to work with other groups.

Sexism

Discussions of misogyny and misandry were focused more specifically on the roots of stereotyping and oppression, but framed as conflicts to working together. Some expressed this by acknowledging their own sexism:

NATE: We were with one of my other friend's female friend, and we were watching a movie, and she let out a really loud belch, which is her personality type. That's normal. She's a loud and crazy person. But this particular friend was really offended by that and thought that was completely disgusting that a girl would burp. But he has guy friends that he hangs out with, and they burp and [do] random bodily stuff all the time, and they're completely fine with it.

REGGIE: I feel like I'm guilty of this, too, throwing around "slut" and "whore." There's a double standard that, obviously, if a woman is scantily clad and ... going out for the night, and she's dressed that way, you'll say that they're being a slut or a whore, but you wouldn't say that about a guy or someone else.

MOD: Would you say that about a gay guy?

REGGIE: I don't think so.

Women brought up the use of misogynistic language as well:

CAROL: The business of gay men calling each other "bitch." I just have to say that drives me bananas ... and women started to call each other bitch. It's like guys, come on. Come on. Come on.

JANE: I make a point to apply the word bitch to straight men all the time.

CAROL: I'm really not sure it's a word that helps any of us. ... It's too easy to co-opt back into a way of disciplining women who get out of line. ... And then it's even easier to say, "Oh, I was just joking. Everybody calls everybody a bitch now. I was just joking when I called you that." Or when women call each other that. It's a subtle way of reminding us to discipline ourselves ... to certain roles. We all have an interest ... in dismantling some of these.

Another man acknowledged his use of such language, but also recognized the problems with it. Similar to treating women instructors differently—as the women had discussed—the self-awareness was heartening, although the fact that the practices continued was disappointing.

JUSTIN: When I think of a women's organization or women in high-position jobs, this is a negative thing, but I usually call them a bitch. ... A guy that is hard, very go-getting and knows what he wants, that's completely normal. But if a woman is like that, then she's classified as a bitch. I would fall along that line. The classifying her as a bitch, and [thinking she would be] not wanting to hire any male because she'd be like, "No, you're a male."

SAM: I'll catch myself sometimes doing that with teachers. The male teacher says, "You have to do this and this and the test is in three days." I'm like, "I hate this guy." But then, if it was a female teacher … I'll still say the same thing, "I hate this class, I hate this teacher," and then I'll say, "She's such a bitch." I won't think that about male teacher.

The men's groups also expressed fears and perceptions of women disliking them for being men, further evidencing the negative stereotypes of feminists.

STEVEN: You get a gay man in there to take control of all them women [at a group meeting], they ain't going to like that.

ANDY: When I'm in gay/lesbian groups … I don't get the feeling that they look at me as a gay man, they look at me as a man. And that's the problem. … Not that I'm a gay man necessarily, just that I'm a man. And I'm coming from a different place than women, particularly lesbian women.

One conversation took this into a complicated level of assumptions and counter-assumptions between gay men and feminist women about male privilege.

NATE: There might also be knowledge [among gay men] of the assumption on the women's part [of male privilege] and, therefore, they might be spiteful. He already thinks that we've accepted his type of attitude. He already knows that he's going to get the job. Or he thinks that he's right for the job. The woman knows that the gay man knows that women know that he probably has the same sensibilities. They begrudgingly want to find flaws because they know he thinks that he's going to get the job. That sense of entitlement as a gay man.

REGGIE: That is my life with my best friend, who is uber feminist. Everything that she does revolves around women's rights. She's getting her masters right now in that, and I always thought that we could commiserate with the hegemonic masculinity. We're both victims. She would just be like, "You don't know what it's like to be a woman, don't try to get to my level." It was almost condescending in ways that she would be like that. But it would only be in the realm of women. When it came to sexuality and gender or gay rights, that's where we could bridge the gap.

Perhaps this suggests that, when forming coalitions, avoid a reductive conflation of oppressions as the same—a very feminist lesson.

Religion

Among the gay men, religion was discussed as a source of homophobia or personal challenge to coming out as LGBTQ. For example, Andy said that "The church is the most discriminatory institution." However, religion was not addressed as a factor in their relationships with feminist women. Among the women, however, it was a source of conflict in working with gay men.

REANNE: I will be honest. I don't believe that the gay lifestyle is right. I'm just going to say the truth. Gay, lesbian, to me, that is not a correct lifestyle. However, I do have a sister whose best friend is gay. He is one of the nicest people I've ever met, and she said that when she gets married, he is actually going to be her man of honor because he's such a cool friend, and I know him. I love him. I like him, but when we get onto his lifestyle, we tell him the truth. We just don't believe that that's what was intended. We do get into some heavy-duty discussions, however, at the end of the day, at the end of the discussion, he is still who he is, and we love him. …

STEPHANIE: I hope that my children … my girls find husbands and my son finds a lovely wife, but in a perfect world, I mean, I have to prepare myself for the day that they might come to me and say that [they are LGBTQ]. I don't ever want them to feel uncomfortable, because what would be worse, having a gay son or having a son that's wanting to kill himself at thirteen years old because he's scared to death of anybody finding out? That's where God comes into my heart and says, Yes, it might not be right for you, but you've got to love.

REANNE: No, and I do love my sister's friend …

STEPHANIE: But I agree with you, I don't feel it's right or what was intended, either.

REANNE: However, reading the Bible, we all know where God's view on that is, and I'm not downing anybody. I'm just saying, if you want education on that, you need to go to the source of it, and it is the Bible. The Bible tells us a lot about gay and lesbian … a whole city was destroyed because of it in there. I'm not knocking it, I'm just saying …

AMY: Well, you do realize that they talk more about bad things about heterosexuality than they do about gay-

REANNE: I'm just, what-

AMY: -queer stuff, and they also … Jesus never once, not once, mentions it.

REANNE: Read your Bible. Read your Bible.

Although never becoming aggressively hostile, this conversation about religion and homosexuality was the moment of greatest tension during all of the focus groups. One woman attempted to steer the conversation into a more secular resolution:

POLLY: Whatever you legislate, on books, on law, is never going to make a gay person straight. That's why we have to have the separation [of church and state], and, like you said, it's not for us to judge. It's for God to judge, if you believe in God. I think we have to understand the separation. What can we legislate, and what is moral? What is in your family? What is in your church?

Another woman specified that religious objection was also connected to the pressure to have children.

STEPHANIE: For my [gay] male friends, they've had more of a hard time in the household with the parents, because in the South, you are raised [with] God made Adam and Eve, not Adam and Adam. In my family, it's mainly about reproduction.

Collaboration

Drawing on commonalities and circumnavigating conflicts, both groups discussed ways in which feminist women and gay men had worked together. The first example both cited was that explored in a previous chapter, women during the AIDS crisis. Unlike the varied representations of lesbians in AIDS cinema, the common narrative here was one of strong collaboration.

AIDS

By the time of the focus groups, AIDS had become a manageable, chronic disease for those who could afford treatment in the United States and other developed nations. No longer its dominating social issue, the LGBTQ rights movement had shifted to priorities such as military service, same-sex marriage, adoption, and immigration, and also engaged more with transgender, asexual, intersex, and other persons under the queer umbrella. However, AIDS was recalled by both groups as a moment of collaboration.

MITCH: That was really bad, in the '70s, when there was a [lesbian] separatism, that was very pronounced. … AIDS pretty much put the kibosh to that because, as gay males died, many, even most of our organizations became lesbian-led. And nobody did more in terms of trying to combat the crisis of AIDS among gay men than lesbians did. We all learned a lot about each other in the process.

NELL: We've been supporting gay men since the first case of AIDS. We have been doing a lot.

TINA: Feminists. …

NELL: I don't know about so much feminists, but in the beginning it was the lesbians supporting men and trying to raise the money and doing the benefits and doing all that. That being said, I think that we support them, whereas I feel they don't support us as well. They're not at our benefits as much.

In contrast, AIDS fatigue was cited as a reason for not being more active now, with women or otherwise.

ANDY: I'm tired. We've fought a lot of battles, and there's nothing, I mean, gay marriage was the biggest thing here in Charleston, but I'm in the year where a lot of my friends died of AIDS, so that took a lot of energy. You kids don't even remember that, don't even know that era occurred. If you saw [the NAMES Project] quilt, how large it was, and the number of people in my age group that names are on it, that died of AIDS, and how our country responded to that, which was pretty pathetic. I guess the cynicism is that I don't see a whole lot of that changing. And I'm old.

However, a legacy of AIDS activism that was cited as a more contemporary collaboration, or at least mutual concern, was in the context of the adult entertainment industry.

SAM: [In] pornography, safe sex is an issue, related to condoms. Guys, gay guys, use it to prevent spreading of STIs [sexually transmitted infections], and girls also [for preventing] STIs and for pregnancy as well. … They use condoms for that exact issue. They can work on [it] together. Whether they're gay or heterosexual, still the same thing, still the chance of passing STIs to each other, and women risk being pregnant.

Same-Sex Marriage

During my focus groups, in the neighboring state of North Carolina, a widely publicized campaign was running for the North Carolina Same-Sex Marriage Amendment, a state constitutional amendment to define marriage as only between a man and a woman, and banning any other form of civil partnership recognition.[3]

TRAVIS: I guess it's tomorrow in North Carolina. I've seen gay and lesbian friends of mine who live in North Carolina, who can vote on that. I've seen stuff on Facebook. I've seen stuff in their political organizations, the gay organization in Charlotte. I've seen them; I've seen conversations. I've seen them kind of rally around that amendment. … A very good friend of mine, who I went to college with, who's my age, and is straight, married, and has several kids, that was her profile picture on Facebook, the voting on that event. She was very outspoken about it. She has a lot of gay friends. I'm trying not to stereotype, but I feel like I'm in the generation that's right in the middle. Things were happening. This disease that nobody knew anything about came out. It was all talked about in college. That was the mid-80s. All of that stuff was happening, and I represent that generation that's right in the middle. We're too young to be old, and we're too old to be young. We've got this part from the past, and we've got everything that we see now coming at us from both sides. … If we could take all of that in, [we could] make a good informed decision about how we feel about gay issues and equality. It was a good place to come from 'cause so much happened so quickly. I have a lot of people my age, who I went to college with, who are straight, but don't have a problem with gay rights at all. It's because we were in that middle, training-ground learning.

STEPHANIE: I think the North Carolina issue is potentially unifying more people because it is bridging that problem with single-parent families and with same-sex families, and how that potential amendment can actually cause immense problems for all of them. I think in that case, the response, at least what I've seen of it, seems to be bringing [people] together a little bit more. … But, that could just be my biased Facebook-influenced perspective.

GINA: Marriage rights [is] something that shouldn't have to continue to be a discussion as far as allowing minorities and individuals, regardless of what's in their trousers, get married, and have access to the rights on top of that.

Indeed, several women mentioned marriage as an issue for gay men, but it was only mentioned once as an issue that impacted feminist women.

POLLY: There's legal problems that the gay community has that women don't have. If a gay couple is married, and it's not recognized, and they go into the hospital when their loved one is dying, oftentimes, they're not allowed in there. So, there are some really tough issues that they have to deal with that women don't.

Electoral Politics and Activism

The focus groups took place during the administration of the first African-American US President, Barack Obama, who was decidedly pro-LGBTQ. Former First Lady Hillary Clinton had served as the first female US Senator from New York for eight years, run for the Democratic Party's nomination for President in 2008, and was, at the time, the US Secretary of State. As evidenced in comments presented previously in this chapter, she was widely expected to run again for President after Obama's tenure was completed. Against this backdrop, the groups discussed collaborating in political activism and elections.

POLLY: I will sign petitions and do whatever I can to help any group. ... We're all human beings. ... Anybody that is not being treated right, I'll stick up for.

BARBARA: I live in Folly Beach, which has always been the refuge in South Carolina for gay people. ... Folly Beach has three churches. It has lots of religious people, but Folly Beach has always been a place that accepts everybody, and it's kind of a fierce thing. ... One guy who is openly gay decided to run for council, and he was told to call me because I'm political. He said, "I'm openly gay. Is that going to hurt me?" I said, "Not in Folly Beach. It will probably help you." But it's the only place in South Carolina where that's true. Then the second thing, which was kind of funny, was four people were running for mayor, and one of them went around telling everybody that another one hated gay people. I was supporting the one who was supposed to hate gay people, and it was a huge crisis in his campaign. What is he supposed to do, go around saying, "No, no, I love gay people?" Finally, he said, "I'm having four fundraisers, and three of them are being given by gay people, so I guess they know I don't hate them." And that was the end of it. But that's not typical of South Carolina.

AMY: I was with Occupy Columbia, and it's a very diverse group of individuals from people like me that are dykes to queer men to Libertarians, Democrats, and Republicans. ... All [of us] came together and did our thing. We had to learn how to work together and realize that everything is all of our problems, and that, just because we're not dealing with it in this exact moment, if it's happening to someone else, then it's happening to us. I think that that is how we were able to work together. We came to that understanding together that no matter how we felt about different issues and different ideas. If we didn't learn to work together, we weren't going to change anything.

Mitch described his background in Washington, DC, local and national politics, and how women had supported him there. Active now in South Carolina local politics, he said:

When Linda Ketner ran as an open lesbian for Congress four years ago, not only did she have strong support from the gay male community, but the bulk of her campaign was gay men. Worked their tails off for her, and they very much saw her as their champion, just as lesbians did, and just as many, many whites did. In 2008, Charleston—city and county—not only voted overwhelmingly for a Black man for president, but they overwhelmingly voted for a lesbian for Congress. It's just that the outlying counties didn't go with her. But Linda carried Charleston solidly, and I knew her campaign really well. There were tons of gay men out there working their tails off for nothing. ... Colleen Collin, or Compton, on the county board here, has tons of gay male support. Charleston is an exception to the rest of the state. Gay men are pretty tightly involved with the political process, the social process here. ... At the national level, most progressive groups try very hard to work together. There is an umbrella group called the Leadership Conference on Civil Rights, the underpinning is the NAACP and various groups like that. Heavy, heavy involvement, surprisingly, with the Catholic Church, which was one of our foremost opponents until we found a way to undercut them. But there is a lot of coordination. Human Rights Campaign [and] National Gay and Lesbian Task Force are now members. It took beating down the door some years ago to do it, but now they're full members. And Hispanic groups, women's groups, Black groups. There are over 100 national organizations involved, and they really work together. That whole network supports our efforts to pass the nondiscrimination bill. We support feminist issues; we support The DREAM Act for undocumented Hispanics. ....

[At another time], I lobbied the Missouri State Legislature on gay rights issues. And we didn't have a formal organization, but we had about 13 of us from various groups: ACLU, women's groups, etc., and me. We would meet in the library of the state capital every morning and coordinate our plans. If two critical hearings were being held at exactly time, maybe one in the House and one in the Senate, we'd share testimony. I'd give testimony for the ACLU person, who would give my testimony at the hearing being held at the opposite location.

TRAVIS: A straight woman, who has worked with the Center for Women, she's worked with We are Family [a support organization for LGBTQ+ youth in Charleston]. She's worked with AFA [Alliance for Full Acceptance, a Charleston LGBTQ organization]. She's worked across all those boundaries. She's had some personal experiences with family members and also friends of hers, or children of friends of hers, who have been discriminated in one way or another. She wanted to be a part of the organizations that were helping those oppressed people.

It seems, in retrospect, an optimistic time. However, the moods I remember from the focus groups were more frustration with the slow pace of progress, disagreement about priorities, fears of generational amnesia, and general uncertainty. There was lingering disappointment with Clinton's failure to secure the presidential nomination, outrage over the pending anti-LGBTQ legislation in North Carolina, and frustration with attacks on reproductive rights. "It's like we just keep repeating things over and over," said Amy. "Didn't we already win the right to have contraception? Didn't we already settle this with the Supreme Court? Well, apparently not now. … I don't think that we've come as far as we'd like to think we have."

While mostly positive discussions, they lacked the galvanizing unity I recalled when faced with previously homophobic administrations, the AIDS crisis, or the blatant sexism and racism of the Clarence Thomas Supreme Court nomination hearings, during which Anita Hill brought sexual harassment into wide public awareness.

Other Collaborations

Several other collaborations were mentioned. While women discussed reproductive rights as a feminist issue, they saw more topics related to existing families as more relevant to gay men. A few women mentioned adoption and "being around children" as issue for gay men. The gay men mentioned several additional examples:

NATE: Shopping for clothes [together] to donate to the poor kids.
JUSTIN: Breast cancer. There was a video [channel] on YouTube, *Ask a Gay Man*, … and he made one about breast cancer awareness. Gay men are more inclined to support breast cancer awareness.
SCOTT: More so than straight men.

NATE: Campus sexual violence. I think that originally started as a response to an article in [our campus paper] that was severely dehumanizing to women. A group of women on our campus gathered to protest that and the views that were culturally against women. I joined in it, and I brought in the whole perspective of violence against men because they're feminist, or feminine in their behavior. They were completely open to that. "Yeah, we understand that that's based on gendered perceptions, and we actually want to address that, too, with our group."

REGGIE: As an undergrad … we had like a month-long celebration of *The Vagina Monologues*. Almost by default, all the gay guys on campus would be the vagina warriors, which is the male version of the people who would help out with *The Vagina Monologues*. It was so much fun, because they would make vagina lollipops, and guys would buy them, and all of that money went to women's shelters. It was a light-hearted way to tackle a serious issue that everybody came together on. It was a really positive experience.

Intellectual Contributions

As discussed in previous chapters, another way in which feminist women and gay men have communicated about and to each other is in the cross-pollinations of women's studies, feminist theory, gender studies, queer theory, LGBTQ studies, and related areas of research and theory. The focus groups demonstrated that this was still ongoing and appreciated. For example, Brent said that he learned about women's issues from "my women's studies class that I'm taking." Another participant described ideas discussed with his feminist roommate, including her critique of gay male preferences for hypermasculinity:

REGGIE: She is into the whole concept of not labeling anyone. It goes into queer theory. … You should be able to experience or construct your own being without having to be broken into either male or female, gay or straight. Just the act of labeling is very limiting to one's individual experience.

NATE: Does that flow from the assumption that masculinity is superior and therefore there's a power structure with male and female?

REGGIE: Yeah. I mean, it's not totally unrelated, so I feel like it does combine.

NATE: 'Cause I don't see the labeling process itself as being hurtful, I think the power structure there and the assumptions behind that is what's supposed to be hurtful.

In such exchanges, one can hear the attempt to use theory to articulate how gay men and feminist women have drawn on each other to understand themselves.

JANE: I've never had a women's studies class that didn't talk extensively about gay and transgender rights, because there seems to be an understanding that we have to talk about masculinity in order to talk about femininity, and then we have to talk about why this dichotomy doesn't actually work.

One gay male instructor talked about his explicit use of feminist history in class:

MITCH: Women are the most discriminated group worldwide throughout history .... I really try to underscore that point, at the end of my Intro to American Government class. ... I always end it with civil rights, civil liberties, and then I show the two-hour video on the women's suffrage movement. Can you imagine anything less controversial today than women's suffrage? Half of the people in the country having the right to vote, and yet it took 72 years of constant struggle for women to win the vote, and they won it by one vote when it came down to the last state. That shocks the hell out of people. I mean, women are just constantly discriminated against.

Some perspectives made clear the dynamic nature of intellectual contributions, although at time sounding something like the more competitive comparisons of two movements.

TINA: Feminism has, for a long time, been much more aware of its need to deal with class, with race, with homophobia, with the intersection of these different things, much more so than those studies have sometimes been willing to think about their need to think about women. Feminism at least has done a pretty good job as an academic discipline. Feminists have long been the ones who were first to think about the intersection of gender issues and gender oppression with other forms, but I don't know what I would say about the other direction.

BARBARA: In many ways, LGBT activism wouldn't be functioning as well as it was if it wasn't after the wake of the feminist movement and the headway that was made there. Maybe sometimes it involves more gay men into that if they can recognize that, Here is a struggle that's occurred and is still occurring, and, once these rights are more established, then we can kind of follow on the heels and continue with that.

However, there was also discussion of the limitations of the classroom, from unintended effects to frustration with students' lack of knowledge.

EVAN: There's, at College of Charleston, a women and gender studies class. I know a lot of friends who take it, a lot of girls. Some of them are very for it, and they enjoy it, and some of them come out of it just absolutely hating it. Hating it, hating it, hating it. They don't like it, or they're like, "I'm anti-feminist." I've heard more women against it, and more against it, than I've heard men having ideas on it.

MITCH: Four years ago on campus, when Obama and Hillary Clinton were running against each other—we all remember how tight and intense that primary

was—overwhelmingly, not only the men, but the women on campus were supporting Obama. The first African-American candidate, this is so historic, da da
da dah. They didn't get it about Hillary. They just were oblivious to the struggle
that women went through, and still go through in terms of winning equality
and their rights. They had no inkling that, when Black men were given the right
to vote, the Fifteenth Amendment of the 1860s, that the leaders of the feminist
suffrage movement pleaded with the House and Senate to be included, that all
people should have the right to vote. They weren't against Black men getting the
vote, they wanted everybody to get it.

Information

Another topic that the gay men discussed, as well as the feminist women, was
acquiring information on gay and/or women's issues. Mainstream media outlets
gay men mentioned included CNN, *The New York Times*, MSNBC, FOX, and
the *Wall Street Journal*. There was also an acknowledgment that gay male representations in mainstream media and popular culture had improved and increased
over the past decades, although some older gay men felt young persons didn't
appreciate this enough. Women also discussed media-related issues of body image
and unrealistic beauty ideals.

Online news aggregators, blogs, and websites mentioned by gay men included the *Drudge Report*, Google News, *Advocate, Huffington Post, Real Clear Politics,
Politico, AfterElton, Human Rights Campaign, OutSports.com, Washington Blade,
World Review Gay*, and *Lesbian World Review*. Reggie suggested that he might be
pulled into reading about a women's issue by a catchy headline, but that he didn't
see women's stories on gay sites very frequently. Women described organizations
with which they were involved, ranging from informal feminist activist collectives
to professional organizations, such as Women Academics Coalition, Association
of University Women, and NOW. Women also mentioned the online accounts of
Human Rights Campaign and the Southern Poverty Law Center.

One subject that came up across the discussions was social media, as a benefi-
cial source of information, amusement, and connection, with the potential to be
a positive tool in social movements. Gay men cited the viral Kony 2012 campaign
as an example of social media's power. They mentioned Tumblr blogs and Twitter
accounts of friends and celebrities, particularly that of a noted feminist educator
who had spoken on campus. Women also mentioned Tumblr, as well as Redditt,
and the blogs *Feministing* and *Autostraddle*. Some described George Takei and
Dan Savage as online sources for news on gay politics.

Overall, Facebook was described as the most common platform for information. Gay men mentioned the Facebook accounts of national organizations, such as HRC, and smaller ones, such as the university's gay-straight alliance, as important information sources. Women cited a recent study of how much news and political information were being shared through Facebook, and mentioned specific Facebook groups, such as Wipeout Homophobia and Gay Wedding Photos.

The viral social media campaign It Gets Better, begun by US gay activist and writer Dan Savage and his husband Terry Miller, presented messages of encouragement for gay youth. Inspired by the suicides of bullied LGBTQ youth, or youth who were thought to be LGBTQ, it became a nonprofit organization and was on the mind of the focus group participants in 2012.

REGGIE: One of the defining things that I've witnessed in my lifetime is It Gets Better and the number of responses that came out with that. It's up to 40,000. You had celebrities, the president, Hillary Clinton, and all of these big-name, big-wig people coming out and creating these videos. It may have been one most inspiring things that I've seen that relates to the gay community. …

PAUL: I liked the ones that came from an athletic program or athletes, because I think that athletics are such a huge part of social life in the US, in schools, [at our university], with our football team, tailgating, and everything. It's such a segregated thing by gender. That's really an awesome place to start sending a message of acceptance and affirmation. The UCLA athletic department just put up a video, UNC Chapel Hill just released a video. Some of that is being influenced by Athlete Allies, Hudson Taylor's organization, and he's straight, that advocates for LGBT inclusion in athletics.

SCOTT: It hits every target audience. It hits businessmen, it hits children, it hits teenagers.

TRAVIS: It Gets Better, the bullying campaign, is ongoing, it's still happening, it's still trying to get better. I saw gay and lesbian women, minorities, Caucasians, all kinds of people come together on that. I actually saw where some churches stepped in.

MOD: Did you see some non-lesbian women?

TRAVIS: Absolutely. … It crosses all boundaries. There are no borders when it comes to bullying. You can be bullied for being female, you can be bullied for being fat, you can be bullied for being gay, you can be bullied for being a feminist, you can be bullied for being a sissy. There are so many reasons that people get bullied. I think they cross all lines.

ERIK: Especially when it has to do with kids.

TRAVIS: Yeah, particularly white kids. …

CURT: It shocked everybody, the fact that there are eighth-graders, and they're bullying children 'til they commit suicide. Teachers and other people are just watching it happen. That is something that does cross borders.

Some women, however, suggested that certain kinds of activism were better handled on an individual level within interpersonal networks of family, friends, churches, and communities, in addition to or integrated with social media.

JANE: [It] is easier to address [political and social issues] in terms of, not organizing, but acting as an individual. Saying to someone, "Hey, just because I'm female doesn't mean that my opinion on feminism is invalid and doesn't mean my opinion on queerness isn't valid." "Hey, wait a minute, that was really kind of homophobic sounding. Can you rephrase that?" I don't think that works institutionally. There's an importance to the individual conversations, and that can happen through Facebook, rather than in person. The "I'd rather you didn't make this kind of comment," my mother-in-law, in my case, "in a public forum, because I feel like this will make some of my Facebook friends really uncomfortable, and I don't want to have to block you." "Grandma, you can't say that about gay families." Those individual conversations can't function on an institutionalized level, or if they can, I would love to hear about it.

In retrospect, it is startling the degree to which such optimism regarding social media has changed. Today many of my students roll their eyes upon hearing the phrase "social media," for numerous reasons. Ongoing public and scholarly debates, including my own, have investigated the utility of networked and social media for politics and activism (e.g., Carty & Barron, 2019; Castells, 2012; Couldry & Curran, 2003; Fuchs, 2012; Kahn & Kellner, 2004; Lindgren, 2019; Scott, 2005, 2007, 2008). Often these debates, and their rehashings, are counterproductive in that they essentialize "the internet" and "social media" into meaningless generalities. As I will describe further in a subsequent chapter, the various online platforms are constantly changing and, even in the moment, can exist in radically different yet simultaneous experiences. Furthermore, I am not trying to suggest this change in zeitgeist is a definitive statement on the nature or function of social media platforms. Whether Twitter or Pinterest, a platform is a tool that can be put to varied uses.

What was significant here was that the affect around social media was generally much more positive and enthusiastic during my focus groups, and students and colleagues in general, in 2012 than when compared to today. Admittedly, while one can cite successes of #MeToo and #BlackLivesMatter, less savory stories are dominant in this, rather dystopian, moment of technological discourses. Most apparently, the United States in currently embroiled in investigations over the role to which foreign actors used social media as part of interference in the 2016 presidential campaign (Linvill, 2019; Linvill, Boatwright, Grant, & Warren, 2019; Ribeiro, Saha, Babaei, Henrique, Messias, Benevenuto, & Redmiles, 2019). The phenomenon of "fake news" sharing is perceived as ubiquitous (Marwick, 2018).

A recent study found evidence of social media campaign manipulation in 70 countries and computational propaganda in 26 authoritarian regimes, with Facebook the most common platform (Bradshaw & Howard, 2019). Additionally, widespread research and news has investigated the privacy abuses by social media companies. Data breaches and leaks of personal information, for commercial gain or personal attack, are regular events. Health reports on social media's negative effects and misuse, of the related devices, fill the news (Scott, 2018). Fatigue runs high as the opportunity to share has evolved into expectations of using social media for self-promotion and branding, and an overall incitement to visibility. Van Dijck (2013) provides an excellent overview of changing social norms reflected in the first ten years of social media; I would suggest that, in the years since, many have shifted from experiencing social media as a toy and entertainment to burden and threat.

I conclude with this chapter as one that is particularly contingent, already dated, and more suggestive of an opportunity and moment than definitive trajectory. Having examined in this chapter gay men and feminist women speaking freely about themselves and each other face-to-face, I turn next to online communication and networking. In the subsequent chapter, I will examine two final questions: How does the general public speak about gay men and feminist women together? Through what networks do the two groups connect to each other? In so doing, my investigation will examine both the moment of the focus groups' 2012 conversations and a re-visitation seven years later, a time of new successes and renewed fears for feminist women, gay men, and others who share their concerns.

Notes

1. A double-space between conversation excerpts indicates they were not continuous.
2. A Georgetown University Law Center student who had made a speech to House Democrats for mandating insurance coverage of contraceptives.
3. On May 8, 2012, the amendment passed, but was overturned in 2014.

References

Barad, K. (2007). *Meeting the universe halfway: Quantum physics and the entanglement of matter and meaning.* Durham, NC: Duke University Press.

Bradshaw, S., & Howard, P. N. (2019). "The global disinformation order: 2019 global inventory of organised social media manipulation." Working Paper 2019.3. Oxford, UK: Project on Computational Propaganda. comprop.oii.ox.ac.uk., 23 pp.

Carty, V., & Barron, F. G. R. (2019). Social movements and new technology: The dynamics of cyber activism in the digital age. In *The Palgrave handbook of social movements, revolution, and social transformation* (pp. 373–397). New York: Palgrave Macmillan.

Castells, M. (2012). *Networks of outrage and hope.* Cambridge, UK: The Polity Press.

Couldry, N., & Curran, J. (Eds.). (2003). *Contesting media power: Alternative media in a networked world.* Lanham, MD: Rowman & Littlefield Publishers.

Douglas, S. J. (1995). *Where the girls are: Growing up female with the mass media.* New York: Three Rivers Press.

Fuchs, C. (2012). Some reflections on Manuel Castells' book "Networks of Outrage and Hope. Social Movements in the Internet Age". *tripleC: Communication, Capitalism & Critique. Open Access Journal for a Global Sustainable Information Society, 10*(2), 775–797.

Kahn, R., & Kellner, D. (2004). New media and internet activism: From the 'Battle of Seattle' to blogging. *New Media & Society, 6*(1), 87–95.

Lindgren, S. (2019). Movement Mobilization in the Age of Hashtag Activism: Examining the Challenge of Noise, Hate, and Disengagement in the# MeToo Campaign. *Policy & Internet, 11*(4), 418–438.

Linvill, D. L. (2019). Addressing social media dangers within and beyond the college campus. *Communication Education, 68*(3), 371–380.

Linvill, D. L., Boatwright, B. C., Grant, W. J., & Warren, P. L. (2019). "THE RUSSIANS ARE HACKING MY BRAIN!" Investigating Russia's Internet Research Agency Twitter Tactics during the 2016 United States presidential campaign. *Computers in Human Behavior, 99,* 292–300.

Marwick, A. E. (2018). Why do people share fake news? A sociotechnical model of media effects. *Georgetown Law Technology Review, 2*(2), 474–512.

Ribeiro, F. N., Saha, K., Babaei, M., Henrique, L., Messias, J., Benevenuto, F., … & Redmiles, E. M. (2019, Jan.). On microtargeting socially divisive ads: A case study of Russia-linked ad campaigns on Facebook. In *Proceedings of the Conference on Fairness, Accountability, and Transparency* (pp. 140–149). ACM.

Scott, D. (2005). Protest email as alternative media in the 2004 US presidential campaign. *Westminster Papers in Communication and Culture, 2*(1), 51–71.

Scott, D. T. (2007). Pundits in muckrakers' clothing: Political blogs and the 2004 US presidential election. In M. Tremayne, (Ed.) *Blogging, citizenship, and the future of media* (pp. 39–57). New York: Routledge.

Scott, D. T. (2008). Tempests of the blogosphere: Presidential campaign stories that failed to ignite mainstream media. In M. Boler, (Ed.) *Digital media and democracy: Tactics in hard times* (pp. 271–300). Cambridge, MA: The MIT Press.

Scott, D. T. (2018). *Pathology and technology: Killer apps and sick users.* New York: Peter Lang.

Van Dijck, J. (2013). *The culture of connectivity: A critical history of social media.* Oxford, UK: Oxford University Press.

5

Queering Networks, Entangled Platforms: Feminist Women and Gay Men in Online Media

A prominent scholar of networks once told me that the structure and function of a network were the only things that mattered in studying them. The specific content of what traveled through a network was irrelevant.

To that scholar, at least. This chapter will follow dynamic, shifting online networks of equality-minded gay men and feminist women, transforming in some cases ultimately to far-right, socially conservative places. My queer methodology resists purely structural approaches by insisting on the importance of the content of networks, while still using them as an analytic. If the driving concern of this project has been the potential connections between feminist women and gay men, then it is ultimately about networking, but networking in which the content of the networks matters to an extreme degree. Here, I turn from the archive and interview rooms to networks and online technologies.[1] However, as discussed in the previous chapter, much has changed for feminist women and gay men since 2012. Therefore, this chapter begins with findings from social media data scraping and network analyses in 2012, then revisits them in 2019. This incorporates temporality into the analysis, but it is not intended to suggest longitudinal research findings. Instead, as part of my research process, I attempted to revisit the topics of the research seven years later. It was not logistically possible to reconvene the four focus groups discussed in the previous chapter; I can merely reflect upon their discussion from today's perspective. However, one can attempt to return to the spaces of online networking of gay men and feminist women, just as one can attempt to return to the women's bookstores listed in the LGBTQ travel guides discussed in an earlier chapter. The stores may be still be there and bustling, or they may be closed.

The Network Society

As discussed previously, Castells describes communication processes as central to global culture. Moreover, these processes take place within the social structure of the network, or, as he names it, the network society. Castells argues, across numerous books and data sets, that the network has become the dominant model of social organization (e.g., 2002, 2004, 2009, 2011a, 2011b, 2015).

What is a network? Castells did not invent the concept, but, as has been noted, he synthesized several areas of research and theory, expanding and developing them significantly (Siapera, 2017). For example, he draws on actor-network theory, which Latour describes as "a simple material argument." In refutation of many social theories, Latour writes that, "Strength does not come from concentration, purity, and unity, but from dissemination, heterogeneity, and the careful plaiting of weak ties" (1996, p. 370). Resisting a reductive technical ontology, Latour defines a network as "not a thing, but the recorded movement of a thing" (1996, p. 378), with movement passing through individuals, institutions, technologies, and other components. All of these have the ability to exert influence, and all are linked in a network of shared objectives.

Castells argues that each network operates under its own processes and organization. Each can reconfigure itself as needed to achieve its goals. All networks, however, traffic in cultural materials: frames, ideas, projects, and visions generate their programs. Programming and switching are the two sources of power in the network society. Programming sets the goals of the network, writing the code of its instructions. In line with Foucault's (1980, 1990, 2001) notions of power as reversible and multiple, programming includes reprogramming and meta-programming. Switching is "the ability to connect and ensure the cooperation of different networks by sharing common goals and combining resources, while fending off competition from other networks by setting up strategic cooperation" (Castells, 2009, p. 45). He defines switching power as "the capacity to connect two or more different networks in the process of making power for each one of them in their respective fields" (2009, p. 427).

To rephrase this in more Foucaultian language, relationships of switching power are those that connect different networks in ways that elevate other power relationships that each are engaged in elsewhere. It is not about sending or distributing power as a concrete thing or message that is (re)distributed, but about altering existing relationships to be able to exercise more power within them. Castells gives the example of Rupert Murdoch as someone in power-switching relationships among media, business, and political networks. Although I am uncomfortable with the language of concrete things Castells uses, his assertion that "programmers and switchers are the holders of power in the network society" (2009, p. 429) is nevertheless useful here. I would rephrase it along these lines: Processes of programming and switching are empowered relations in a networked society. Being in a relationship in which one can switch and program puts one in a position to assert one's will over others: a position of power.

Castells writes that

> Networks are complex structures of communication constructed around a set of goals that simultaneously ensure unity of purpose and flexibility of execution by their adaptability to the operating environment. They are programmed and self-configurable at the same time. Their goals and operating procedures are programmed, in social and organizational networks, by social actors. Their structure evolves according to the capacity of the network to self-configure in an endless search for more efficient networking arrangements. (2009, p. 21)

Networks have several defining characteristics. They are *binary* in that you are either in the network or not, and networks are either connected to each other or not.[2] Networks are similarly binary in their relationships to one another: They cooperate or compete with one another. Networks are *flexible, scalable,* and *survivable* (their decentralized structure allows them to persist and reconfigure when nodes are lost); they are malleable and dynamic, with no fixed, permanent boundaries. Their values are not universal but vary depending on the programming of each. They are "*communicative* structures" in social life (Castells, 2009, p. 21), which include both multimodal mass media and interactive online and wireless communication technologies, the blending of which Castells refers to as "mass self-communication" (2009, p. 4).

Networks are not unique to the twenty-first century. Their study and use as an analytic have antecedents reaching into the nineteenth century (Castells, Monge, & Contractor, 2011; Coward, 2018). Network analyses have expanded into rich fields of study, such as multidimensionality, ambiguity, and exclusion (Castells et al., 2011), and organizational studies (Clegg et al., 2016).

Networks do "constitute the fundamental pattern of life, of all kinds of life" (Castells, 2009, p. 21). Yet, in the past, they simply were not as dominant a social model as hierarchical bureaucracies, not until the emergence and global spread of electronic communication technologies. These communication technologies, particularly once digitized, structured—but did not determine, as Castells takes care to point out—"a new form of society, the network society, made up of specific configurations of global, national, and local networks in a multidimensional space of social interaction" (2009, p. 19). The network society is also notable for new social divisions of labor: more working, and work has been divided into types that are autonomous or "self-programmable." The vastly more common generic labor, which cannot set its own goals (2009, p. 30), is valued less and disposed of easily. This division is typically gendered, with more women employees but also valued feminized characteristics, such as adaptability and flexibility, which come to structure even male-dominated work. Another hallmark of the network society is a reorganization of space and time into the "space of flows"—noncontiguous simultaneity, or what technology scholars refer to as synchronous mediated communication, e.g., chatting online with someone far away—and "timeless time"—the breakdown of previous sequential chronologies, such as the nonlinear experience of the database that Lev Manovich (2001) describes as the paradigmatic form of new-media narrative, or the dispersed infiltrations of labor into all hours of the day that break down the previous sequence of rest/work/leisure into "always on."

Drawing on Foucault (1980, 1990, 2001), power here is conceived in his modern sense as dispersed, multiple relations rather than a thing possessed by any particular entity or group, and power is also conceived of as inextricably linked with knowledge. The power relationships of feminist women and gay men are connected to their knowledges of each other and the broader society's knowledges of them. In the network society, power is exerted in four ways: (1) networking power, that of the actors at the core of global networks, (2) network power, that of standards and rules of inclusion, (3) networked power, that of social actors over others within a particular network, and (4) network-making power, the power to program networks and switch different networks through strategic alliances (Castells, 2011b, p. 773). Network-making power is of key interest here, as "programmers and switchers are those actors and networks of actors who, because of their position in the social structure, hold network-making power—the paramount form of power in the network society" (Castells, 2011b, p. 777). For feminist women and gay men, these roles are crucial to efforts at counterpower, "enacting the interests and values of those in subordinate positions in the social organization" (Castells, 2011b, p. 773–774).

If "networks are powerful carriers of new social norms, values, and practices" (Clegg et al., 2016, p. 281), their importance for social movements is vital. Castells conceptualizes social movements as "the producers of new values and goals around which the institutions of society are transformed to represent these values by creating new norms to organize social life" (2015, p. 9). This is distinct from insurgent politics, which are "processes aiming at political change (institutional change) in discontinuity with the logic embedded in political institutions" (2009, p. 300). Both, however, are forms of reprogramming social networks. For social movements, the two mechanisms of counterpower are the same two mechanisms that constitute power in general in the network society: programming and switching.

> Counterpower, the deliberate attempt to change power relationships, is enacted by reprogramming networks around alternative interests and values, and/or disrupting the dominant switches while switching networks of resistance and social change. (Castells, 2015, p. 9).

This requires creating autonomous communication channels for planning action and debating ideals, such as the LGBTQ community media examined previously or, in this chapter, online communications.

Social movements can introduce new codes into networks and reprogram them with new fundamental kernels: introducing a new issue into a political campaign, such as the introduction of student debt to debates about wealth disparity, or redefining a fundamental issue, such as measuring company success by social contribution rather than profit. They can also switch power between existing networks, but also unswitch them, for example, filing a lawsuit that prevents a state from enacting legislation that prohibits same-sex marriage, or severing the networked power between political and social institutions and actors.

Fuchs (2012) situates Castells within an ongoing debate among communication and technology scholars about the relations between social media and politics, arguing that he perpetuates a technological optimism, if not determinism. "Castells' model is simplistic: social media results in revolutions and rebellions" (Fuchs, 2012, p. 781). Indeed, it is important to avoid over-emphasizing the technological components of networks. Social movements may utilize Twitter or Facebook, but they are not created by social media platforms. Additionally, social movements do not live by technology alone. Castells acknowledges this when he proposes that they "are networked in multiple forms," creating a multimodal networking form that

> Includes social networks online and offline, as well as pre-existing social networks, and networks formed during the actions of the movement. Networks are within the movement, with other movements around the world, with the Internet blogosphere, with the media and with society at large. (2015, p. 249)

Castells does not, however, extend his analyses to the dyadic and small-group relationships of Social Network Analysis (SNA), a field he largely neglects (Anttiroiko, 2015). Another critique of Castells' work is that he neglects social theory and critical theory (Fuchs, 2012). My agreement with this, and, given the topics of this book, are why I have used him as a conceptual tool, rather than explanatory model, particularly in this final chapter.

In terms of the specific social movements under review here, feminism is not a major social movement examined by Castells, although he does describe the impact of women moving into the workforce as a structural change in the network society: "Professional women have reached a higher level of connectivity into what used to be called old boys networks" (2009, p. 31), while other gendered changes have affected the structure of male labor as well. Gay men, however, were the explicit subject of his initial research: Urban gay male communities were one of the early examples of networks Castells investigated (1983).

Essentialism lingers in some feminist and LGBT scholarship and theory (even if of strategic or conditional nature). Theories of networks offer some amends while, admittedly also introducing new problems. In the limited discussion of feminist women and gay men, especially in the common reductive form of solely talking about lesbians, the implicit suggestion is of natural, fixed identities: they *are* enemies or allies. Gay men *are* sexist; feminist women *are* homophobic. This is reinscribed by the focus on individual political leaders and, to a certain degree, by the focus on events. If gay men are targeted during the AIDS crisis, then lesbians come to the join the fight because they also *are* homosexuals.

Castells, however, reframes network relations in terms of collaboration and competition, which allows for greater recognition of contingency and moves further away from essential identities. Under the right circumstances, any two groups can be competitors or collaborators (as indeed, should be apparent from anti-porn feminists' collaboration with Christian conservatives, as well as gay rights activism for marriage and military service). This more pragmatic view also defuses some of the highly charged language of sexism and homophobia. Competition does not necessarily imply hatred or dislike. You can compete in a race with your best friend. Your goals merely are not aligned. This takes some of the personal emotion of identity politics out of the discussion. However, such depersonalization and evacuation of affect have been a critique of network theories. Indeed, several scholars have moved to center emotion through studies of networked affect (Hillis, Paasonen, & Petit, 2015; Papacharissi, 2015). Part of my move in queering network analysis in this chapter is to include quotes from social media postings so that their affect shines through clearly.

Another critique of network analysis has been that the emphasis on connection deprioritizes the connection points or nodes. As Coward argues,

> A correlate of this prioritization of links is that nodes are understood to have no substantive content. The interconnections of the network are constitutive of the nodes that they connect. The node is treated as a black box with little analytic value. Thus, it is not so much the individual that matters, but how they are related to others. Put differently, an individual node has no specific characteristics or interest for the researcher until they are linked into a network. (2018, p. 452)

Along with this, Coward says, nodes are "disembodied from surrounding, continuous matter and relationships" (p. 452). Similarly, Szulc calls for a move from quantitative mapping of networks to more qualitative analysis of, for example, hyperlinking politics, choices, and implications: "We need not only to identify where hyperlinks lead to but also what for and in what way" (2015, p. 3). Such critiques inform my approach in this chapter to examine networks in a manner in which their contiguous cultures and communities are foregrounded. Moreover, individual nodes and their characteristics will be presented here as of analytic importance, particularly as the chapter moves to examine changes over time.

Caveats

One must add some caveats when dealing with quantitative data in social media, even if merely descriptive. First, the social categories of "feminist," "woman," "gay," and "man" are conceived of as discursively constituted and highly contingent, even if treated here as fixed. One of the reasons this project does not extend further back in time is to resist a presentist extension of contemporary conceptions of identity into the past. It is fully acknowledged that these categories are largely socially constructed yet also, out of political necessity, must be treated as stable, essential identities and, indeed, in many ways in social life are felt and experienced as exactly that.

Additionally, both feminist and gay-related social media posts were dominated by Twitter. Yet, a single, impulsively composed, short (re)tweet and a single, carefully argued, lengthy blog post are clearly not the same thing, even if quantified as such. Therefore, I have resisted the false certainty and comparisons of numeric totals in this section. One person posting to their personal blog with no followers or comments is not the same as a major political commentator posting on a commercial blog housed with a major news outlet. Such issues of influence and engagement are significant, and I will turn to them later.

Social Media Snapshot: 2012

To mine social media regarding the two groups, a graduate student and I used Saleforce's Radian6 software for data-mining and sentiment analyses. "Sentiment" refers to determining whether a post or utterance is positive, neutral, or negative based on keywords in the text (Newton, 2009). (See methodological discussions in Basich, 2010; Bell, 2011; Newton, 2009; Rasmussen, 2009; Solis, 2012). Blogs, blog aggregators and comments; tweets and other micromedia, Facebook and MySpace posts, and discussion forums and replies were searched for the month of March, 2012, for keywords related to gay men ("gay(s)/bisexual(s)/homosexual(s)/queer(s)/pansexual(s)" and "man/men/transman/transmen/FTM/FTMs") and feminist women ("women/women's" and "rights/equality/liberation," "rights," "feminism, feminist OR feminists"). Sexual keywords ("xxx/anal/fisting/hardcore/fetish") were excluded to skip pornography sites. Among each of these two groups, a subset of posts were identified in which the other group was also mentioned. In other words, a pool of gay-related posts was identified, then within that pool we searched for feminist keywords. The software at the time did not allow us to search directly for posts in which any one or more of the gay keywords appeared along with any one of the feminist keywords. Therefore, we repeated the process: a pool for feminist-related posts was also identified, and we searched within that pool for gay-related posts. Ostensibly, these pools should have mirrored each other. If you imagine the pools of posts as a Venn diagram, the overlap between the two pools should have been the same regardless of from which direction we entered the diagram. The subset of A that included B should be the same as the subset of B that included A. Sentiment analyses were then conducted to see if, when people talked in social media about feminist women *and* gay men, their sentiment was generally positive or negative.

If this book has described the received view of what was spoken about when gay men and lesbians were linked, how would that compare to discourses in social media? If the historiographic discourse of the two groups was minimal and limited, would the social discourse be the same? Clearly, these were apples and oranges in many ways. Social movement scholars and authors are not the same as the free-for-all of social media. Nevertheless, given that social movements are concerned with changes to society as a whole, what insights could be gleaned from investigating discourses in social media? What could a network data mining perspective suggest, unlike issue- and individual-driven historiography, or group conversations?

Minimal Linkage

First, social discourse suggested a similarly minimal linkage of the two groups. Many people were posting in social media using the keywords related to gay men or feminist women. However, there were very few posts that had both: at least one gay-male-related keyword and one feminist-related keyword. Depending on how one interpreted the meanings and uses of the keywords (e.g., "gay" as synonym for "stupid"), the exact percentage of posts linking the two groups varied, but never rose above one percent. As with the famous Ferdinand de Saussure quote, this tool was approached as a bulldozer, capable of broad, sweeping assessments. Therefore, I have limited my analyses here to such generalizations: People definitely spoke in social media about gay men and feminist women in 2012, but it was comparatively very infrequent when they spoke about the two at the same time. This suggests that the popular discourse was not unlike the scholarly and historic discourses: generally, the two groups were not connected, despite the arguments and advancements of queer and gender studies.

Sentiments – 2012

Our next question was, then, when people connected or juxtaposed the two groups, what were they saying? When using the sentiment analysis feature to determine the emotional tone of posts that included both gay men and feminist women, the results were mostly negative. For approximately 70% of all posts mentioning both groups, the sentiment was negative. This degree of consistency was across all keyword combinations: when most people talked about gay men and feminist women, they were not expressing happiness or pleasure. Furthermore, given that pejorative terms were not included as keywords, it can be assumed that the actual number of negative posts may have been higher. However, this did not *necessarily* mean that they were describing a negative relationship between the two groups (e.g., "As a gay man, I hate feminists") or toward the two groups (e.g., "Homosexual men and feminists are evil"). It meant the emotional tone in posts that mentioned both groups was largely negative. But, this could be toward the two groups (e.g., "Gay men and feminists are all stupid and I hate them") or in regard to others' feelings about the two groups (e.g., "Rednecks don't like queers and women's liberation. That's stupid.")

Therefore, investigating the content of the posts themselves was used to determine sentiment themes. Rather than simply positive or negative—which are meaningless categorizations without context or elaboration—a systematic random sampling of posts was examined to determine frequent themes. Keywords were then used to verify potential themes. Themes were narrowed into those that expressed some clear opinion on feminist women and gay men, not merely having a co-occurrence of keywords with a conceptual connection expressed.

Scroll down to examine a sample:

Allies, Kinship. As seen in previous chapters, a natural association between feminist women and gay men was at times evidenced:

HJAYBEE:	RT Most of the men I know that are vehemently for women's rights are gay. So gay men love the wimminz more than straight men
GHOSTANGEL:	This is one of those days where it is incredibly awkward to be a gay man in a female body and still be a feminist. Bad headspace.
RUNRYLANRUN:	I like to consider myself a gay man who is a feminist. Its a shame feminism has gained a bad connotation.
RUSTYBOYROBOT:	RT Dear gays: remember, we would be up shit creek if it weren't for the Women's Movement … so hug and thank a Feminist today! #IWD #canqueer

Victims of Common Oppressors. The association could extend to their victimhood. Here, for example, negative posts criticized those who oppressed feminist women and gay men:

ENIGMA:	One of the major problems that I've outlined before for the gaming community is sexism, and to the same degree, racism and homophobia. Because these form a spectrum, rarely will you find someone who isn't one or more of these things. You'll be hard pressed to find "just a sexist", because odds are, they're likely a homophobe and racist, too. These kinds of people form a notable segment of the video game, table-top game, card game, speculative fiction, and comic book communities.

JENNNQ:	I have seen feminism be left at the fringes. It became something left to intellectuals, nerds, punks, extremist, or, that most right-wing threatening group of all; gays.
KT:	[In a news post on Victoria's Secret announcing an upcoming line of men's lingerie] The gay community is thrilled with the decision as are feminist groups, while conservatives have expressed overall disgust.
KISSTHEDWARFOH:	Xtians blame the alleged demise of the Family on everyone but themselves. The gays are out there ruining familes according to them. Secularists are out in the RV's traipsing from town to town ruining their Families. Feminists are out there indoctrinating girls to their evil ways, and emasculating Xtian males.

Intellectual Contributions. While explicit discussions of academic theory were not common, the cross-pollination between groups could be evidenced when they were positioned as components or markers of broader social changes. TRANS-MEDITATIONS posted her experiences as a transwoman with 20 years of experience witnessing divisions between transgender groups and feminist groups, which she now saw as having much better understandings: "Queer, feminist and trans movements and theoretical schools are revolutionary, and each compliments [sic] the other in helping scholars and activists alike to pose pivotal, critical questions about the nature of gender and sexuality in this society." REINADELAISLA tweeted, "Just like I must be gay if I support gay marriage. And I must hate men if I'm a feminist. lol ok?" In another example, ERINHORAKOVA posted:

Idk, maybe we should run a better 'this is the history of what we've been up to' crash course for wee Post-AIDS gays and allies than 'Wilde-->Stonewall-->RENT the musical-->Marriage?!' But also the 'how could u not want marriage?!' is a bit generally naive. No group/movement is completely homogenous in their goals, or that unilaterally committed to one scheme of achieving their goals, even if they are clear on exactly what shape those goals will take. See also: feminism, labor, black rights (oh god, DEF go look up the divides in the aims of Civil Rights campaigners), everything ever.

Conflicts. Other times, the association between the groups was that of inherent opposition. TNOPPER tweeted that, "Many straight women and male feminists analytically forget abt gays and lesbians unless talking abt DADT [the former military policy of Don't Ask, Don't Tell], gay marriage, or hate crimes." Similarly, TGODTAYLORJON tweeted, "I'm pretty sure she's real brah. Mormon Feminist who hates gays. Surprise?" Sometimes this was less essentializing and more particular, as when CHARJONES21 tweeted, "'After uni LIFE GETS HARD' 'just because you're gay doesn't mean you can touch me up, I'm a women with rights'

#quotesoftheevening" or EGABBERT's tweet "even by feminists, like there is a fear of anything womanly (or gay) being seen as weak."

Disliked. Familiar forms of negative associations combined the two groups as objects of hate or distaste. ITWERK4SKITTLES retweeted, "@Dull_Antsy: Feminists are the most annoying creatures on earth," replying, "Either them or flaming gay men." LABESFORDAYS tweeted, "Anyway feminism is gay and trans people are disgusting and moewytch is a stupid cunt!!!! bye!!!!"

Disliked Subsets. Sometimes dislike was framed in terms of their roles as subsets within larger disliked groups:

TC: ALL law firms -as prime pushers of the feminist-faggot rot that is destroying Americans and the rest of the human race- should be put out of business, as should the adolescent fools on Wall Street and those fools in the oil, gas, coal, chemical … industries. For they are responsible for global warming and all its associated problems/disasters as well as the cancers, heart and lung disease, genetic disease, obesity.

Co-conspirators. In comparison to previous chapters, collaboration here could also be seen as a negative, in that both groups were described as actually political pawns, interest groups aligned in often unwitting or subversive power politics.

SWORDMAIDEN_MONICA: Re: MRA? More Like "Anti-Women's/Gay/Non-Whit Rights Activists" The inevitable curse that many advocacy movements with good intentions succumb to, a curse that has befallen many of those that championed racial minorities and feminism as well, seems to have taken hold quite early in the men's rights movement. Just like it helped the NAACP and several women's groups to become little more than left wing mouthpieces, this one seems to have let itself become just another gun platform for right wing conservatives and what can only be described as genuine misogynists.

BUCK47:   Gay rights, women's rights, minority rights, all nonsense. What we need is a set of comprehensive HUMAN rights, without all the labels.

SHELLI_EATON: Left tried race card, feminism card, gay card & class warfare card, but it's not working like they wanted. You've been PLAYED. What's next?

Influencers and Switchers: 2012

Evidence from data-mining, historiographies, archives, representations, and focus groups had suggested that links existed between these two groups both politically, historically, and popularly, but that they were limited and/or under-represented. Wanting to zoom in on those links to explore the idea of switching—of gay and feminist networks connecting for counterpower—my research assistant and I then began the process of identifying major nodes in online networks of feminist women and gay men, specifically blogs with high degrees of influence.[3] "Influence" was conceptualized as a blog's ability to share a conversation, particularly in terms of provoking measurable effects and behaviors online. In an attempt to measure the three dimensions of influence—reach, relevance, and resonance—influence was also seen as taking into consideration the amount of "buzz" a host generated, as well as the number of "eyeballs" accrued (Basich, 2010; Solis, 2012; see methodological discussions in Gillian, n.d.; Rubenstein, 2011; Stansberry, 2011).

We focused on blogs in order to achieve some consistency regarding the issues of posts' length and quantity. We identified potential influencer blogs based on several criteria: total recent post count, Technorati ranking, Ice Rocket ranking, self-promoted analytics, awards, Twitter followers, Facebook members/likes, Flickr account, YouTube subscribers, and YouTube total views. From this process, we identified 12 feminist blogs and 13 gay blogs who warranted consideration as influencers. Using a data-scraping software that was then known as Radian6, we ran its Influencer Viewer tool on gay-related and feminist-related posts coming from all blogs online. This process identified a new influencer for both groups, the women's blog *Jezebel*, which was the third-highest gay-related blog influencer and highest feminist-related blog. We then included *Jezebel* with our other influencer blogs. We also included a major LGBTQ advocacy organization, Human Rights Campaign (HRC), and a major feminist organization, NOW. Our resulting list of influencer blogs, or nodes in online networks of feminist women and gay men was:

> *AfterElton* http://www.afterelton.com/
> *American Blog Gay* http://gay.americablog.com/
> *The Bilerico Project* http://www.bilerico.com/
> *Bitch Magazine* http://bitchmagazine.org/blogs
> *Box Turtle Bulletin* http://www.boxturtlebulletin.com/
> *Fem2.0* http://www.fem2pt0.com/
> *Feminist Philosophers* http://feministphilosophers.wordpress.com/
> *Feministing* http://feministing.com/
> *Feministe* http://www.feministe.us/blog/
> *FemMedia* http://www.jmkeep.com/blog/
> *Finally, A Feminism 101 Blog* http://finallyfeminism101.wordpress.com/
> *Gay Patriot* http://www.gaypatriot.net/

Gay Politics http://www.gaypolitics.com/
GeekFeminism http://geekfeminism.org/
The Girl Who http://thegirlwho.net/
The Gist http://www.signorile.com/
Human Rights Campaign http://www.hrc.org/
I Blame the Patriarchy http://blog.iblamethepatriarchy.com/about-the-blog/
Jezebel http://jezebel.com/
Joe.My.God. http://joemygod.blogspot.com/
National Organization for Women http://www.now.org/
Our Bodies Our Blog http://www.ourbodiesourblog.org/
Queerty http://www.queerty.com/
Queers United http://www.queersunited.blogspot.com/
Racialicous http://www.racialicious.com/
Rex Wockner http://wockner.blogspot.com/
Towleroad http://www.towleroad.com/

Having identified these influencers, we then proceeded to then examine the networks they formed.

Interactor Link Analysis. We used the open-source IssueCrawler webtool (www.issuecrawler.net, see also Stansberry, 2011) to see what connections were made by these influencers. In interactor analysis, IssueCrawler took the influencer URLs with which we provided it (the "starting points") and captured their outlinks—the pages or sites to which the influencers were linking. It then removed all outlinks that were not to another starting point. In other words, it found how these networks of influencers linked to each other or not ("isolates").

From this analysis, *Jezebel* and the gay blog *Bilerico* were seen as both linking to and receiving links from feminist *and* gay blogs. In other words, they were switching power through communication between these networks. *Bitch* magazine received several links from our feminist blogs, and linked to a few gay male blogs, but did not receive any links from them. *Queers United* linked out to both gay and feminist blogs, but only received links from gay blogs. *Rex Wockner, The Gist*, and *AfterElton* were isolates, as were *Geek Feminism, JMKeep.com, Finally Feminism 101*, and *Feminism 2.0*.

Interestingly, when this crawl was run—and these crawls do not represent a longitudinal portrait—the major organizations of these two groups did not appear as switchers. We had thought that the Human Rights Campaign Fund and NOW might provide switching by virtue of being major entry points into these networks. However, interactor analysis showed HRC and NOW as more peripheral recipients of outlinks rather than themselves linking to many other influencers. Indeed, among our group of influencers, NOW linked only to HRC—who did not return the favor. This suggested that, online at least, more switching was taking place among individualistic social media outlets rather than national political organizations.

During this crawl, *Bilerico* had the most links within the network, driven by a 2011 article on Ken Mehlman, former chair of the Republican National Committee, who had come out as gay the year before and was now lobbying on behalf of marriage equality. Many bloggers and media pundits had been debating whether or not to "forgive" Mehlman for his affiliation with the traditionally anti-gay Republicans. An article in *Gawker* had pointed out that, while campaign manager for George W. Bush in the 2004 presidential election, the Republican Party worked to put out measures in 11 states making same-sex marriage illegal. Considered a conservative get-out-the-vote tactic, the laws passed in all states. The author suggested that, to punish him, "every gay man in the world (or at least America) should pledge that they will never sleep with Ken Mehlman" (Moylan, 2011, paragraph 7). However, *Out*, "*The Advocate*'s sister magazine praised Mehlman as a 'stealth activist' who was 'quietly instrumental' in passing marriage equality in New York," and, therefore, was worthy of inclusion in their annual list of 100 inspiring and motivating persons (Grindley, 2011, paragraph 3).

Traffic was also being generated at *Jezebel* due to a feature story on the need for gender-neutral student housing on college campuses to prevent homophobic violence (Baker, 2012). Gay students felt they would be safer rooming with women than straight men: "'I've always gotten along better with girls. Why couldn't they just let me live with a girl?'" (paragraph 3). Although directly illustrating an issue of gay-male connection with women, the article surprisingly did not discuss the implications for transgender students or if this could prevent problems in making women more vulnerable to campus violence. The stereotypical assumption seemed to be that gay men would not ever commit violence against women; yet, this issue was not allowing co-ed housing only if the occupants were of different sexual orientations. It was gender-neutral housing, which could allow heterosexual, opposite-sex couples. A Google search for the article headline found it reposted across over 50 unique locations, including blogs, news, aggregators, and Twitter and Facebook accounts.

Colink Analysis. Switcher nodes could be individual accounts or a particular media outlet, if not a medium in general (i.e., an individual or group of bloggers, a specific blog, but not blogging in general). For example, Facebook and Twitter emerged as central switchers between gay and feminist clusters in colink analysis.

Colink analysis looked at everything the influencers or starting points were link-ing to, then narrowed this down to links shared by at least two starting points. In other words, it identified things to which more than one of our influencers were linking. Although, at this level of analysis of link depth, this did not reveal the specific Facebook or Twitter accounts being linked to, it did point to social media in general as switching posts, with Facebook and Twitter being the respective leaders of each, as switching points.

Aside from social media, where were our blogs linking? The top 20 colinks were:

Add This, a social bookmarking and tools site addthis.com/
Advocate advocate.com
AfterEllen afterellen.com
Angry Black Bitch angryblackbitch.blogspot.com
Blabbeando blabbeando.blogspot.com
Comedy Central's political coverage site indecisionforever.com
The Daily Beast's blog by Andrew Sullivan andrewsullivan.thedailybeast.com
Feministe feministe.us
Feministing feministing.com
Gawker gawker.com
Gay and Lesbian Alliance Against Defamation glaad.org
Human Rights Campaign hrc.org
Huffington Post huffingtonpost.com
Joe. My. God. joemygod.blogspot.com
The LOGO cable network logotv.com
Ms. Magazine msmagazine.com
MSNBC msnbc.msn.com
Queerty queerty.com
Questioning Transphobia questioningtransphobia.com
Racialicious racialicious.com

Several of these were sites that had been mentioned by our focus groups conduct-ed at the same time. Note, however, that what we saw here was predominantly blogs and niche media, with the exception of MSNBC. We also saw two major LGBTQ organizations appear, GLAAD and HRC, and one major feminist pub-lication, *Ms.* However, when exploring linkages further, we found an increase in linking to mainstream media.

Snowball Analysis. Whereas colink analysis found sites to which two or more of our influencers were linking, snowball analysis started by finding, first, sites linked to by any one of our influencers, then found to where those sites linked. In other words, where were our influencer blogs linking, and to where were their link recipients subsequently linking?

Twitter dominated, with Facebook close behind. Facebook destinations ran the gamut of the platform, from events and groups to individual accounts, news accounts, and the accounts associated with the original blogs. Twitter links were similarly diverse.

Aside from those two social media platforms, the top 20 now included more mainstream news outlets and additional social media platforms. This suggested that online networks, as they expanded, did not reinforce themselves more strongly, but circled back to the mainstream media. The top twenty here were:

America Blog, a liberal news aggregator americablog.com
Babble, a parenting site babble.com
Babble's hosted blogs blogs.babble.com
BBC bbc.co.uk
CNN cnn.com
A *CNN* subdomain edition.cnn.com
Feministing feministing.com
Guardian guardian.co.uk
Human Rights Campaign hrc.org
Huffington Post huffingtonpost.com
Joe.My.God joemygod.blogspot.com
Just Jared justjared.com
Los Angeles Times latimes.com
MSNBC msnbc.msn.com
National Review nationalreview.com
Reuters' blogs blogs.reuters.com
Washington Post washingtonpost.com
Wikipedia en.wikipedia.org
What I Am I Said whattamisaid.com
YouTube youtube.com

As you see in the list above, our gay and feminist blogs were linking heavily to social media, but also to mainstream news sources. This phenomenon of bloggers functioning often as media pundits rather than original reporters or content creators has been noted in earlier research of mine (Scott, 2007, 2008).

Queer Networks and Entangled Platforms

Revisiting data, such as social media scraping and network analyses, brings to light the dynamic nature of networks. The actors themselves changed. Facebook was described previously as a network node or switch in 2012. One may ask, Is it still? Was it always? However, this would be something of a misleading perspective, because Facebook today is not the same Facebook it was in 2012. As Van Dijck (2013) and others have described, social media platforms are constantly changing. Their role in a network may change or be stable over time, but their ontology is not. Network theory captures the dynamism of changing relationships between actors and nodes, but it does not provide a useful tool for conceptualizing the changes in the qualitative essences or attributes of those actors or nodes. One needs to queer network theory, to bring in a feminist-queer understanding of actors as fluid, unstable, and constantly changing. Just as the socially constructed dimensions of the categories of biological sex, gender, and sexuality are constantly changing—for example, the addition of identities such as pansexual and gender-fluid not appearing in archival materials—so, too, are communication platforms. To refer to Karen Barad again, they are ongoing processes of constant (re) becoming.

Facebook, like other platforms, is constantly experimenting with new features and interface redesigns. Not only does it change over time, it simultaneously offers different experiences to different users. Facebook on an Apple laptop running an outdated version of the Mac OS operating system with a Chrome web browser on satellite internet in rural Kansas is not the same as the Facebook and Messenger mobile applications running on a Google Pixel 4 phone running Android OS with the Google Fi mesh network combining cellular carriers across Los Angeles.

Additionally, the cultural meanings of a technology or medium are also in flux. When, and for whom, did Facebook change from a fun social network to an obligatory communication chore, haunted by grandparents and trolls? When does technological cool dissipate? Moreover, platforms do not exist in isolation. They mutually influence and constitute one another; they are entangled, to use another term of Barad's. Facebook and Twitter changed when Instagram and Snapchat came along. Not merely in their functionality—for example, Facebook added a stories feature—but also in their very constitutive phenomena. For example,

Instagram was a photo-sharing platform, like Flickr. This was in contrast to the processes of social sharing and connections of Facebook. And yet, Instagram also became more of a life-broadcasting platform; it became more like Facebook, and Facebook (re)became less unique, less "Facebook." Twitter became less quotidian life-casting "microblogging" and more a network of conversations and reactions. Tumblr went from blogging to photo-sharing to porn-centric to porn-scrubbed to porn archives and ghostly clones. My young focus group participants in the previous chapter had been enthusiastic about Tumblr as a communication tool in 2012. However, a few years later, a student told me they would be embarrassed if anyone saw Tumblr on their phone because, by that time, many associated it with sharing adult content, which it would ban in December 2018. At this time, its traffic had already been in decline, and this decision led many users who posted or supported the right to post pornographic, erotic, and sex-related content, especially queers and artists, to abandon the platform. I and other instructors have continued to use the platform in course assignments, and it remains ranked seventh in social media platforms worldwide, but its global traffic has declined by almost half since July of 2018 (Clement, 2019).

The tools used to measure social media and networks can change as well. In May of 2014, Salesforce released Social Studio, which took Radian6 and combined it with publishing tool Buddy Media (Kanaracus, 2014). A mere six months later, they unveiled the "next generation" of Social Studio, featuring "a completely re-built social listening engine that will unlock the power of Radian6 to a broader audience than ever before" (Ball, 2014, "Integrated Listening" section, paragraph 1). In the available online release notes from Salesforce, between January 2018 and August 2019, nine releases of Social Studio included over 70 new features significant (or marketable) enough to promote, ranging from "Engage with Facebook Brand Mentions" to "Keep Employee Data Private in Social Studio" ("Release Notes," 2019). This only suggests the amount of changes to programming and algorithms that occurred between 2012 and 2019.

When examining my early screenshots of Radian6, notes, and memories, what I noticed was that many aspects of the interface changed for searching, analysis, and visualization of results. Meanwhile, sources of data—such as open public comments sections and discussion forums—had been increasingly shut down or limited by many media sources and individuals. IssueCrawler had changed as well. Although its functionality and interface were largely the same, clicking some options returned blank screens, caused browsers to freeze, or simply did not offer results, making some direct comparisons impossible. To return to Barad, not only were the process of measurement and phenomena being measured constantly changing, they were also entangled in each other's mutual, ongoing processes of (re)becoming.

Such changes are not meant to invalidate data from such tools, but I describe them here as an important caveat to the authority often bestowed upon quantitative information and automated tools. "Big data," although the subject of much critique, also continues to generate a great deal of scholarly excitement and research funding. Thus, instability and, therefore, interpretation, are present in this chapter, just as they were in discussing historic artifacts from South Carolina. I foreground this perspective as a jab at queering the objective authority of big data tools and network analyses.

Seven Years Later

In "The Transformative Power of Network Dynamics: A Research Agenda," Clegg et al. (2016) cite critiques of organizational studies that treat networks as fixed and stable, arguing instead:

> It is only by turning our attention to the processes that account for the appearance and disappearance of ties and the larger networks in which they are embedded that we can begin to understand how collective action is organized and with what consequences. (p. 286)

Reflecting their call for a more dynamic and transformative approach to examining networks, I now present a revisitation to the social media snapshot of gay men and feminist women. Here, I have attempted to replicate the previous examination seven years later, in 2019. This was intended to foreground the dynamic nature of online networks. This was also intended to support Coward's critique of by providing a "thicker, more culturally attuned" (2018, p. 458) network description through, not only examining contiguous cultures and communities, but also how they changed over time. In other words, the description of these networks was here thickened by adding a context of temporality.[4]

Minimal Linkages

In 2019, when harvesting a month of social media conversations that used the same gay-related and feminist-related keywords we had used in 2012, each brought back large amounts of results. However, conversation posts containing both groups were comparatively rare. It was impossible to say, given the changes in the scraping software, whether any of the conversations—conversations speaking of gays, feminists, or both—were of greater or lesser number than in 2012. However, the conversations which did link the two groups made up a vastly smaller proportion that either of the conversations discussing them separately. As a broad generalization, then, social media discussions from both years remained similar to those of historiographic discourses discussed at the beginning of this book, the archival evidence from women's and LGBTQ groups in South Carolina, and the mutual representations of feminist women and gay men in theory and cinema, respectively, as previous chapters have explored. That is, very limited. Despite the readily apparent commonalities, as discussed in the focus groups, social media conversations had continued to rarely put the two groups together.

However, the association still existed, even if in only a few conversations a day. Rather than treat these conversations as outliers, perhaps they could be thought of as seeds to be nurtured or opportunities to be explored. Indeed, the activist dimension of this book has been, not only to investigate what has been said and is being said regarding the two social movements, but, by virtue of this investigation across its multiple forms, to enact a forced juxtaposition of the two: a discursive formation, an agential cut. Rather than dismiss a few references in books, archives, or social media posts, I have been underlining those references, turning up the high-contrast filter, in order to think about their potential: potential realized, as well as potential lost.

Sentimental Themes

Sentiment analysis is a rough and unreliable tool. Moreover, the sentiment analysis function in the data scraping software had also changed significantly. If one made repeated measurements with a flawed tool, at least there was the possibility of consistency. However, if the tool is flawed and changes itself, it makes the results largely meaningless. For example, the categories of "somewhat negative" and "somewhat positive" were no longer options, replaced by "neutral" and "mixed."

Therefore, in revisiting sentiment analysis, I began with the categories returned and examined each, either the entire category or using systematic random sampling when the results were large. I also searched for specific keywords related to the 2012 themes among all posts. In this way, I aimed to see which of the 2012 themes were still present, and if there were new ones. For the most part, the themes had persisted, although with some new nuances. The persistence of these themes, listed below, provided a stronger suggestion that they offered understandings of the ways these two social movements were associated, and opportunities for building upon useful associations or trying to challenge negative ones.

Victims of Common Oppressors. Opening a discussion thread titled, "Which political ideology has the most dorks/losers/neckbeards in it?" BeuclairDrunk wrote, "Alt Righters are similar to Libertarians as in most of them don't have a life outside of social media so they think the biggest threat facing the planet are purple haired feminists and social justice warriors putting gay characters into video games." Additional examples illustrate this theme:

Dragonlady:	I have never understood how ANY woman could vote Republican, or gays or blacks for that matter. How can you vote for a party that doesn't want women to have equal rights?
Aponi:	Yea I think so then why do so many conservatives want to kill living people like gays, dems, liberals, progressives, atheists, muslims, feminists ....? Anynameyouwish: It's a terrible combination of ignorance and evil. Both of which Republicans have an abundance of.
CBLOOMFIELDVT:	Anti-SJW politics is just far-right social conservative boomer politics rebranded for millennials and younger. If you listen to a Rush Limbaugh rant about feminists and gays from the 90's, it's identical to current anti-SJW politics with just a couple jargon substitutions.

Co-conspirators. This theme persisted in the new political context.

PMS SHOCKER:	There are so many levels of Trump Derangement Syndrome that are afflicting the left leaning, progressive, PC faggots, lesbian feminist bull dykes, slow thinkers, criminals and minorities that think they are 'Woke'- Truth be told your fucking stupid and uneducated full of hate
WORKINDAWG:	Dems are a loose confederation of groups who have nothing in common and are often opposed. They can't survive in their current form. Give to the blacks, upset the gays. Help labor (men) upset the feminists. It can't work.

Disliked. Hate is alive.

Omega Hunter:	Yes they should have the rights of everyone else in a free society. However feminism is a cancerous plague on our society and gays as a class have a higher standard of living then your average American so I would hardly call them "marginalized."
Ratko_Falco:	no one is going to listen to gay men (unless they fake a hate crime) and the women will just go goo goo muh feminism so islam.

Disliked Subsets. Sonnysunshine described groups, traditionally within the left moving to the right, tweeting, "People have been brainwashed into thinking they are guilty and need to kiss ass. But there has been a growing (and just) backlash to this. I've seeing more women, minorities and even gays speaking against this crap." Meanwhile, FROSTBITE positioned herself within and among numerous identity categories: "I don't have a preference over cishet BM vs WM vs MoC as a bi/ace nb femme. Both actively attempt to erase my existence or kill me so it's a no win. I would have to find a queer/trans/nb person to be with or a cishet man that is hella left & in tune with black feminism/womanism"

Components of Broader Social Change, Markers. Dave Fiorazo addressed changing definitions of marriage in his blog post:

> In order to eliminate natural marriage in society, it must first be rendered mean-ingless. How could that happen? You might say 'gays and lesbians pushing same-sex marriage for several decades', and you'd only be partially right. Many factors lead to marriage being redefined. ... The Feminist movement and cry for wom-en's liberation and equality sounded good in its early stages, but it is no longer about equal pay or equal rights. It has become a liberal, anti-family, socialist movement detrimental to God-ordained, natural marriage and healthy families.

Meanwhile, BEYONDTHEBILLBOARD critiqued the recently released film *Isn't It Romantic?* from a civil rights perspective, noting that it "tries to deliver a message to female audiences by citing the failures of other films in the genre and how they treat women and gay men. What *Isn't It Romantic?* doesn't acknowledge is how the genre treats people of colour, something this film doesn't correct."

Conflicts. BIGGIRLPANTS2 put feminists in competition with gay men, tweet-ing that heterosexual men were being attacked. "They're being emasculated by the feminists and left. Gay men have come a long way (♥ This fact) and are now more embraced than a masculine, heterosexual man when it comes to the dems. Am I right?!' "

Starletka quoted Shinshini, continuing the debate around pornography in relation to the two groups, writing, "Porn is not oppressing woman, men with a lack of education and a socially conservative society does. Gay porn has the same aggressive narrative, yet you can hardly claim watching gay porn makes me regard other gay men as sex objects." Here one could see the debates around pornography, discussed in a previous chapter, revisited. Although porn was not positioned as causing women's oppression, it still had an "aggressive narrative," whether gay or straight. However, porn by and for women was not mentioned, suggesting the topic remained a conflictual separation between feminist women and gay men.

Fading Influencers and Sustained Switchers: Where Are They Now?

My next goal was to determine the status of our previously identified influencers. I chose to do this, rather than identify new influencers, for two reasons. One was that the assessment tools would be inevitably inconsistent from those used previously. Another was, What had become of previous influencers? Much analysis of social media is anchored in the present; instead I chose to examine how influence lasts. Here, then, is our original pool of influencer blogs, with current status updates:

American Blog Gay http://gay.americablog.com/
The LGBTQ-tagged posts from the progressive news and information site had remained very active.
AfterElton http://www.afterelton.com/
The gay culture blog had been owned by the LGBTQ-centric cable television channel Logo since 2006. In 2013, it renamed itself as *The Backlot*, which then merged with Logo's *NewNowNext* website in 2015.
The Bilerico Project http://www.bilerico.com/
The URL now redirected to the Commentary section of LGBTQ Nation, an active news and politics website owned by Q.Digital, an employee owned media company in San Francisco.
Bitch Magazine http://bitchmagazine.org/blogs
It had expanded into the *Bitch Media* website.
Box Turtle Bulletin http://www.boxturtlebulletin.com/
Its last post had been from December 2016.
Fem2.0 http://www.fem2pt0.com/
Its most recent post had been from November 2016.
FemMedia http://www.jmkeep.com/blog/
The original link no longer worked, and the associated webpage and alternate blog now focused on fantasy-related fiction. The most recent post had been from January 2017.
Feminist Philosophers http://feministphilosophers.wordpress.com/
It had been closed as of May 2019 but available as an archive.
Feministe http://www.feministe.us/blog/
The blog was no longer online, but the associated Twitter account was still active.
Feministing http://feministing.com/

It was still active, but was posting infrequently. The most recent posts had been from four, five, and six months previous.

Finally, A Feminism 101 Blog http://finallyfeminism101.wordpress.com/
Its most recent post had been from June 2014.

Gay Patriot http://www.gaypatriot.net/
"The internet home for American gay conservatives" was still active.

Gay Politics http://www.gaypolitics.com/
This website was now a small collection of heterosexual articles and ads on dating and sex tips.

GeekFeminism http://geekfeminism.org/
It had been closed as of February 2018 but was available as an archive.

The Girl Who http://thegirlwho.net/
It had no posts since April 2014.

The Gist http://www.signorile.com/
It was still active, but posts were now summary descriptions of the long-time author and activist's program on SiriusXM satellite radio.

Human Rights Campaign http://www.hrc.org/
Still active.

I Blame the Patriarchy http://blog.iblamethepatriarchy.com/about-the-blog/
It had information but no posts. The Home page for the blog led to a blank page with only this text: "May 3, 2006 Greetings, blamers. Naturally I have fucked up the upgrade. The database is in limbo, or possibly has moved straight on down to Hell. Please stand by." The author's linked Twitter account had been still active, but covering a variety of topics, and was not exclusively focused on feminist concerns.

Jezebel http://jezebel.com/
It was active and had become a website with multiple sections of content. Significantly, *Jezebel* had been from its beginnings part of a media company, Gawker, and was now owned by Univision.

Joe.My.God. http://joemygod.blogspot.com/
It was still active, although the blog had moved in 2015 to a new address at https://www.joemygod.com/

National Organization for Women http://www.now.org/
Still active.

Our Bodies Our Blog http://www.ourbodiesourblog.org/
Still active.

Racialicous http://www.racialicious.com/

Its blog was no longer at this address, having moved to Tumblr. However, there had been no posts there since October 2016. The associated Twitter account had been active, although linked to the inactive blog address. The associated Facebook page had no posts since January 2018. However, multiple authors had been posting with Racialicious as a tag at *Jezebel*.

Rex Wockner http://wockner.blogspot.com/

After a July 2013 post, long-time gay journalist Wockner had not posted at this blog until March 2019, when he posted his professional biography. The following month, he had posted an update to "LGBT Antidiscrimination Laws in U.S. States and Territories," and, in June 2019, had updated the blog's survey of marriage equality around the world, although it was not clear whether Wockner or his assistants credited on the post had done the update. So, although not inactive, it was not being frequently updated or posting entirely new content. Wockner, however, remained active on Twitter.

Towleroad http://www.towleroad.com/

Still very active.

Queers United http://www.queersunited.blogspot.com/

The top post, from March 2011, could be glimpsed before the site redirected automatically to a 2019 commercial phishing page.

Queerty http://www.queerty.com/

Very active across multiple platforms, they were also owned by Q.Digital.

Interactor Link Analyses: 2019

With so few sites still active, it would seem that there would be few links among these mostly former influencers. However, because many were still online, if not active, their links still existed. A skeleton of the network was still there, about a tenth of the links among the blogs found in 2012. However, many of these were links to inactive or removed sites, and likely little traffic was traveling through the links of the inactive blog archives. The active blogs were only slightly more linked to than the inactive blogs. The most linked-to node in the network was now an organization, the Human Rights Campaign. NOW, however, had not increased, with relatively few links.

As noted, many of the blogs had changed addresses or moved their activity to other platforms. This is not to say that the authors of these social media outlets were no longer having influence. It did, however, point to the ephemerality of online networks and the relatively stability of organizations. While social media and individual influencers may have possessed immediacy and agility that organizations lacked, their status was dynamic as well, waxing and waning for various reasons. An organization was more likely to hire a replacement Executive Director than an independent blogger was likely to replace themselves.

Colink Analysis: 2019

Among the original network influencers, a few were still active in 2019. Where to, then, were they linking? The list was shorter, given the decreased activity of the network. Moreover, it no longer included any members of the original network or mainstream media. However, one of the feminist blogs mentioned in the 2012 focus groups, *Autostraddle*, was now present. In fact, the only site consistent between the two crawls was <u>*Blabbeando*</u>, a gay blog that had last posted in April 2016. Twitter was there, which had been seen in the 2012 snowball analysis, but Facebook was not. The complete list was:

Apple, apple.com

The *Audre Lorde Project* remains an active LGBTQ community organizing center in New York City, alp.org

Autostraddle autostraddle.com

Blabbeando blabbeando.blogspot.com

blogACTIVE, "direct action tools from the nation's capital," was no longer online blogactive.com

Gay Politics gaypolitics.com

Good As You, an active LGBTQ blog, goodasyou.org

Join the Impact, an LBGTQ online activism blog jointheimpact.com

No On Proposition 8, an LGBTQ political action blog whose URL has since been populated with home décor and cooking articles noonprop8.com

LGB *Servicemembers Legal Defense Network*, sldn.org, now had merged with Modern Military Association of America at https://modernmilitary.org/

Twitter twitter.com

Unite the Fight, an active LGBTQ politics blog, unitethefight.blogspot.com

Waking Up Now, a leftist political blog that had last posted in September 2017, and has since been removed, wakingupnow.com

Snowball Analysis: 2019

When the search was expanded to snowball analysis, an exact ranking of actors could not be retrieved from IssueCrawler. However, the tool did produce a network visualization, which was compared to the 2012 visualizations.

Again, Twitter dominated by far, and the mix included other platforms, such as YouTube and Wikipedia. Mainstream media were also present, such as CNN, the *National Review*, and the *Washington Post*. However, none of the original network influencers appeared. What was new, however, were several conservative news and opinion sources: *FoxNews.com, MichelleMaklin.com, PajamasMedia. com, DrudgeReport.com, PJMedia.com, Breitbart.com*, and others. This further indicated the dynamic transformations of the original network. A group of influential gay and feminist bloggers, and their two leading national organizations, had connected to networks that evolved and changed such that, in a mere seven years, the vestiges that remained took one to several of the very sites representing the ideologies of their common oppressors.

This does not mean that online networks of gay men and feminist women did not continue to operate in support of their respective social movements, and provide switching points between their networks. *Jezebel*, for example, still evidenced that role. What this chapter does suggest, however, is that the dynamism of social media and online networks has both strengths and weaknesses. It can be marshaled to link networks, communicate power, channel energy, and more. However, this dynamism is also ephemeral: networks move, change, and reconfigure. Influencers rise and fall. Actors come and go. While this is a strength in the sense of adaptability and responsiveness, it raises issues with regards to stability and permanence.

Conclusion

In this chapter, we have seen that despite many advances for LGBTQ persons and women in the United States, the minimal linkage of the two social movements has remained. When they are discussed in social media, just as when they were mentioning each other in their histories with which this book began, it was infrequent and limited. However, when they were posted about together, a variety of themes and ideas and appeared. The associations both reflected the early themes of commonality, competition, and contributions, but also expanded upon them in new and intriguing ways. As with the focus group discussions, there was rich material to build upon when examining how people think about gay men and feminist women with regards to each other. Indeed, we have also seen how they were included in larger discussions of identity politics, electorates, and social changes, suggesting the potential for amplifying these connections to larger coalitions. New collaborations could be formed, and new strategies could be developed by resonating strategies and tactics based on these associations.

Not that they were all positive. Conceptual associations are like the links in a network in that varying kinds of sentiment can flow through them. Content matters. They can be populated by actors with different ideologies and agendas. A switcher can connect, but the intention of that connection can vary widely. Therefore, the negative associations are of use as well, as tools to identify resistance and blockages to these social movements. They can potentially help us ascertain the arguments, logics, and associations used to justify not supporting movements for social justice and equality. This nuanced information can be of vital importance and has more potential for use than just dismissing them as forces of hate.

This research has demonstrated that feminist women and gay men had, if not a stronger association in both popular thinking and historic practice than the received view would suggest, more kinds of associations. The question for these and other social movements then becomes, what impedes and what accelerates collaboration? I argue that a discursive theorization is useful to surpass impediments based on essentialist assumptions, such as "gay men *are* inherently sexist, apolitical, and feminine; feminist women *are* essentially homophobic, humorless, and masculine." A network conceptualization reminds us that *anything* can travel through a link: connections can be positive *or* negative. Connections can be collaborative *or* competitive. Indeed, what may be more productive for social movements is, not to determine the essential truth of whether or not they essentially *are* allies or enemies, but to identify how they are discursively linked (or not). Start with the *perception* of connection then, using switchers, reframe that connection into something that can achieve the desired social goals. Coalition, from a network perspective, is not about identifying your allies. It is about networking with your collaborators. Ultimately, social acceptance comes, not when dominant society recognizes you as a member or friend, but when it connects to marginal groups as possessing the same goals and ideals. And, if not, Castells and Foucault both argue for the possibility of change: the networks must be reprogrammed with new goals, and discourses must reconfigure into new forms of power-knowledge. However, this cannot be done until one links into the network. The challenge then becomes how to facilitate, argue for, and demonstrate that linkage.

For example, feminist women and gay men can be conceived of as stable identities both struggling for their piece of the equality pie. Maybe these separate pieces come together to form a coalition, a larger piece with more political clout. However, it could be also framed differently: Feminism is the genesis of LGBT movements (via the separation of biological sex and gendered actions) and thereby a theoretical foundation which could unite not only gays and lesbians, but also all women, and transgendered persons, and other sex, gender, and filial minorities, including like-minded heterosexual men. All could be united under the conceptual umbrella of sexism, the critique of which includes all sexed, gendered, and romantic behaviors, structures, and relationships.

Notes

1. I acknowledge the false dualism of online/offline, and that the spaces of corporeal and mediated existence are not separate but ongoing, fluid, and entangled processes of being.
2. Concepts from the field of Computer-Mediated Communication soften this binary logic somewhat. One can be "in" a network to degrees: through weak or inactivated, latent ties. For example, I am in the network of an email listserv but never read its messages. I am networked to the neighbors in my building, but many of them I have never met. Particularly with the networks I am examining, I would amend this binary logic of included/excluded to be extremely dynamic and fuzzy.
3. We were aware of complications that Search Engine Optimization and other promotional tactics (e.g., blog rolls, creating fake blogs to comment on personal content and use of advisements to connect blogs) had in the perception of influencers online. Furthermore, we acknowledged that social media monitoring, or listening, was not uniform in method or even access in professional or scholarly environments. There was, especially at the time, a lack of precedent for an ideal descriptive data set surrounding the monitoring of phenomena online.
4. The section is not intended as a longitudinal comparison. In fact, I have removed specific numbers and quantities from the previous section that were used when it was originally presented at a conference. Although useful at the time, here I find it misleading. Inevitably, listing quantities from two different years would invite perception of claims regarding increases and decreases, and that is not what I am arguing here.

References

"Release Notes" (2019). Salesforce. Retrieved from https://help.salesforce.com/articleView?id=mc_rn_april_2018_social_studio_web.htm&type=5

Anttiroiko, A. V. (2015). Castells' network concept and its connections to social, economic and political network analyses. *Journal of Social Structure, 16*(11), 208–219.

Baker, K. J. M. (2012, May 9). The red state fight for co-ed housing on campus. http://jezebel.com/5904173/the-red-state-fight-for-gender+neutral-housing-on-campus

Ball. (2014, Nov. 19). Salesforce unveils the next generation of Social Studio. *Salesforce.com*. Retrieved from https://www.salesforce.com/blog/2014/11/salesforce-unveils-the-next-genera-tion-of-social-studio.html

Basich, T. (2010). Social media measurement and analysis. Available from http://www.radian6.com/blog/2010/03/social-media-measurement-analysis/

Bell, L. (2011). The future of analytics. Available from http://www.radian6.com/blog/2011/08/the-future-of-analytics/

Castells, M. (1983). *The city and the grassroots: A cross-cultural theory of urban social movements.* Berkeley: University of California Press.

Castells, M. (2002). *The Internet galaxy: Reflections on the Internet, business, and society.* Oxford, UK: Oxford University Press on Demand.

Castells, M. (2004). *The network society: A cross-cultural perspective.* Cheltenham, UK: Edward Elgar.

Castells, M. (2009). *Communication power.* Oxford, UK: Oxford University Press.

Castells, M. (2011a). *The rise of the network society.* Hoboken, NJ: John Wiley & Sons.

Castells, M. (2011b). A network theory of power. *International Journal of Communication, 5,* 15.

Castells, M. (2015). *Networks of outrage and hope: Social movements in the Internet age.* Hoboken, NJ: John Wiley & Sons.

Castells, M., Monge, P., & Contractor, N. (2011). Prologue to the special section | Network multi-dimensionality in the digital age. *International Journal of Communication, 5,* 6.

Clegg, S., Josserand, E., Mehra, A., & Pitsis, T. S. (2016). The transformative power of network dynamics: A research agenda. *Organization Studies, 37*(3), 277–291.

Clement, J. (2019, Aug. 20). Tumblr—statistics & facts. Statista. Retrieved from https://www.statista.com/topics/2463/tumblr/

Coward, M. (2018). Against network thinking: A critique of pathological sovereignty. *European Journal of International Relations, 24*(2), 440–463.

Foucault, M. (1980). *Power/knowledge: Selected interviews and other writings, 1972–1977.* New York: Pantheon.

Foucault, M. (1990). *The history of sexuality Volume One An introduction.* New York: Random House.

Foucault, M. (2001). *Power.* New York: The New Press.

Fuchs, C. (2012). Some reflections on Manuel Castells' book "Networks of Outrage and Hope. Social Movements in the Internet Age." *tripleC: Communication, Capitalism & Critique. Open Access Journal for a Global Sustainable Information Society, 10*(2), 775–797.

Gillian, K. (Producer). (n.d., May 9, 2012) Exploring hyperlink networks with Issue Crawler: Methodological issues. PowerPoint presentation deck. Retrieved from http://www.socialsciences.manchester.ac.uk/ricc/projects/MDMN/workshop/documents/gillan-is-sue-crawler.ppt

Grindley, L. (2011, Nov. 5). Forgiven? Picks Ken Mehlman among 100 who inspire. *The Advocate.* Retrieved from https://www.advocate.com/news/daily-news/2011/11/05/forgiven-out-picks-ken-mehlman-among-100-who-inspire

Hillis, K., Paasonen, S., & Petit, M. (Eds.). (2015). *Networked affect.* Cambridge, MA: The MIT Press.

Kanaracus, C. (2014, May 6). Salesforce unveils SocialStudio, which combines Radian6 and Buddy Media. *ComputerWorld.* Retrieved from https://www.computerworld.com/article/2489068/salesforce-unveils-social-studio--which-combines-radian6-and-buddy-media.html

Latour, B. (1996). On actor-network theory: A few clarifications. *Soziale Welt, 47*, 369–381.

Manovich, L. (2001). *The language of new media.* Cambridge, MA: The MIT press.

Moylan, B. (2011, Nov. 4). Don't forgive gay traitor Ken Mehlman. *Gawker.* Retrieved from https://gawker.com/5856577/dont-forgive-gay-traitor-ken-mehlman

Newton, C. (2009, May 9). On automated sentiment analysis. http://www.radian6.com/blog/2009/12/on-automated-sentiment-analysis/

Papacharissi, Z. (2015). *Affective publics: Sentiment, technology, and politics.* Oxford, UK: Oxford University Press.

Rasmussen, R. (2009, May 9). Making social media measurement meaningful. Zocalo Group. Retrieved April 15, 2020 through Wayback Machine at https://web.archive.org/web/20110702230627/http://www.zocalogroup.com/2009/07/making-social-media-measurement-meaningful.html

Rubenstein, P. (2011). Why (and how) the growth of social media has created opportunities for qualitative research in organizational development. *The Industrial-Organizational Psychologist, 49*(2), 19–26.

Scott, D. T. (2007). Pundits in muckrakers' clothing: political blogs and the 2004 US presidential election. In M. Tremayne (Ed.), *Blogging, citizenship, and the future of media* (pp. 39–57). New York: Routledge.

Scott, D. T. (2008). Tempests of the blogosphere: Presidential campaign stories that failed to ignite mainstream media. In M. Boler (Ed.), *Digital media and democracy: Tactics in hard times* (pp. 271–300). Cambridge, MA: The MIT Press.

Siapera, E. (2017). Network society: Networks, media, and effects. *The International Encyclopedia of Media Effects*, 1–12.

Solis, B. (2012). *The rise of digital influence: A "how-to" guide for businesses.* Altimeter Group.

Stansberry, K. (2011). Mapping mommy bloggers: Using online social network analysis to study publics. *PRism, 8*(2). Retrieved from http://www.prismjournal.org/fileadmin/8_2/Stansberry.pdf

Szulc, L. (2015). The hyperlinked identities of LGBTQ websites: Towards a qualitative hyperlink analysis. Presentation to the International Communication Association, San Juan, Puerto Rico.

Van Dijck, J. (2013). *The culture of connectivity: A critical history of social media.* Oxford, UK: Oxford University Press.

Conclusion: Creative Destruction

In an earlier chapter, I mentioned Tim Edwards' *Erotics & Politics: Gay Male Sexuality, Masculinity and Feminism* (1994). One of the ways in which Edwards' feminism resonated with me was in his reflexivity, incorporating subjective asides that positioned himself as a writer and challenged the masculinist mode of scholarly objectivity. The last such section, which ends his book, is particularly poignant:

> During the writing of this book, I have felt increasingly torn: torn between seeing gay men as profoundly oppressed yet equally creative opposers, victims and survivors of (post)modern society; and seeing gay men as more like men than straight men themselves, swilling around, literally sometimes, in undiluted misogyny. Yet it is a misogyny and full of self-loathing, long-lost yearnings and groveling, not some swaggering, patriarchal trip over women. I suspect some gay men will loathe this book for dragging up all those uncomfortable issues they hoped they had buried years ago and no doubt some women will groan that it doesn't go nearly far enough. The frustration and the grief lie in listening to these shouting voices who just cannot or will not listen. It's high time they started. (p. 158)

On one hand, the process of writing this book has been my act of listening to and sharing the voices of feminist women and gay men. It has been a response to

Ward's (2000) call for conducting empirical research on gay men's involvement in, and attitudes about, feminism.

However, as suggested in the last two chapters, much has changed over the eight years I have been working on this project. As I write this now, the current US President, Donald J. Trump, is, by his own words, a sexual predator. He is the subject of numerous lawsuits by women and, if actions are character, a male chauvinist pig. Surely, there have been worse representatives of patriarchy in our nation's highest office, but has there been one whose sexism, racism, ableism, transphobia, infantile narcissism, and outright cruelty were not only clearly evident during the campaign, but also perhaps components of his success? Even if one acknowledges that he lost the popular vote, and that he clearly had illegal campaign help, it does not make his success any less stunning. The fact that he advanced past the initial primaries, where he stalled out previously, let alone became President, is mind-boggling.

My academic "mother," the feminist scholar Sarah Banet-Weiser, describes the current moment as one of popular feminism and popular misogyny (2018). Feminism has been reclaimed and touted boldly in popular culture. My students no longer treat "feminism" like a dirty word. At the same time, explicit sexism and misogyny have become flagrant and acceptable in a way I could never have imagined. In the nomination hearings for US Supreme Court Justice Brett Kavanaugh, the Clarence Thomas hearings repeated themselves, and, in some ways, were even worse.

If we are living in a time of popular feminism, it is also a time of popular gays. I am writing this a month after the fiftieth anniversary of the Stonewall riots. I am legally married to a man. My students often seem to be generally excited about having an out, gay professor, and my Southern conservative university has supported me with tenure and housing, with my husband, as Faculty in Residence. RuPaul is ubiquitous. Musicians and actors don't come out; they are out to begin with, and it seems to garner less and less notice. There is a gay man running for the Democratic nomination for President.

However, I am a white, cisgender man. While the Trump administration insults me, to mention just one example, with lack of recognition of LGBTQ Pride Month, I am nowhere near as directly attacked as women and transgendered persons have been. While this may not be a moment of popular gay bashing, at least in the United States, it remains a moment of popular misogyny and popular racism. Perhaps nowhere is this contradiction more evident than in the success of films such as *Tangerine* and Academy-Award winner *Moonlight*, which tell stories of queers of color in the generation after *Chocolate Babies*. But their flickering, as they stream from laptops, mobile devices, and giant wall screens, grows cold against the continued murders of transwomen of color.

Before academia, I was actively working as a fiction writer. Having gone to art school from 1987–1991, my understanding of creative work was as a political act. This was not only because of the contemporary AIDS crisis and government attacks on funding for queer artists, but also my studying of and exposure to feminist art and art theory. My writing about gender and sexuality was creative expression, but also intended as a contribution to and intervention in debates around masculinity, sexuality, gay identity, and queer politics.

In the 1990s, I attended several conferences for LGBTQ writers. At one, I took a break from the often feisty, debate-charged panel discussions to take a lakeside stroll with two other writers, also gay men in their twenties. We were bantering and gossiping in what one of RuPaul's drag queens might refer to as a kiki. One writer was Dale Peck, who was receiving acclaim for his novel *Martin and John*. The other writer, unfortunately, I cannot remember. Peck made a rather cutting remark, and the other writer told him, "If you were nicer, you might have a boyfriend." To which Peck replied, "If you weren't so nice, you might have a career."

In my focus groups from 2012, described in a previous chapter, recall how one woman predicted that the US would see a gay male president before a female president. At the time I, and, the group, were dubious. As I write this now, a gay man, Pete Buttigieg, mayor of South Bend, Indiana, is running for the 2020 Democratic presidential nomination, rising from self-described "total obscurity" to becoming a "star" (McAfee, Gomez, Coburn, & Rivas, 2019, paragraph 1).

In an essay critical of Buttigieg, Peck, who has since established himself as a somewhat notorious literary critic—his 2005 nonfiction collection is titled *Hatchet Jobs*—writes that he wants to tell Buttigieg

> to take a good hard look at his world, at his experiences and his view of the public good as somehow synonymous with his own success, and I want him to reject it. I want to do this not because I have any particular desire to hurt his feelings, but because I made a similar journey, or at least started out from a similar place, and I was lucky enough to realize (thank you, feminism; thank you, ACT UP) that the only place that path leads is a gay parody of heteronormative bourgeois domesticity. (Peck, 2019, ¶10)

Although I am, at the time of writing, indifferent to Buttigieg—perhaps uninspired by would be more accurate—I was heartened to see a one-time peer such as Peck cite feminism and ACT UP among their formative influences. Peck's political critique is that "Mary Pete [a gay version of Uncle Tom] is a neoliberal and a Jeffersonian meritocrat, which is to say he's just another unrepentant or at least unexamined beneficiary of white male privilege" (paragraph 7).

However, Peck marries this with a gay critique. As a gay man, Peck distrusts Buttigieg because Buttigieg is a gay man who came out late in life. In his essay, Peck trashes him in the manner of a private conversation between gay men:

> He's been out for, what, all of four years, and if I understand the narrative, he married the first guy he dated. And we all know what happens when gay people don't get a real adolescence because they spent theirs in the closet: they go through it after they come out. And because they're adults with their own incomes and no parents to rein them in they do it on steroids (often literally). … Mary Pete was never a teenager. But you can't run away from that forever. Either it comes out or it eats you up inside. It can be fun, it can be messy, it can be tragic, it can be progenitive, transformative, ecstatic, or banal, but the last thing I want in the White House is a gay man staring down 40 who suddenly realizes he didn't get to have all the fun his straight peers did when they were teenagers. I'm not saying I don't want him to shave his chest or do Molly or try being the lucky Pierre (the timing's trickier than it looks, but it can be fun when you work it out). These are rites of passage for a lot of gay men, and it fuels many aspects of gay culture. But like I said, I don't want it in the White House. I want a man whose mind is on his job, not what could have been—or what he thinks he can still get away with. (paragraph 13)

Peck's essay immediately drew fire, including accusations of homophobic language, and *The New Republic* quickly removed it from its website "in response to criticism of the piece's inappropriate and invasive content" (The New Republic, 2019, paragraph 1).

How can coalitions form when gay men are busy attacking each other for their own version of gayness? I am reminded at this moment of the struggles over lesbians within the mainstream feminist movement. Divide and conquer.

The Incitement to Network: Depathologizing Separatism

A presumption of this book has been the model of individuals with a common identity forming groups to achieve political power, and then collaborating with groups sharing similar goals to form coalitions of greater power. To amend

Foucault, one could call this widespread perception an "incitement to network." But, as recent events have shown, networking can bring together coalitions of any political stripe or ideological practice. As discussed in the last chapter, the content of a network matters.

However, there has been an alternate tactic, one pathologized in the data throughout this project. The process by which individuals, who belong to a disenfranchised and marginalized social group, withdraw from society, then reform into new collectives, with the intent to change the social order, is called separatism. One of the most demonized such groups, typically painted as monstrous, angry, and destructive, has been lesbian separatists. Numerous sources in this project have cited feminist and lesbian separatism as problems that prevented gay men from working with feminist women.

Generally speaking, lesbian separatists are not seen as a success story of social progress, unlike Foucaultian homosexuals. Even among progressives, they are typically suggested as a misdirected extreme, a dead end to be avoided in future social movements. They did not "succeed" in the sense of establishing a plethora of powerful separatist communities, and arguments have been made that the "lavender menace" even contributed to certain defeats in the women's movement, such as the Equal Rights Amendment.

I wish, however, to argue for the success of lesbian separatists. Virginia Woolf famously argues for the importance of solitude in her extended essay, *A Room of One's Own* (2004). Although Woolf is speaking of the importance of the need for privacy, workspace, and freedom from distraction in order to facilitate women's creation of great literature, she nevertheless articulates one example of a broader equation of solitude and equality. Growth—be it of literary skills, personal subjectivity, or a collective movement—needs a nurturing environment, which often necessitates distancing from factors that hinder such growth. Although Woolf's analysis of the difficulty of women writing literature also includes financial dependence, social discouragements, and other factors, it is solitude that titles her famous essay. It is, moreover, a singular solitude.

Lesbians did not invent separatism, but drew on precedents of female separatism as a feminist strategy dating back into the nineteenth century (Freedman, 2006). Perhaps the most famous statement of lesbian separatism is the collective Radicalesbians' essay of 1970, "The Woman-Identified Woman" (1997), which argued that the success of a revolutionary women's movement would require women to develop consciousness distinct from that developed within a misogynistic, sexist, and patriarchal culture. "What is crucial is that women begin disengaging from male-defined response patterns," reads the statement. "In the privacy of our own psyches, we must cut those cords to the core" (p. 156). Separation was not merely physical and institutional but also psychic: interior and private spaces. The statement concludes with a justification for separatism that begins to speak in broader, more general terms:

> Together we must find, reinforce, and validate our authentic selves. ... We find receding the sense of alienation, of being cut off, of being behind a locked window, of being unable to get out what we know is inside. We feel a real-ness, feel at last we are coinciding with ourselves. With that real self, with that consciousness, we begin a revolution to end the imposition of all coercive identifications, and to achieve maximum autonomy in human expression. (p. 157)

In both urban and rural environments, lesbian-separatist feminists did exactly that, with mixed results. In her 1976 essay, "Learning from Lesbian Separatism," Charlotte Bunch (1987) clarifies a misperception of lesbian separatism as escape from men to some kind of Amazonian utopia. Instead, a major factor was escape from heterosexual women in the feminist movement who, as many have described, were largely hostile and unsupportive toward lesbian feminists (Radicalesbians, 1997). "We must not lose sight of why separatism happened in the first place," Bunch writes. "It happened because straight feminists were unable to allow lesbians to grow—to develop our personal lives and out political insights" (p. 190).

Separation is not necessarily an act of hostility toward the group one from which one is removing oneself (although bad feelings certainly may be involved), it is a necessary act to allow for nurturing self-awareness and political consciousness denied by the group being left. Separatism can be less a rejection of the dominant and more a strategic creation of safe space free from it, a secure place in which new insights, political understandings, social structures, and institutions can be developed that, as Bunch describes, ultimately serve to benefit any social justice movement: "Separatism is a dynamic strategy to be moved in and out of whenever a minority feels that its interests are being overlooked by the majority, or that its insights need more space to be developed" (p. 190). Indeed, writing a few years before the rise of lesbian separatism, Valarie Solanas' infamous, yet continually popular, *S.C.U.M. Manifesto* linked explicitly, for example, female separation with another progressive movement, organized labor:

> If a large majority of women were SCUM, they could acquire complete control of this country within a few weeks simply by withdrawing from the labor force.
> ... If all women simply left men, refused to have anything to do with any of

them—ever, all men, the government, and the national economy would collapse completely. (2009, Disease and Death section, paragraph 19)

In the 1980s and 1990s, lesbian separatism fell under heavy criticism, one critique being that it posited an essential lesbian identity unacceptable to the rising popularity of post-structural and postmodern theory. However, ethnographic research on separatist communities suggests this was inaccurate and that, instead, a great diversity flourished, with no universal or coherent lesbian identity articulated from community to community, nor even an agreement on how to best implement separatism (Cheney, 1985; Valentine, 1997).

However, a more trenchant critique was that any process of categorical (re) definition necessarily involved new exclusions and thereby hierarchies. Drawing a new circle still involved the drawing of lines, and critiques from lesbian feminists of color pointed this out, most famously in "A Black Feminist Statement" by the Combahee River Collective (1997). This argued that, although separatism was consolidation of difference, there were multiple differences, and therefore separatism necessarily chose to prioritize certain vectors of difference over others. When sex and sexuality were prioritized, race, ethnicity, and, to varying degrees, class, were neglected. Moreover, disconnection from heterosexuality and men hindered the very solidarity efforts that were needed in other social justice movements, such as anti-racism and labor organizing. Feminist responses to such critiques theorized women's consciousness and subjectivity as multiply constituted through gender, sexuality, sex, race, class, geography, and other factors (Anzaldúa, 1994; Crenshaw, 1994; hooks, 2000; Mohanty, 2003).[1]

Such experimentation, deliberation, theorizations, writings, and debates were in many ways ultimately productive for the intellectual and social health of the women's movement. The fact that such criticisms were still heeded by even contemporary advocates of separatism as a strategy for building coalitions of difference (Freedman, 2006) evidences, not the failure of lesbian separatism but, on the contrary, its success. For, we see the goal of separatism—expanded consciousness in support of more equitable world-changing along multiple vectors of difference—precisely in the critiques and challenges it inspired. Its "failures" or limitations can be seen as, instead, quite productive in their provocations and responses.

Questioning Identity in the Trump Era

Am I advocating for some new form of separatism? Not necessarily. I am more provoking reflection on some of the assumptions built into this project and its sources. When it comes to recommending applications of scholarly insights, I am skeptical of the academic-as-policymaker. As Foucault explained,

> My position is that it is not up to us [intellectuals] to propose. As soon as one "proposes"—one proposes a vocabulary, an ideology, which can only have effects of domination. What we have to present are instruments and tools that people might find useful. By forming groups specifically to make these analyses, to wage these struggles, by using these instruments or others: this is how, in the end, possibilities open up.

> But if the intellectual starts playing once again the role that he has played for a hundred and fifty years—that of prophet in relation to what "must be," to what "must take place"—these effects of domination will return and we shall have other ideologies, functioning in the same way. (Foucault, 1988, p. 197)

My project here intentionally has used fixed categories to, somewhat perversely, force an expansive vision of multiplicity. My agential cut, my intervention in forcing this juxtaposition, has been a journey which led to, not the tidy answers or stories I was once seeking as a graduate student, or that a graduate student once sought from me, but instead many more avenues of potential exploration. A ripe peach might appear solid, but, when squeezed, many colors of pink, red, white, and yellow appear. Its solid sphere gives way to multiple states of solid, liquid, and in-between. This book has been something of an act of creative destruction. The identities of gay men and feminist women, and the stories of their histories, narratives, and networks, have emerged messier than when I began. Messier and multiplied.

The Trump era, along with nationalist, "alt right," and populist movements around the globe, has seen identity politics used in a dual motion. In one direction, identity categories are used to marshal affect and action. National identities, racial and ethnic identities, gender identities and religious identities have been harnessed in appeals to mobilize voters, but from the opposite end of the political spectrum. It is an identity politics of Western national purity and origin, White supremacy, masculinity, heterosexuality, cisgenderism, and Judeo-Christianity. The urgency and effectiveness of these appeals has come from positioning them as victims. Of what? Of identity politics. The identity-based political coalitions that brought about social changes, particularly since the feminist second wave and rise of the modern LGBTQ rights movement, have been positioned as oppressors. Today, as I write this, the *National Review*—a conservative publication but at least, in the new normal, one that challenged rather than blindly kowtowed to Trump—ran a story titled "The Overreach of LGBTQ Activism" (Kearns, 2019).

This, when we still lack national hate crime laws, adoption rights, and basic discrimination protection.

Such rhetoric casts a troubled shadow over this project. I began wondering about feminist women and gay men. As I learned there was no readily available story, I thought that, by researching their stories—whether as common allies, collaborators, competitors, or in conflict—I could find lessons on coalition. Stories of failure can be just as useful, and sometimes more so, than stories of success. Now, however, I wonder if these foundational concepts of identity groups and coalitions have become broken.

Social media, championed in its initial years for what was thought to be their inherently democratizing potential, have been used to undermine US democracy. Many believe they were part of a larger effort that succeeded. The tools of the Arab Spring are also the tools of Pepe the Frog. Tumblr has banned adult content. YouTubers have lost their accounts for racism, sexism, and homophobia. Social media giants flounder in the face of investigations into privacy abuse, monopolization, and political manipulation.

Which is not to say that social media and identity politics are wholly ineffectual. Coming-out videos and feminist blogs can still have a powerful effects. Working at a rural, Southern university, I am deeply aware of how the progress of social movements is varied and contingent. Moreover, in defense of Buttigieg, coming out—as gay or feminist—or coming into political awareness, happens in unique and individual ways for each person, which should be respected rather than used in judgment. Therefore, I do not intend "creative destruction" to be taken absolutely but more as a provocation for deep reflection and reconsideration, a call to see what could be gained from imagining a blank slate.

Could identity politics be a similar political tool as separatism? It clearly seems now to be capable of being used for, not only progressive goals, but also the most regressive ideologies possible. Perhaps it is time to squeeze the peach of identity. Not to destroy it or abandoned it, but to see what other textures, gradations, and scents it holds. This project was originally conceived as being about the successes or failures in attempting to build communicative connections. I finish it wondering about how we can rebuild ourselves.

Note

1. Arguably, queer theory's attempts to distance or separate from all positions reliant on definitional categories and practices of differentiation can be seen as a related extension or perhaps inverse of this intellectual lineage.

References

Anzaldúa, G. (1994). "La Conciencia de la Mestiza: Towards a new consciousness" from Borderlands/ La Frontera: The New Mestiza. In W. K. Kolmar & F. Bartkowski (Ed.), *Feminist theory: A reader* (pp. 420–425). New York: McGraw-Hill.

Banet-Weiser, S. (2018). *Empowered: Popular feminism and popular misogyny*. Durham, NC: Duke University Press.

Bunch, C. (1987). Learning from lesbian separatism. In C. Bunch (Ed.), *Passionate politics: Feminist theory in action* (pp. 182–191). New York: St. Martin's Griffin.

Cheney, J. (Ed.). (1985). *Lesbian land*. Word Weavers.

Combahee River Collective, T. (1997). A black feminist statement. In L. Nicholson (Ed.), *The second wave: A reader in feminist theory* (pp. 63–70). New York: Psychology Press.

Crenshaw, K. (1994). Intersectionality and identity politics: Learning from violence against women of color. In W. K. Kolmar & F. Bartkowski (Ed.), *Feminist theory: A reader* (pp. 533–542). New York: McGraw-Hill.

Edwards, T. (1994). *Erotics and politics: Gay male sexuality, masculinity and feminism*. New York: Routledge.

Foucault, M. (1988). *Confinement, psychiatry, prison in politics.‖ Philosophy, culture: Interviews and other writings 1977–1984*. Ed. Lawrence D. Kritzman. New York: Routledge.

Freedman, E. B. (2006). *Feminism, sexuality, and politics: Essays*. Greensboro: University of North Carolina Press.

hooks, bell. (2000). *Feminist theory from margin to center*. Cambridge, MA: South End Press.

Kearns, M. (2019, July 5). The Overreach of LGBTQ Activism. Retrieved July 14, 2019, from *National Review* website: https://www.nationalreview.com/2019/07/lgbtq-activism-overreach/

McAfee, M., Gomez, J., Coburn, L., & Rivas, A. (2019). Pete Buttigieg on police shooting of a black man in South Bend. Retrieved July 14, 2019, from ABC News website: https://abcnews.go.com/Politics/pete-buttigieg-talks-rising-stardom-police-shooting-black/story?id=64273694

Mohanty, C. T. (2003). *Feminism without borders: Decolonizing theory, practicing solidarity*. Durham, NC: Duke University Press.

Peck, D. (2019, July 13). My Mayor Pete Problem. *The New Republic*. Retrieved July 14, 2019, from Archive.is website: http://archive.is/Tz45f

Radicalesbians. (1997). The woman identified woman. In L. Nicholson (Ed.), *The second wave* (pp. 153–157). New York: Psychology Press.

Republic, T. N. (2019, July 12). Editor's note. *The New Republic*. Retrieved from https://newrepublic.com/article/154457/editors-note

Solanas, V. (2009). *S.C.U.M. Manifesto*. Retrieved from http://www.womynkind.org/scum.htm

Valentine, G. (1997). Making space: Separatism and difference. In H. J. Nast, John PaulJones, & Susan M. Roberts (Eds.), *Thresholds in feminist geography: Difference, methodology, representation* (pp. 65–75). Lanham, MD: Rowman and Littlefield.

Ward, J. (2000). Queer sexism: Rethinking gay men and masculinity. *RESEARCH ON MEN AND MASCULINITIES SERIES, 12*(152–175), 56.

Woolf, V. (2004). *A room of one's own [eBook edition]*. Retrieved from http://ebooks.adelaide.edu.au/w/woolf/virginia/w91r/

Index

CULTURAL MEDIA STUDIES

Leandra H. Hernández and Amanda R. Martinez
Series Editors

In the past few years, our political, cultural, and media landscapes have cultivated a sharp, notable rise of media activism, more representations of diverse groups and characters, and the need for intersectional approaches to media studies. The #MeToo campaign, the 2017 and 2018 Women's Marches, Black Lives Matter marches, cross-border anti-feminicide activist marches, immigration marches, and increased representation of diverse sexual identities, racial/ethnic groups, and gender identities are evidence of the need for continued research on cultural media studies topics.

The Peter Lang Cultural Media Studies book series is accepting book proposals for both proposed book and fully developed manuscripts on a rolling basis for media studies books that explore media production, media consumption, media effects, and media representations of feminism(s), race/ethnicity, gender, sexuality, and related topics.

For additional information about this series or for the submission of manuscripts, please contact:

Peter Lang Publishing
Acquisitions Department
29 Broadway, 18th floor
New York, NY 10006

To order other books in this series, please contact our Customer Service Department:

peterlang@presswarehouse.com (within the U.S.)
order@peterlang.com (outside the U.S.)

Or browse online by series:

www.peterlang.com

www.ingramcontent.com/pod-product-compliance
Lightning Source LLC
Chambersburg PA
CBHW050644280326
41932CB00015B/2775